OVERCOMING
LOW SELF-ESTEEM

2nd Edition

*A self-help guide using
Cognitive Behavioural Techniques*

OVERCOMING

MELANIE FENNELL

ROBINSON

ROBINSON

First published in Great Britain in 2016 by Robinson

10

A CIP catalogue record for this book
is available from the British Library.

Important Note
This book is not intended as a substitute for medical advice or treatment.
Any person with a condition requiring medical attention should consult a
qualified medical practitioner or suitable therapist.

ISBN: 978-1-47211-929-2

Typeset in Bembo by Initial Typesetting Services, Edinburgh
Printed and bound in Great Britain by Clays Ltd, Elcograf S.p.A.

Papers used by Robinson are from well-managed forests
and other responsible sources

Robinson
An imprint of
Little, Brown Book Group
Carmelite House
50 Victoria Embankment
London EC4Y 0DZ

An Hachette UK Company
www.hachette.co.uk

www.littlebrown.co.uk

Dr Melani　　　　　　　　of *Overcon* *Low Self-Esteem*, the *Ov* *ing Low Self Esteem* *elf-Help Course, Boost Your Confidence* and *Talks With Your Therapist: Overcoming Low Self-Esteem* (audio). She was a pioneer of cognitive behavioural therapy (CBT) in the UK, and is a Founding Fellow of the Oxford Cognitive Therapy Centre, an internationally recognised centre of excellence in CBT training, where she developed and led courses at Diploma and Masters level, as well as presenting many workshops and papers at major international conferences. As a member of research teams in the Oxford University Department of Psychiatry, Melanie has contributed to the development and evaluation of cognitive behavioural therapy for a range of emotional problems, especially depression. Her interest in low self-esteem grew out of this work. *Overcoming Low Self-Esteem* has become a classic of self-help literature, winning acclaim for its practical and user-friendly approach, and recommended by 'Reading Well', the UK National Health Service's 'Books on Prescription' self-help scheme. In July 2002, Melanie was voted 'Most Influential Female UK Cognitive Therapist' by the membership of the British Association for Behavioural and Cognitive Psychotherapies, and in 2013 she was awarded an Honorary Fellowship by the Association.

The aim of the **Overcoming** series is to enable people with a range of common problems and disorders to take control of their own recovery programme.

Each title, with its specially tailored programme, is devised by a practising clinician using the latest techniques of cognitive behavioural therapy – techniques which have been shown to be highly effective in changing the way patients think about themselves and their problems.

Many books in the Overcoming series are recommended by the UK Department of Health under the Books on Prescription scheme.

Other titles in the series include:

OVERCOMING ANGER AND IRRITABILITY, 2ND EDITION
OVERCOMING ANOREXIA NERVOSA
OVERCOMING ANXIETY, 2ND EDITION
OVERCOMING BODY IMAGE PROBLEMS INCLUDING BODY DYSMORPHIC DISORDER
OVERCOMING BULIMIA NERVOSA AND BINGE-EATING, 2ND EDITION
OVERCOMING CHILDHOOD TRAUMA
OVERCOMING CHRONIC FATIGUE
OVERCOMING CHRONIC PAIN
OVERCOMING COMPULSIVE GAMBLING
OVERCOMING DEPERSONALIZATION AND FEELINGS OF UNREALITY
OVERCOMING DEPRESSION, 3RD EDITION
OVERCOMING DISTRESSING VOICES
OVERCOMING GRIEF
OVERCOMING HEALTH ANXIETY
OVERCOMING HOARDING
OVERCOMING INSOMNIA AND SLEEP PROBLEMS
OVERCOMING MILD TRAUMATIC BRAIN INJURY AND POST-CONCUSSION SYMPTOMS
OVERCOMING MOOD SWINGS
OVERCOMING OBSESSIVE COMPULSIVE DISORDER
OVERCOMING PANIC AND AGORAPHOBIA
OVERCOMING PARANOID AND SUSPICIOUS THOUGHTS, 2ND EDITION
OVERCOMING PERFECTIONISM
OVERCOMING PROBLEM DRINKING
OVERCOMING RELATIONSHIP PROBLEMS
OVERCOMING SEXUAL PROBLEMS
OVERCOMING SOCIAL ANXIETY AND SHYNESS, 2ND EDITION
OVERCOMING STRESS
OVERCOMING TRAUMATIC STRESS
OVERCOMING WEIGHT PROBLEMS
OVERCOMING WORRY AND GENERALISED ANXIETY DISORDER, 2ND EDITION
OVERCOMING YOUR CHILD'S FEARS AND WORRIES
OVERCOMING YOUR CHILD'S SHYNESS AND SOCIAL ANXIETY
OVERCOMING YOUR SMOKING HABIT

Contents

PART ONE

WHAT IS LOW SELF-ESTEEM?
An introduction to this book

1 What is low self-esteem?   3

PART TWO

UNDERSTANDING LOW SELF-ESTEEM

2 How low self-esteem develops   39
3 What keeps low self-esteem going   75

PART THREE

OVERCOMING LOW SELF-ESTEEM

4 Checking out anxious predictions   101
5 Questioning self-critical thoughts   147
6 Enhancing self-acceptance   193
7 Changing the Rules   245
8 Creating a new Bottom Line   301
9 Planning for the future   356

Useful books and addresses 387
Appendix 393
Index 409

PART ONE

WHAT IS LOW SELF-ESTEEM?

An introduction to this book

1

What is low self-esteem?

What do we mean by 'low self-esteem'?

Self-image
Self-concept
Self-perception
Self-confidence
Self-efficacy
Self-acceptance
Self-respect
Self-worth
Self-esteem

All these words refer to aspects of the way we view ourselves, the thoughts we have about ourselves, and the value we place on ourselves as people. Each has a slightly different shade of meaning.

'Self–image', 'self-concept' and 'self-perception' all refer to the overall picture a person has of him- or herself. These terms do not necessarily imply any judgement or evaluation, but simply describe a whole range of characteristics. For example:

- National, and perhaps regional, identity (e.g. 'I am English', 'I come from New York')
- Racial and cultural identity (e.g. 'I am black', 'I am Jewish')
- Social and professional role (e.g. 'I am a mother', 'I am a policeman')
- Life stage (e.g. 'I am just thirteen', 'I am a grand-parent')
- Physical appearance (e.g. 'I am tall', 'I have brown eyes')
- Likes and dislikes (e.g. 'I love football', 'I can't stand spinach')
- Regular activities (e.g. 'I play baseball', 'I use a computer')

and

- Psychological qualities (e.g. 'I have a sense of humour', 'I lose my temper easily')

'Self-confidence' and 'self-efficacy', on the other hand, refer to our sense that we can do things successfully, and perhaps to a particular standard. As one self-confident person put it, 'I can do things and I know I can do things'. For example:

- Specific competencies (e.g. 'I am good at maths', 'I can catch a ball')
- Social relationships (e.g. 'When I meet new people, on the whole I get on well with them', 'I am a good listener')
- General coping ability (e.g. 'If I set out to get something, I usually get it', 'I am a good person to turn to in a crisis')

'Self-acceptance', 'self-respect', 'self-worth' and 'self-esteem' introduce a different element. They do not simply refer to qualities we assign to ourselves, whether good or bad. Nor do they simply reflect things we believe we can or cannot do. Rather, they reflect the overall opinion we have of ourselves and the value we place on ourselves as people, our fundamental sense of worth. The tone of this may be positive (e.g. 'I am good', 'I am worthwhile') or negative (e.g. 'I am bad', 'I am useless'). When the tone is positive, this reflects broadly healthy self-esteem. But when the tone is negative, we are talking about low self-esteem.

What is healthy self-esteem?

People sometimes mistake the term 'self-esteem' for something just as extreme and unrealistic in a positive direction as low self-esteem can be in a negative one. Naturally enough, this does not sound like an attractive option – no one likes people who are self-important, convinced of their own perfection, feel entitled to have life go their way at all times, always put their own needs ahead of the wellbeing of others, and constantly congratulate themselves on their extraordinary gifts.

This is not what healthy self-esteem means, nor is it the intention of this book to take you in this equally unhelpful direction. By 'healthy self-esteem', I mean a broadly positive sense of your worth, reflected in *a balanced view of yourself.* In low self-esteem, your view of yourself is biased heavily towards the negative – your flaws, your weaknesses, your mistakes, the times when you fall short. Your strengths, talents and good qualities tend to be ignored or discounted. In excessively positive self-esteem, the reverse is true: the positive alone occupies centre stage, and the shortcomings that are an inevitable and natural part of being a normal, imperfect human being are ignored or discounted.

The intention of this book is to help you to cultivate healthy self-esteem – a fundamental acceptance of yourself just as you are, warts and all. So, yes, like every other human being who ever lived, you have weaknesses, you get things wrong, you do things you later regret, and there are things about you that you would like to change. And you also have strong points, lovely qualities, skills and achievements, and these deserve equal attention and value. This is what is meant by a balanced view. At its heart is the sense that it's OK to be you.

How do I know if I have low self-esteem?

Take a look at the ten questions below. Put a tick next to each question, in the column that best reflects how you feel about yourself. Be honest – there are no right or wrong answers here, simply the truth about how you see yourself.

If your answers to these questions are anything other than 'Yes, definitely', then this book could be useful to you. If you are generally comfortable in accepting yourself as you are, if you have no real difficulty in respecting and appreciating yourself, if you see yourself as having intrinsic value and worth despite your human weaknesses, and feel at ease with taking up your space in the world and enjoying its riches, then you have the gift of healthy self-esteem. You may still find ideas in this book that will interest you or open up avenues that you have not previously thought of, but any changes you make will be built on a solid foundation of self-acceptance. If, on the other hand, you feel your true self to be weak, inadequate, inferior or lacking in some way, if you are troubled by uncertainty and self-doubt, if your thoughts about yourself are often unkind and critical, or if you have difficulty in feeling that you have any true worth, or that you deserve to enjoy the good things in life, these are signs that your self-esteem is low. And low self-esteem may be having a painful and damaging effect on your life.

	Yes, definitely	Yes, mostly	Yes, sometimes	No, mostly	No, not at all
My experience in life has taught me to value and appreciate myself					
I have a good opinion of myself					
I treat myself well and look after myself properly					
I like myself					
I give as much weight to my qualities, skills, assets and strengths as I do to my weaknesses and flaws					

I feel good about myself	I feel worthy of other people's attention and time	It's OK for me to care for myself and to enjoy the good things in life	My expectations of myself are no more rigid or exacting than my expectations of other people	I am kind and encouraging towards myself, rather than being self-critical

The impact of low self-esteem

'Self-esteem', then, refers to the overall opinion we have of ourselves, how we judge or evaluate ourselves, and the value we attach to ourselves as people. We will now consider in more detail the kind of impact low self-esteem can have on a person's life. This will give you an opportunity to reflect on your own opinion of yourself, and what sort of value you place on yourself, as well as considering how your opinion of yourself affects your thoughts and feelings and how you operate on a day-to-day basis.

The essence of low self-esteem: Your central beliefs about yourself

At the heart of self-esteem lie your central beliefs about yourself and your core ideas about the kind of person you are. These beliefs normally have the appearance of statements of fact ('I am …'). They look like straightforward reflections of your identity, pure statements of the truth about yourself. Actually, however, they are more likely to be opinions than facts – summary statements or conclusions you have come to about yourself, based on the experiences you have had in your life, and in particular the messages you have received about the kind of person you are. So, to put it simply, if your experiences have generally been positive, your beliefs about yourself will probably be broadly positive, too. If your experiences have been pretty mixed (as most people's are), then you may have a range of different ideas about yourself, and apply them flexibly according to the circumstances in which you find yourself. However, if your experiences have been generally negative, then your beliefs about yourself are likely to be equally negative. Negative beliefs about yourself are the essence of low self-esteem. And this essence may have coloured and contaminated many aspects of your life.

The impact of low self-esteem on the person

Negative beliefs about the self – which form the essence of low self-esteem – express themselves in many ways.

To get a sense of this, it may be useful to think about someone you know who you think has low self-esteem. Of course, if you think *you* have low self-esteem, you could consider yourself at this point. But you may find it easier at first to consider another person. This is because if you try to look at yourself, it is often difficult to obtain a clear view – you are too close to see clearly. Think now about the person you have chosen. Remember recent times when you have met. What happened? What did you talk about? How did your person look? What did they do? How did you feel with them? Try to get a really clear picture of them in your mind's eye, see if you can hear their voice. Now the question is: How do you know that this person has low self-esteem? What is it about them that tells you they have a problem in this area?

Jot down as many things as you can think of that give the game away. Look for clues in what your person says. For example, do you hear a lot of self-criticism, or apologies?

What does this tell you about how your person thinks about him- or herself? Look at what your person does, including how he or she gets along with you and other people. For example, is he or she characteristically quiet and shy in company? Or perhaps the opposite — always rather pushy and self-promoting? What does this tell you? And what about self-presentation (posture, facial expression, direction of gaze, tone of voice)? Does he or she, for example, tend to adopt a hunched, inward-turned posture and avoid meeting others' eyes? Again, what does this tell you about how he or she sees him- or herself? Think too about your person's feelings and emotions. How does it feel to be him or her? Does he or she seem sad? Or fed up or frustrated? Or shy and anxious? What bodily sensations or changes might go with those emotions?

You will probably discover that clues are to be found in a number of different areas.

THOUGHTS AND STATEMENTS ABOUT THE SELF

Negative beliefs about the self find expression in what people habitually say and think about themselves. Look out for self-criticism, self-blame and self-doubt — the sense that the person does not place much value on him- or herself, discounts positives and focuses on weaknesses and flaws.

BEHAVIOUR

Low self-esteem is reflected in how a person acts in everyday situations. Look out for telltale clues like difficulty in asserting needs or speaking out, an apologetic stance, avoidance of challenges and opportunities. Look out too for small clues like a bowed posture, downturned head, avoidance of eye contact, hushed voice and hesitancy.

EMOTIONS

Low self-esteem has an impact on emotional state. Look out for signs of sadness, anxiety, guilt, shame, hopelessness, frustration and anger.

BODY STATE

Emotional state is often reflected in uncomfortable body sensations. Look out for signs of fatigue, aches and pains, low energy or tension.

What you have noticed in this person you know shows how holding a central negative belief about yourself reverberates on all levels, affecting thinking, behaviour, emotional state and body sensations. Now consider how this may apply to *you*. If you were observing yourself as you have just observed someone else, what would you see? What would be the telltale clues in your case?

The impact of low self-esteem on life

Just as low self-esteem is reflected in many aspects of the person, so it has an impact on many aspects of life. This in turn may feed into even lower self-esteem.

SCHOOL AND WORK

There may be a consistent pattern of underperformance and

avoidance of challenges, or perhaps rigorous perfectionism and relentless hard work, fuelled by fear of failure. People with low self-esteem find it hard to give themselves credit for their achievements, or to believe that their good results are the outcome of their own skills and strengths. They may drop out of school early without qualifications – and later on, this impacts on working life. They may end up earning less and spending more time unemployed.

PERSONAL RELATIONSHIPS

In their relationships with others, people with low self-esteem may suffer acute (even disabling) self-consciousness, over sensitivity to criticism and disapproval, excessive eagerness to please – even outright withdrawal from any sort of intimacy or contact. Some people adopt a policy of always being the life and soul of the party, always appearing confident and in control, or always putting others first, no matter what the cost. They believe that if they do not put on this sort of front, people will simply not want to know them.

LEISURE ACTIVITIES

How people spend their leisure time can also be affected. People with low self-esteem may avoid any activity in which there is a risk of being judged (art classes, for example, or competitive sports), or may believe that they do not deserve rewards or treats or to relax and enjoy themselves.

SELF-CARE

People with low self-esteem may not take proper care of themselves. They may struggle on when they feel ill, put off going to the hairdresser or the dentist, not bother to exercise or eat a healthy diet, rarely buy new clothes, drink excessively or smoke or use street drugs. Or, in direct contrast, they may spend hours perfecting every detail of how they look, convinced that this is the only way to be attractive to other people.

Variations in the role and status of low self-esteem

Not everyone is affected to the same extent by central negative beliefs about the self. The impact of low self-esteem depends in part on its exact role in your life.

1. Low self-esteem can be an aspect of current problems

Sometimes a negative view of the self is purely a product of current mood. People who are clinically depressed almost always see themselves in a very negative light. This is true even for depressions that respond very well to antidepressant medication, and for those that have a strong biochemical basis. These are the recognised signs of clinical depression:

- Low mood (feeling consistently sad, depressed, down or empty)
- A general reduction in your capacity to experience interest and pleasure
- Changes in appetite and weight (marked increases or decreases)
- Changes in sleep pattern (again, marked increases or decreases)
- Being either so fidgety and restless that it is difficult to sit still, or slowed down compared to your normal speed of going about things (this should be visible to others, not just a feeling inside yourself)
- Feeling tired and low in energy
- Feeling extremely guilty and worthless
- Difficulty concentrating, thinking straight, making decisions
- Feeling that things are so bad that you might be better off dead, thinking of hurting yourself or even perhaps planning to do so

To be recognised as part of a depression that deserves treatment in its own right, at least five of these symptoms (including low mood or a general loss of pleasure and interest) should have been present consistently over an extended period (two weeks or more). That is, we are not talking here about the fleeting periods of low mood that everyone experiences from time to time when things are rough, but rather about a mood state that has become persistent and disruptive.

If your current poor opinion of yourself started in the context of this kind of depression, then seeking treatment for the depression in its own right should be your first priority. Successfully overcoming the depression could even restore confidence in yourself without you needing to work extensively on self-esteem. That said, you may still find some of the ideas in this book useful: especially Chapters 5, 6 and 7, which discuss how to tackle self-critical thoughts, how to focus on positive aspects of yourself, give yourself credit for your achievements and treat yourself with kindness and compassion, and how to change unhelpful Rules for Living. You may also find it helpful to consult another book in this series, Paul Gilbert's *Overcoming Depression*.

2. Low self-esteem can be a consequence of other problems

Loss of self-esteem is sometimes a consequence of some other problem which causes distress and disruption in a person's life. Long-standing anxiety problems, for example, such as constantly worrying or apparently uncontrollable panic attacks, can impose real restrictions on what a person can do, and so undermine confidence and lead to feelings of incompetence and inadequacy. Similarly, people who suffer from depression often see it as a reflection of personal weakness (rather than a normal human response to adversity and loss), and may even feel too ashamed to admit it to anyone.

Enduring relationship difficulties, hardship, lasting severe stress, chronic pain and illness can have a similar impact. All of these difficulties may result in demoralisation and loss of self-esteem. In this case, tackling the root problem may be the most helpful thing to do. People who learn to manage panic and anxiety, for example, are often restored to previous levels of confidence without needing to do extensive work on low self-esteem in its own right. If this is your situation, and your low self-esteem developed as a consequence of some other problem, you may nonetheless find some useful ideas in this book to help you to restore your belief in yourself as swiftly and completely as possible. It could also be worth your while consulting other titles in this series to see whether any of them address your other difficulties directly.

3. Low self-esteem can create vulnerability to other problems

Sometimes low self-esteem, rather than being an aspect or consequence of current problems, seems in fact to be the fertile soil in which they have grown. It may have been in place since childhood or adolescence, or as far back as the person can remember. Research has shown that low self-esteem (lasting negative beliefs about the self) may contribute towards a range of difficulties, including depression, suicidal thinking, eating disorders, substance abuse and social anxiety (extreme shyness). If this is true for you, and your current difficulties seem to reflect or spring from an underlying sense of low self-esteem, then working with those difficulties will undoubtedly be useful in itself, but it will probably not produce significant or lasting changes in your view of yourself. And unless the issue of low self-esteem is tackled directly, in its own right, you are likely to remain vulnerable to future difficulties. In this case, you could benefit greatly from using this book as a guide to working consistently and systematically on your beliefs about yourself, undermining the old negative views and building up new and more helpful perspectives.

Variations in the impact of low self-esteem

Whether low self-esteem is an aspect or consequence of other difficulties, or a vulnerability factor for them, the extent to which it impinges on life will vary from person to person. This point is illustrated on the following scale:

Low Self-esteem: Variations in Impact

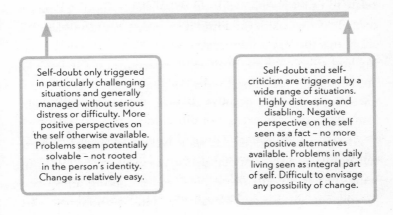

Self-doubt only triggered in particularly challenging situations and generally managed without serious distress or difficulty. More positive perspectives on the self otherwise available. Problems seem potentially solvable – not rooted in the person's identity. Change is relatively easy.

Self-doubt and self-criticism are triggered by a wide range of situations. Highly distressing and disabling. Negative perspective on the self seen as a fact – no more positive alternatives available. Problems in daily living seen as integral part of self. Difficult to envisage any possibility of change.

A person with low self-esteem might fall anywhere on this scale. At the left-hand end would be found people who experience occasional moments of self-doubt, usually under very specific conditions (for example, a job interview or asking someone out on a first date). Such doubts interfere only minimally with people's lives. They might feel mildly apprehensive in a challenging situation, but would have no real trouble managing the apprehension, would give it little weight, would find it easy to reassure themselves, and would not be held back from meeting the challenge successfully. When people like this have difficulties in life, they tend to see them straightforwardly as problems to be solved, rather than as a sign that there is something fundamentally wrong with them as a person. In addition to the negative perspective on the self triggered by challenges, they probably have other more positive and constructive alternative views, which influence how they feel about themselves most of the time. They may well find it easy overall to relate to other people, and feel comfortable about asking for help. Such people should find it relatively easy to isolate the situations in which they experience self-doubt, consolidating and strengthening positive perspectives on the self that are already in place, and learning quite rapidly to question anxious predictions about performance and to answer self-critical thoughts.

At the other end of the scale would fall people whose self-doubt and self-condemnation were more or less constant. For them, no more kind and accepting alternative perspective on the self is available. This is simply the way things are. The slightest trigger is enough to spark off a torrent of self-critical thoughts. They find it hard to believe in their capacity to deal with any of life's challenges or to achieve lasting closeness to other people. Their fears and their negative beliefs about themselves may be powerful enough to cause widespread disruption in how they go about their lives – opportunities missed, challenges avoided, relationships spoiled, pleasures and achievements sabotaged, and self-defeating and self-destructive patterns of behaviour in many areas. When people at this end of the scale have difficulties, rather than seeing these as problems to be solved, they tend to view them as central to their true selves ('This is me', 'This is how I am'). So it is hard to step back far enough to see things clearly, or to work systematically to change things for the better without outside help. Even then, making progress can be tough, because it is difficult to have confidence in the possibility of change or to persist if improvement is slow in coming.

Most of us fall somewhere between these two extremes. This book may have limited relevance for people falling at the left-hand end, though it could still be a useful source of handy tips for fine-tuning an already robust sense of self-confidence and self-worth. For those who fall at the far right-hand end of the scale, using the book on its own may not be enough. It could, however, be helpful as part of a programme of therapy with a cognitive behavioural therapist. Its main use will be for the people who fall in the broad middle area of the continuum – people whose low self-esteem is problematic enough for them to wish to do something about it, but who have enough freedom of movement to be able to stand back from how they habitually see themselves and search for alternative perspectives.

How to use this book

You may be a person who is generally self-confident but suffers from occasional moments of self-doubt in particularly challenging situations. Or you may be someone who is plagued by self-criticism and finds it hard to think of anything good about yourself. The chances are, you are somewhere in between. Whatever the intensity and breadth of impact of your particular brand of low self-esteem, this book provides your road map for a journey towards self-knowledge and self-acceptance. It is intended to help you to understand the origins of your poor opinion of yourself, and to discover how unhelpful thinking habits and self-defeating patterns of behaviour keep that poor opinion going in the present day. You will learn how to use close self-observation as a basis for learning to question your negative sense of yourself and to develop a new, more kindly, respectful and accepting view.

A number of things may help you on your journey, and are explained in more detail below. They are:

- Being open to new possibilities
- Taking things step by step

- Being willing to experiment with putting new ideas and skills into practice
- Making a commitment to yourself
- Writing things down
- Being prepared for ups and downs

Being open to new possibilities

Human beings are learning animals − it's how we have evolved as a species, and how as individuals we continue to grow and develop throughout our lives. The problem is that sometimes, things we learn at particular times and under particular (often painful) circumstances can become long-term fixtures which resist change. Low self-esteem can be an example of this.

You do not have to believe that this book will revolutionise your life and make a new person of you. Rather, the important thing is to tune in to and make the most of that amazing human capacity to learn. Keep an open mind, be alert to new possibilities (rather than letting old thinking habits automatically shut them out), and see if you can bring a sort of friendly curiosity to your investigations.

Taking things step by step

Throughout the book, you will find plenty of opportunities to think about how you developed your poor opinion of yourself, and to reflect on how low self-esteem is affecting you on a daily basis. There are lots of practical exercises and worksheets that will help you apply what you read to your own personal situation. Exactly how you use the book will be up to you. You may decide to skip quickly through it, picking up one or two handy tips. Or you may decide, after you have skimmed the chapter headings, that it would be worth investing time and effort in working through the book systematically, carefully observing how you react in situations that trouble you so that you can change old patterns, rethink your normal strategies for getting by, undermine old, negative beliefs about yourself, and replace them with more helpful and realistic alternatives.

If so, you may find it most helpful to work with one chapter at a time, since each introduces ideas and skills that will be useful to you as you proceed, and each is built on the foundations of the last. In this case, first read the chapter through quite quickly, to give yourself a general sense of what it is about. You can use this overview to notice stories and examples that ring bells for you, and to begin to consider how the chapter is relevant to *you* personally – after all, you are the expert on yourself. Then go back and read the chapter more carefully, in detail, completing the exercises as you go.

Do not move on to the next chapter until you feel you have a good grasp of the change methods introduced – a sense that you understand what they are and how to use them, and that you are beginning to get results. If you rush on, you risk completing nothing properly and the ideas presented will not be able to have any significant impact on how you feel about yourself. It takes the time it takes – and you are worth it. Think of this work as a gesture of respect and kindness towards yourself, a step towards self-acceptance and self-esteem.

Being willing to experiment with putting new ideas and skills into practice

You will learn most if questioning and rethinking your old ideas runs hand in hand with a willingness to try things out in practice. The most powerful learning is learning through direct experience. This doesn't mean just thinking afresh and perhaps discussing things with another trusted person, but being willing to put your money where your mouth is and to test your new ideas out in the real world. This takes courage, of course, but there is no doubt that experience will be your best teacher.

Making a commitment to yourself

If you do decide to work through the book systematically, it will take time. You will probably get most out of it if you set aside a certain amount of time every day (say, 20–30 minutes) to read, write, reflect, plan what to do and review your records. This is undoubtedly a real commitment, particularly as the book will sometimes ask you to think about events and issues that may be painful to you. However, especially if your doubts about yourself are long-standing and if they distress you and restrict your life, the commitment could have a substantial payoff. There may be times when you get stuck and can't think how to take things forward, or can't find alternatives to your usual way of thinking. Or you may sometimes feel impatient or discouraged because things are not moving as fast as you want them to or think they should. Don't get angry with yourself or give up – put your work to one side for a time and come back to it later, when your mind has cleared and you are feeling more relaxed.

You may also find it helpful to work through the book with a trusted friend or supporter. Two heads are often better than one, and your stuck points may not be the same as his or hers. You may even be able to help each other out, encouraging one another to persist, supporting each other to make the most of real-life experiments in new ways of operating, sharpening your focus on your strengths and good qualities, and thinking creatively about how to be a good friend to yourself; in other words, how to treat yourself like someone you value, love and respect.

Writing things down

It is important to keep a record of what you do. Throughout the book (and the accompanying 'Overcoming' website), you will find worksheets designed to help you to identify, rethink and test out old, unhelpful patterns of thought. These are intended to help you to go about your investigations step by step, in a systematic, structured way. Bear in mind that our memories are unreliable. We may think of memories as being reproductions of what actually happened. But in fact memory does not so much reproduce as reconstruct – recreate, even. The reconstructions can be influenced by, for example, what has happened since the original events, things we may have heard about what took place, and our mood at the time of remembering. If you are feeling low, for example, it will be very easy to remember difficult and painful experiences and much harder to remember good times and things that have gone right. This means that new learning and important insights can fade, change shape or disappear over time. Your records will act as reminders of the work you have done and the new ways of thinking and acting that you are developing. Such reminders can be especially helpful at times when you are under pressure, feeling tired or low, or when your confidence has taken a knock.

Being prepared for ups and downs

Particularly when your self-esteem has been low for some time, you will almost certainly experience ups and downs as you work through the book. Fortunately, you will find much valuable learning in both. Your successes will demonstrate the value of going about things in a new way and strengthen new ideas and skills. Downs, meanwhile, offer further opportunities to observe your low self-esteem doing what it does, right in front of your very eyes, and to discover how best to tackle it. So there is no need to be disheartened when you hit a rough patch.

A note of caution

This book will not help everyone who has low self-esteem. Sometimes a book is not enough. The most common way of dealing with things that distress us is to talk to someone else about them. Often, talking to a loved family member or a good friend is enough to relieve distress and move us forward. Sometimes, however, even this is not enough. We need to see a therapist, someone professionally trained to help people in distress (see pages 387–92). If you find that focusing on self-esteem is actually making you feel worse instead of helping you to see clearly and think constructively about how to change things for the better, or if your negative beliefs about yourself and about the impossibility of change are so strong that you cannot even begin to use the ideas and practical skills described, then it may be that you would do well to seek professional help. This is especially true if you find yourself becoming depressed in the way that was described earlier or too anxious to function properly, or if you find yourself starting to contemplate self-defeating and self-destructive acts.

There is nothing shameful about seeking psychological help – any more than there is anything shameful about taking your car to a garage if it is not running properly, or going to see a lawyer if you have legal problems you cannot resolve. The decision to seek help is both wise and courageous. It opens the door to the possibility of a different future. It means taking your journey towards self-knowledge and self-acceptance with the help of a concerned and friendly guide, rather than striking out alone. If you feel comfortable with the approach described in the book, its practical focus and emphasis on personal empowerment through self-observation and systematic change, then your most helpful guide might be a cognitive behaviour therapist.

The approach: Cognitive behavioural therapy

'Cognitive behavioural therapy' (CBT) is a form of psychotherapy that was originally developed in the United States by Professor Aaron T. Beck, a psychiatrist working in Philadelphia. It is an evidence-based approach with a solid foundation in psychological theory and clinical research. It was first shown to be effective as a treatment for depression in the late 1970s. Since then, it has broadened in scope, and is now used successfully to help people with a much wider range of problems. These include: anxiety, panic and worry; relationship difficulties, sexual difficulties; body-image problems; eating problems (like anorexia and bulimia nervosa); insomnia and chronic fatigue; chronic pain; compulsive gambling, alcohol and drug dependency, and post-traumatic stress (including recovery from childhood trauma). You will find other books in the 'Overcoming' series that deal with some of these problems.

CBT is an ideal approach for low self-esteem, because it focuses on thoughts, beliefs, attitudes and opinions (this is what 'cognitive' means) and, as we have already noted, a person's opinion of him- or herself lies right at the heart of low self-esteem. CBT provides an easily grasped framework for understanding how the problem developed and what keeps it going. It shows how your fundamental sense of yourself shapes everyday life – how it influences how you think and feel and what you do from moment to moment. Do not assume, however, that understanding and insight alone are enough. CBT offers practical, tried-and-tested and effective methods for producing lasting change. It invites us to step back from old thinking patterns and teaches us to see them as mental habits, some of them acquired many years ago and no longer useful or relevant. It shows us how to observe and question our thinking, rather than automatically assuming our thoughts and beliefs must be true. CBT is not just a 'talking therapy', however. It encourages you to take an active role in overcoming low self-esteem, to find ways of putting new ideas into practice in everyday situations, at work, with your friends and family, and in how you treat yourself, even when you are at home all on your own. You will learn how to experiment with acting differently and observing the impact of doing so on how you feel about yourself (this is the 'behavioural' element).

So, to summarise, CBT is a commonsensical, practical, down-to-earth approach to fundamental issues. It empowers you to become your own therapist – developing insight, planning and executing change, and assessing the results for yourself. The new skills you develop and practise will continue to be useful to you for the rest of your life.

The end result could be changes in all the areas we identified at the beginning of the chapter:

- A more balanced *perception of yourself*, able to see all sides of you, not simply focusing on the negative and screening out the positive.

- A more balanced *self-image* or *self-concept*, which appreciates and celebrates you in the round, warts and all, as you really are – in a word, *self-acceptance*.

- Increased *self-confidence* and *self-efficacy* – you have a less restricted view of your abilities, your qualities, assets, skills and strengths, and consequently your *self-respect* has grown.

- A new, enhanced sense of *self-worth* and *self-esteem*, a knowledge of your intrinsic value, the ease and confidence to enjoy your life to the full and to treat yourself with the same affectionate attentiveness you would give to another person you cared about.

The shape of the book

Chapter 2 explores in greater detail where low self-esteem comes from. It will allow you to consider what experiences in your life have contributed to how you see yourself, to understand how the view you have of yourself makes perfect sense, given what has happened to you.

Chapter 3 homes in on what keeps old negative perspectives going in the present day, and how out-of-date thinking habits and unhelpful patterns of behaviour work together in a vicious circle to block the development of healthy self-esteem.

Chapter 4 suggests a first way of breaking out of the circle, showing you how to become aware of, question and test negative predictions which make you anxious, restrict what you can do, and so contribute to low self-esteem.

Chapters 5 and 6 complement one another. Chapter 5 will teach you how to catch and answer self-critical thoughts, undermining your negative perspective on yourself. Chapter 6 offers ways of actively creating and strengthening a new, more kindly and accepting perspective.

Chapter 7 moves on to consider how to change your Rules for Living, the strategies you have adopted to compensate for low self-esteem.

Chapter 8 discusses ways of working directly on the negative beliefs about yourself which lie at the heart of low self-esteem.

Finally, Chapter 9 suggests ways of summarising and consolidating what you have learned, and how you might go about taking things further if you wish to do so.

You will notice that direct methods for changing your beliefs about yourself come last. This may seem odd. Surely shifting your negative beliefs about yourself should be the first thing you do? In fact, it is usually easiest to change long-standing beliefs if you start by considering how they operate in the present day. It is interesting and useful to understand how they developed, but what most needs to change is what keeps them in place. Changing a fundamental view of yourself (or indeed of anything else) may take weeks or months. So, by starting work at this broad, abstract level, you would be attempting the most difficult thing first. This could slow you down and might even be rather discouraging.

In contrast, changing how you think and act from moment to moment can have an immediate impact on how you feel about yourself. It may be possible to make radical changes within days. Working on your thoughts and feelings in everyday situations will help you to clarify the nature of your beliefs about yourself, and the impact they are having on your life. It will form a firm foundation for dealing with the bigger issues at a later stage. It may well also have an impact on your central negative beliefs about yourself, even before you begin to work on them directly. This is particularly likely to be the case if, as you work to change the specific thoughts and unhelpful behaviours that come up in particular situations, you keep asking yourself questions like:

- What are the implications of this for my beliefs about myself?
- How does this fit (or not fit) with my poor opinion of myself?
- What changes might follow from this in how I see myself as a person?

You may well find that small changes you make in your thinking and behaviour will gradually chip away at the boulder of your central negative beliefs about yourself. You may even find that by the time you reach Chapter 8 the boulder will be too small to need anything more than a few final blows. Even if you have not reduced it to this extent, the work that you have done in undermining negative thinking and focusing on new, kinder perspectives will stand you in good stead when you come to tackle the big, abstract issues. Chapter 8 quite explicitly draws on the work that has been undertaken earlier in the book. This means that you will get most benefit from it when you have absorbed the ideas and skills covered in earlier chapters.

Good luck. Enjoy your journey!

Chapter summary

1. *Your self-esteem reflects how you think about yourself, how you judge yourself, and your sense of your value or worth.*

2. *'Low self-esteem' means thinking badly of yourself, judging yourself unfavourably and feeling you have little or no worth or value.*

3. *In contrast, 'healthy self-esteem' means having a balanced view of yourself, one which recognises and accepts your human weaknesses, but also appreciates your strengths and good qualities.*

4. *Negative beliefs lie at the heart of low self-esteem. These shape your everyday thoughts, feelings and actions and can have a painful and disabling impact on many areas of your life.*

5. *The role of low self-esteem varies — it can be an aspect or a consequence of current problems, or it can be something that has made us vulnerable to a whole range of other difficulties. Either way, the extent to which it disrupts daily life varies from person to person.*

6. *This book offers a cognitive behavioural understanding of how your low self-esteem developed and what keeps it going. Understanding is the foundation for rethinking old, unhelpful negative beliefs and discovering a new, kinder and more accepting perspective.*

PART TWO

UNDERSTANDING LOW SELF-ESTEEM

2

How low self-esteem develops

Introduction

At the heart of low self-esteem lie negative beliefs about the self. These may seem like statements of fact, in the same way that your height and weight and where you live are facts. Unless you are lying (e.g. you would like people to think you live in a more desirable part of the city) or not in possession of the information you need to give an accurate account (e.g. you have only just moved to a new home and have trouble recalling the address), then statements of fact like these are indisputable – and, indeed, their truth can easily be checked and verified by you and other people.

The same is not true of the judgements we make about ourselves and the worth we place on ourselves as people. Your view of yourself – your self-esteem – is a learned opinion, not a fact. And opinions can be mistaken, biased and inaccurate – or indeed, just plain wrong. Your ideas about yourself have developed as a consequence of your experiences in life. If your experiences have largely been positive and affirming, then your view of yourself will probably also be positive and affirming. If, on the other hand, your experiences in life have largely been negative and undermining, then your view of yourself will also probably be negative and undermining.

This chapter will explore how experience leads to low self-esteem and reinforces it. The processes involved in the development of low self-esteem are illustrated in the flow chart on page 42 (the top half of the flow chart, in bold type, is our focus in this chapter). The flow chart shows how low self-esteem can be understood from a cognitive behavioural perspective. Keep it in mind as you read through the chapter. And, as you read, think about how the ideas outlined here might apply to you personally. What fits? What does not fit? What helps you to make sense of how you feel about yourself? Which of the stories told in the chapter ring bells for you? What are the experiences that have contributed to low self-esteem in your own case? What is your Bottom Line? What are your Rules for Living?

You may find it helpful to keep a sheet of paper or a notebook (or the electronic equivalent) beside you, and note down anything that occurs to you as you read – ideas, memories, hunches. The aim is to help you to understand how it is that *you* view yourself as you do, and to identify and map the experiences that have contributed to your low self-esteem. You will discover that the idea you have of yourself is an understandable reaction to what has happened to you – probably anyone who had your life experience would hold a similar view.

This understanding is the first step to change. You will begin to see how conclusions you reached about yourself (perhaps many years ago) have influenced how you have thought and felt and acted over time. The next chapter will help you to understand how the way you operate now keeps your self-esteem low — how well-established reaction patterns prevent you from changing your opinion of yourself.

Mapping the territory of low self-esteem in this way allows you to take a vital first step towards transformation. You will be able to use your map to investigate your reactions on a day-to-day basis. Once you understand how the problem works, you can watch it do what it does in real time, as it actually happens. You will begin to see how these compelling, painful ideas are in fact nothing more than unhelpful old habits of thought. You learn to say to yourself, 'Oh, there it is again', rather than accepting without question that the voice of low self-esteem tells the truth. And if you can say, 'There it is again', you are no longer quite so lost in your own painful thinking patterns. You have stepped back from them a little, and begun to discover that you need no longer engage with them, or get sucked into them, or believe what they say.

That is the main implication of this new understanding: opinions can be changed. The remaining chapters provide more detailed ideas about how to bring about change, how to undermine the old negative view of yourself and how to establish and strengthen a more positive, kindly, accepting alternative.

Figure 1. Low Self-esteem: A Map of the Territory

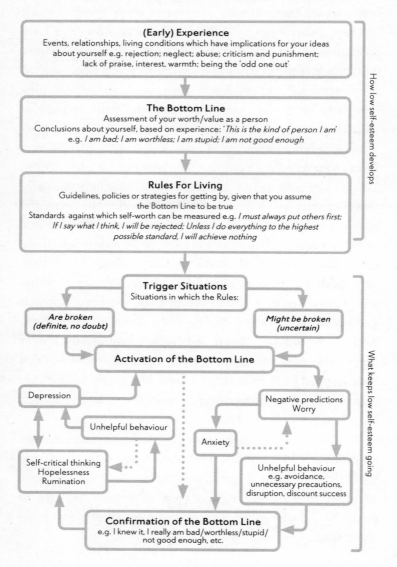

(Early) Experience
Events, relationships, living conditions which have implications for your ideas
about yourself e.g. rejection; neglect; abuse; criticism and punishment;
lack of praise, interest, warmth; being the 'odd one out'

The Bottom Line
Assessment of your worth/value as a person
Conclusions about yourself, based on experience: 'This is the kind of person I am'
e.g. I am bad; I am worthless; I am stupid; I am not good enough

Rules For Living
Guidelines, policies or strategies for getting by, given that you assume
the Bottom Line to be true
Standards against which self-worth can be measured e.g. I must always put others first;
If I say what I think, I will be rejected; Unless I do everything to the highest
possible standard, I will achieve nothing

How low self-esteem develops

Trigger Situations
Situations in which the Rules:

*Are broken
(definite, no doubt)*

*Might be broken
(uncertain)*

Activation of the Bottom Line

Depression

Negative predictions
Worry

Unhelpful behaviour

Anxiety

Self-critical thinking
Hopelessness
Rumination

Unhelpful behaviour
e.g. avoidance,
unnecessary precautions,
disruption, discount success

Confirmation of the Bottom Line
e.g. I knew it, I really am bad/worthless/stupid/
not good enough, etc.

What keeps low self-esteem going

How experience leads to low self-esteem

CBT is based on the idea that beliefs about ourselves (and indeed about other people and about life) are all learned. They have their roots in experience. Your beliefs about yourself can be seen as conclusions you have come to on the basis of what has happened to you. This means that, however unhelpful or outdated they may now be, they are nonetheless understandable – there was a time when they made perfect sense, given what was going on for you.

Learning comes from many sources – direct experience, observation, the media and social media, listening to what people around you say and watching what they do. Experiences that lead to negative beliefs about the self often (though not necessarily) occur early in life. What you saw and heard and experienced in childhood in your family of origin, in the society in which you lived, at school and among your peers will have influenced your thinking in ways which may have persisted to the present day. A range of different experiences may have contributed to thinking badly of yourself. Some of these are listed below. Each is then explored in more detail.

Systematic punishment, criticism, neglect or abuse

Your idea of yourself and sense of your own worth may be a result of how you were treated early in life. If children are treated badly, they often assume that this reflects something bad in themselves – they must somehow have deserved it. If you were frequently criticised or punished (especially if the criticism or punishment was excessive, unpredictable or made no sense to you), if you were neglected, abandoned or abused, these experiences will have left psychological scars. They will have influenced how you see yourself.

Briony, for example, was adopted by her father's brother and his wife after both her parents were killed in a car crash when she was seven. Her new step–parents already had two older daughters. Briony became the family scapegoat. Everything that went wrong was blamed on her. She could do nothing right. Briony was a loving little girl, who liked to please people. She tried desperately to be good, but nothing worked. Every day she faced new punishments. She was deprived of contact with friends, made to give up music – which she loved – and was forced to do more than her fair share of work around the house. Briony became more and more confused. She could not understand why everything she did was wrong.

One night, when she was eleven, Briony's stepfather came silently into her room in the middle of the night. He put his hand over her mouth and raped her. He told her that she was dirty and disgusting, that she had asked for it, and that if she told anyone what had happened, no one would believe her, because they all knew she was a filthy little liar. Afterwards, she crept around the house in terror. No one seemed to notice or care. Briony's opinion of herself crystallised at that point. She was bad. Other people could see it, and would treat her accordingly.

Figure 2. Experiences Contributing to Low Self-esteem

Early experiences:

- Systematic punishment, criticism, neglect or abuse

- Failing to meet parental standards or being unfavourably compared to others

- Failing to meet peer group standards

- Being on the receiving end of bullying or cyber bullying

- Being on the receiving end of other people's stress or distress

- Being part of a family or social group struggling with adversity (eg. financial hardship, illness, being a target for prejudice or hostility)

- Lacking what you needed in order to develop a secure sense of self-worth (eg. praise, affection, warmth, interest)

- Being the 'odd one out' at home

- Being the 'odd one out' at school

Later experiences:

- Workplace intimidation or bullying, abusive relationships, persisting stress or hardship, exposure to traumatic events

- Gradual changes in things that were important to your identity (eg. losing health, good looks, or earning capacity)

Failing to meet parental standards, being unfavourably compared to others

Briony's experiences were extreme. It is not necessary to be systematically abused in this way to develop a poor opinion of yourself. Much less extreme punishment and criticism will also leave a mark. If others treated you as though nothing you did was good enough, focused on your mistakes and weaknesses at the expense of your successes and strengths, teased or ridiculed you, put you down or made you feel small, all these experiences (even if much less intense) may have left you with the sense that there was something fundamentally wrong with you or that you were lacking in some way.

Rajiv's father worked in a bank. He had never realised his ambitions to rise to a manager's position, and put this down to the fact that his parents had failed to support him during his years at school. They had never seemed particularly interested in what he was doing, and it was easy to skip school and neglect his homework. He was determined not to make the same mistake with his own children. Every day, at the supper table, he would interrogate them about what they had learned. Everyone had to have an answer, and the answer had to be good enough.

Rajiv remembered dreading the sight of his father's car in the drive when he came home. It meant another grilling. He was sure his mind would go blank and he would be unable to think of anything to say. When this happened, his father's face would fall in disappointment. Rajiv could see that he was letting his father down. He felt he fully deserved the close questioning that followed. 'Why can't you be more like your cousin?,' his father would say. 'If you can't do better than this, you'll never get anywhere in life.' In his heart of hearts, Rajiv agreed. It was clear to him that he was not good enough: he would never make it.

Failing to meet peer group standards

Children and young people can be powerfully influenced, not only by their parents' explicit or implied standards, but also by the demands of others of the same age. Particularly during adolescence, when the sense of oneself as an independent person is coming into being, and when sexual identity is developing, the pressure to conform can be very strong. It may be reinforced by idealised images of celebrity constantly promoted by the popular press and social media. This is how you should look, what you should buy, what you should aspire to. Seeing yourself as failing to make the grade in relation to these standards can be a painful experience, with lasting implications for self-esteem.

Evie, for example, was an attractive, sturdy, energetic girl who enjoyed sport and loved dancing. She grew up at a time when the ideal body shape for women was to be tall and extremely slender. Although she was not at all overweight, Evie's natural body shape was not even close to this fashionable ideal. Her mother tried to boost her confidence by telling her that she was 'well built'. This clumsy attempt to help her to feel OK about herself backfired. 'Well built' was not what she was supposed to be. Evie was ignored by the popular girls at school. She knew about other girls who had been cyberbullied for their looks, and hardly dared to look at social media. Even her friends all bought into the airbrushed celebrity look. They were passionate about fashion and spent hours shopping and trying on clothes. Evie would join them but felt excruciatingly awkward and self-conscious. Every mirror showed to what extent her body failed to meet the ideal. Her broad shoulders and rounded hips were just completely wrong.

Evie decided to diet. In the first couple of weeks, she lost several pounds. Her friends thought she looked great. Evie was delighted. She continued to restrict her eating and to lose weight. But somehow, no matter how she tried, she could never be thin enough. And she was constantly hungry. In the end, she gave in and began to eat normally again, and indeed to overeat. This was the beginning of a lifelong pattern of alternating dieting and overeating. Evie was never happy with her physical self. As far as she was concerned, she was fat and ugly.

Being on the receiving end of bullying or cyberbullying

The sense that you do not measure up to the standards of your peers, that it is not OK to be you, is amplified if you have the misfortune to become a target for bullying, face-to-face or online. Evie's concerns about social media were not misplaced. Face-to-face bullying can do lasting damage to a person's self-esteem – and cyberbullying even more so. This can be true at any stage of life – even highly successful adults are sometimes targets for vicious, anonymous online abuse. But young people whose adult identities are still 'under construction', especially perhaps those who already doubt their worth and worry about what others think of them, may be especially vulnerable.

The internet and social media are a marvellous resource, for exploring and learning, for playing, for staying connected with those we care about when they are not with us, and for 'meeting' a huge diversity of people, worldwide. But their impact can be toxic in a number of different ways:

- They can generate a pressure to create (and constantly edit) a false, perfect online identity – a fictional cool, exciting life with numerous friends that will attract admiration and envy.
- They can encourage the idea that your worth is dependent on what other people think of you, rather than an inner capacity to accept and value yourself just as you are.
- Shame and humiliation are intensified when abusive messages are not confined to a small number of people you know (e.g. your schoolmates, people in your workplace), but shared with hundreds, perhaps thousands, of people – most of them complete strangers, people who have no idea who you are or your circumstances, yet feel free to judge you and write you off. This is perhaps even more the case when intensely personal and private information (including images) is spread abroad.

- Online bullying is invasive. On your phone or computer, you can be reached no matter where you are, at any hour of day or night. There is no escape.

- Anonymity allows viciousness full rein, often free of consequences. Research has shown that in cyberspace it is easier for people to lose their inhibitions, to speak out without any sense of empathy for their unfortunate victims, and to behave as they would not dream of doing face to face.

- You may be too hurt and ashamed to seek help and support, and this will make it even harder to realise that what is happening says more about the bully or abuser than it does about you.

The consequences of cyberbullying and abuse are already evident in the mental health of young people. In a survey of 5,000 teenagers from eleven different countries, one in five reported being targeted. Of these, nearly half were left feeling depressed and helpless. Even more distressingly, one in five felt suicidal. Tragically, a small number did in fact end their lives.

Being on the receiving end of other people's stress or distress

Even in fundamentally loving families, with parents who at heart truly appreciate and value their children, changes in circumstances can sometimes create pressure and distress which have a lasting impact on children. Parents who are stressed, unhappy or preoccupied may have little patience for normal naughtiness, or the natural lack of self-control and skill that are a part of early childhood.

Jack, for example, was an energetic, adventurous, curious little boy. As soon as he could walk, he had his fingers in everything. Whenever something caught his eye, he would run off to investigate it. He had very little fear and even as a toddler was climbing trees and plunging into deep water without a second thought. His mother used to say she needed eyes in the back of her head to keep track of him. Jack's parents were proud of his adventurousness and enquiring mind, and found him funny and endearing. When he was three, however, twin babies arrived. At the same time, Jack's father lost his job and had to take work at a much lower rate of pay. The family moved from their house with its little garden to a small apartment on the fourth floor of a large block. With two new babies, things were chaotic. Jack's father felt his job loss keenly, and became morose and irritable. His mother was constantly tired. In the confined space of the apartment, there was nowhere for Jack's energy to go, and his interest and curiosity only created mess.

He became a target for anger and frustration. Because he was only little, he did not understand why this change had happened. He tried hard to sit quietly and keep out of trouble, but again and again ended up being shouted at and sometimes smacked. It was no longer possible to be himself without being told he was a naughty, disobedient boy and uncontrollable. Even into adulthood, whenever he encountered disapproval or criticism, he still felt the old sense of rejection and despair – in short, all wrong.

Your family's place in society

It may be that your beliefs about yourself are not simply based on how you personally were treated. Sometimes, low self-esteem is more a product of the way a person and his or her family lived, or his or her identity as a member of a group. If, for example, your family was very poor, if your parents had serious difficulties that caused the neighbours to look down on them, or you were a member of a racial, cultural or religious group which was a focus for hostility and contempt, you may have been contaminated by these experiences with a lasting sense of inferiority to other people.

This was true for **Aaron**, whose story shows how a feisty, attractive child can come to believe he has nothing to contribute because his family group is rejected by the society in which he lives.

Aaron was the middle of seven children, in a family of travellers. He was brought up by his mother and his maternal grandmother and had no consistent father figure. Life was tough. There were constant financial strains, and little permanence of any kind. Aaron's grandmother, a striking woman with brightly bleached hair, coped by drinking. Aaron had clear memories of being rushed through the streets to school, his grandmother pushing two babies crammed into a buggy, the older children and another whining toddler trailing behind. Lack of money meant that all the children wore second-hand clothes, which were passed down from one to the next. Their sweatshirts were grubby, their shoes scuffed, their faces smudged, their hair standing on end. Every so often, the grandmother would stop and screech at the older children to hurry up.

What stuck in Aaron's mind were the faces of people coming in the opposite direction as they saw the family approaching. He would see their mouths twist, their frowns of disapproval, their avoidance of eye contact. He could hear their muttered comments to one another. The same happened when they reached the school. In the playground, other children and parents gave the family a wide berth.

Aaron's grandmother, too, was well aware of other people's stance. She was fiercely protective of the family, in her own way. She would begin shouting and swearing, calling names and screaming threats.

Throughout his schooldays, Aaron felt a deep sense of shame. He saw himself as a worthless outcast, whose only defence was attack. He was constantly fighting and scuffling, failed to engage in lessons, and as a consequence left with no qualifications, and became involved with other young men operating on the fringes of the law. The only time he felt good about himself was when he had successfully broken the rules – stolen without being caught or beaten someone up without reprisals.

Lacking what you needed in order to develop secure self-esteem

It is easy to see how painful experiences like those described above could contribute towards feeling bad, inadequate, inferior, weak or unlovable. Sometimes, however, the important experiences are less obvious. This may make how you feel about yourself a puzzle to you. Nothing so extreme happened in your childhood – how come you have so much trouble believing in your own worth?

It could be that the problem was not so much the *presence* of dramatically bad things, but rather a *lack* of the day-to-day good things that you needed in order to feel good about yourself. Perhaps, for example, you did not receive *enough* interest, *enough* praise, *enough* encouragement to express yourself, *enough* warmth and affection, *enough* comfort and reassurance when things went wrong, e*nough* loving care and attentiveness when you were ill or upset – in short, *enough* messages that you were loved, wanted and valued for being exactly who you were. Or perhaps your parents were very protective, sheltered you from challenges and upsets, and did everything for you. Even if they did so out of concern for your wellbeing, you may not have had the opportunities you needed to develop courage, resilience and the sense that you had what you needed to deal independently with life's ups and downs. Any of these experiences could have influenced your ideas about yourself.

Kate, for example, was brought up by elderly parents from a strict middle-class background. At heart, both were good people who tried their best to give their only daughter a good upbringing and a sound start in life. However, the values they had grown up with meant that both of them had difficulty in openly expressing affection. Their only means of showing how much they loved her was through caring for her practical needs. So, they were good at ensuring that

Kate did her homework, in seeing that she ate a balanced diet, that she was well dressed and had a good range of books and toys.

As she grew older, they made sure she went to a good school, took her to girl guides and swimming lessons, and paid for her to go on holiday with friends. But they almost never touched her – there were no cuddles, no kisses or caresses, no pet names. At first, Kate was hardly aware of this. But once she began to see how openly loving other families were, she began to experience a sad emptiness at home. She did her best to change things. She would take her father's hand as they walked along – and noticed how he would drop it as soon as he decently could. She would put her arms round her mother – and feel how she stiffened. She tried to talk about how she felt – and saw how awkward her parents looked, and how they swiftly changed the subject.

Kate concluded that their behaviour towards her must reflect something about her. Her parents did their duty by her, but no more. It must mean she was fundamentally unlovable.

Being the 'odd one out' at home

Another more subtle experience that can contribute to low self-esteem is the experience of being the 'odd one out'. I mean by this being someone who did not quite 'fit' in your family of origin. Perhaps you were an artistic child in an academic family, or an energetic, sporty child in a quiet family, or a child who loved reading and thinking in a family who were always on the go. Or perhaps you realised as you grew up that your sexual orientation might not be accepted or approved of by your more conventional parents and siblings. In each case, there was nothing particularly wrong with you, or with them, but for some reason you did not match the family template or fit the family norm. It could be that you were never subject to anything more than good-natured teasing or perhaps mild puzzlement. But sometimes people in this situation take away a sense that to be different from the norm means to be odd, unacceptable or inferior.

Lin was an exceptional artist. Both her parents, however, believed that to achieve academically was the most important thing in life. They were plainly delighted with her two older brothers, who did very well at school, moved on to do well at university, and became a doctor and a lawyer. Lin, however, was an average student. There was nothing particularly wrong with her schoolwork – she simply did not shine as her parents hoped she would.

Her real talent lay in her hands and eyes. She could draw and paint, and her collages were full of energy and colour. Lin's parents tried to appreciate her artistic gifts, but they saw art- and craftwork as essentially trivial – a waste of time. They never openly criticised her, but she could see how their faces lit up when they heard about her brothers' achievements and could not help but contrast this with their lack of enthusiasm when she brought her artwork home. They always seemed to have more important things to do than look carefully at what she had done ('Very nice, dear').

Lin's conclusion was that she was inferior to other, cleverer people. As an adult, she found it difficult to value or take pleasure in her gifts, tended to apologise for and downgrade her work as an artist, and fell silent in the company of anyone she saw as more intelligent or educated than herself, preoccupied with self-critical thoughts.

Being the 'odd one out' at school

In the same way that not fitting into one's family of origin can make it difficult to feel good about oneself, so being in some way different from others at school can lead people to see themselves as weird, alien or inferior. As we saw earlier in the case of Evie, school can be a demanding environment. We have to fit in and get along with all sorts of new people, whether we like them or not. We have to cope with tests and homework. We have to wear the right clothes, have the right haircut, listen to the right music – and these pressures are intensified by images of ideals of how to look and what life to aspire to in the popular press and on social media.

Children and young people who stand out in some way from the group can be cruelly teased, bullied and excluded, face to face or online. For many children, to be different is to be wrong. This can be true for differences in appearance (e.g. skin colour, wearing spectacles), differences in psychological make-up (e.g. shyness, sensitivity), differences in behaviour (e.g. having a different accent, being openly affectionate to parents beyond the age where this is considered cool) and differences in ability (e.g. being obviously intelligent and good at schoolwork, or being slow to learn). Being the odd one out in any of these areas can leave children feeling there must be something wrong with *them* – they just don't measure up.

Tom's early childhood was happy. But he began to experience difficulties as soon as he went to school, because of undiagnosed dyslexia. While all the other children in the class seemed to be racing ahead with their reading and writing, he lagged behind. He just could not get the hang of it. He was assigned a teacher to give him special help, and had to keep a special home reading record which was different from everyone else's.

Other children started to make fun of him and call him names. He compensated by becoming the class clown. He was the one who could always be relied on to get involved in silly pranks. The teachers too began to lose patience with him, and to label his difficulties laziness and attention-seeking. When his parents were summoned to the school yet again to discuss his behaviour, his comment to them was, 'What can you expect? I'm just stupid.'

Late onset

Although low self-esteem is often rooted in experiences a person has had in childhood or adolescence, it is important to realise this is not necessarily the case. Even very confident people, with strong favourable views of themselves, can have their self-esteem undermined by things that happen later in life, if these are sufficiently powerful and lasting in their effects. Examples include workplace intimidation or bullying, being trapped in an abusive marriage, being ground down by a long period of relentless stress or material hardship, exposure to traumatic events. Other less dramatic changes can also impact on self-esteem, if they involve the loss of things that have been an important part of a person's identity (e.g. deteriorating health, fitness, looks or capacity to earn, if these have been central to feeling good about yourself).

Mike's story illustrates how solid self-confidence can be undermined in this way. Mike was a fireman. As part of his job, he had attended many accidents and fires, and had been in a position on more than one occasion to save lives. He had a stable, happy childhood and felt loved and valued by both his parents. He saw himself as strong and competent, able to deal with anything life might throw at him. This was why he was able to succeed and remain outgoing and cheerful despite his tough, risky and demanding job. One day, as he was driving down a busy street, a woman stepped off the pavement immediately in front of him and was caught under the wheels of his car. By the time he was able to stop, she had been fatally injured. Mike always carried a first aid kit, and he got out of the car to see what he could do. After a while, however, during which other people had called an ambulance and gathered round to help, he began to feel increasingly sick and shocked and retreated to his car.

Like many people who have suffered or witnessed horrific accidents, Mike later began to suffer symptoms of post-traumatic stress. He kept replaying the accident in his mind. He found the victim was 'haunting' him – he didn't seem to be able to get her out of his mind, asleep or awake. He was tormented by guilt – he should have been able to stop the car, he should have stayed with the victim to the bitter end. He was constantly tense, irritable and miserable – not at all his usual self.

Mike's usual way of coping with difficulties was to tell himself that life goes on, that he must put it behind him and live in the present. So he tried not to think about what had happened, and to suppress his feelings. Unfortunately, this made it impossible for him to come to terms with what had happened. He began to feel that his personality had fundamentally changed, and for the worse. The fact that he had not been able to prevent the accident, that he had withdrawn to the car, and that he could not control his feelings and thoughts meant that far from being the strong, competent person he had believed himself to be, he was actually weak and inadequate – a pathetic wreck.

Experiences in later life that affect self-esteem do not have to be as sudden and dramatic as this. More gradual losses and changes too can have a substantial impact, if what is lost or changed is something on which a person has based their sense of worth. **Mary**, for example, was a thoughtful, sensitive person, very attuned to the needs of others and glad to help. She was always the one who took care of everybody else. She was praised as a child for being so thoughtful, and came to see it as the essence of who she was. In fact, she loved doing it, and her caring nature and kind deeds were deeply appreciated by everyone who knew her. But as she grew older, her health, her strength and her energy gradually declined. She became less and less able to care for her family, friends and neighbours in the practical ways she had done in the past. Rather than realising that, because of her kind heart, she still had much to offer in terms of attentive listening and loving support, Mary felt more and more downhearted. What use was she now? None whatsoever.

Bridging the past and the present: The Bottom Line

These stories all show how experience shapes self-esteem. As people grow up, they take with them the voices of people who were important to them. These need not be parents' voices. Other family members (grandparents, for example, or older siblings), teachers, child minders, friends and schoolmates – all can have a major impact on self-confidence and self-esteem. We may criticise ourselves in their exact sharp tones, call ourselves the same unkind names, and make the same comparisons with other people and with how we ought to be. That is, the beliefs we hold about ourselves in the present day often directly reflect the messages we received as children.

Along with this, we may re-experience emotions and body sensations, and see images in our mind's eye that were originally present at a much earlier stage. Lin, for example, when she submitted a painting for exhibition, would hear her mother's patient voice ('Well, I suppose if *you* like it, dear') and experience the same sinking feeling in her stomach that she experienced as a child. Jack, when in the best of spirits and full of energy and ideas, would suddenly catch a flash in his mind's eye of his father's distorted, shouting, angry face and feel instantly in the wrong, inappropriate and deflated. Flashbacks like these, fed by painful memories, can be so vivid, so real, that it is as if what we experienced so long ago is happening all over again, right here and now, proving that nothing has changed; what we have always thought of ourselves is indeed true.

Why is this? Life goes on, after all. We are no longer children. We have adult experience under our belt. So how come these events, so long ago, still influence how we operate in the present day?

The answer lies in the way that our experiences have created a foundation for general conclusions about ourselves, judgements about ourselves as people. We can call these conclusions the 'Bottom Line'. The Bottom Line is the view of yourself that lies at the heart of low self-esteem. The Bottom Line can often be summed up in a single sentence, beginning with the words, 'I am . . .' Look back over the stories you have read on the last few pages. Can you spot the Bottom Lines of the people described there?

Figure 3. The Bottom Line

Briony	I am bad
Rajiv	I am not good enough
Evie	I am fat and ugly
Jack	I am all wrong
Aaron	I am worthless
Kate	I am unlovable
Lin	I am not important I am inferior
Tom	I am stupid
Mike	I am strong and competent → I am pathetic
Mary	I am kind and caring → I am completely useless

The distressing ideas that these people have developed about themselves flow naturally from the experiences they have been exposed to. Their opinions of themselves make perfect sense, given what has happened to them. But, when you read their stories, did you agree with those opinions? Did *you* think that Briony was bad, that Rajiv was not good enough, Evie fat and ugly, Jack all wrong? In *your* opinion, was Aaron worthless, did he deserve to be an outcast? Did *you* agree that Kate was unlovable, Lin unimportant and inferior, Tom stupid, Mike pathetic and Mary completely useless?

As an outsider, you could no doubt see that Briony was not responsible for what was done to her, that Rajiv's father's own needs were clouding his judgement, that Evie's only shortcoming was not meeting a false ideal, that Jack's parents changed towards him because their difficult circumstances made them lose sight of his lovable qualities and made his strengths into sources of stress. It was probably clear to you that the disapproval Aaron attracted was no fault of his own, that the limitations of Kate's parents restricted how loving they could be with her, that Lin's parents' narrow standards prevented them from enjoying her gifts, that Tom's slowness to learn was nothing to do with stupidity. Similarly, you could probably see that Mike's distress was a normal and understandable reaction to a horrific event, and not a sign of weakness, and that Mary was still the same kind and caring person even if her health prevented her from expressing it as she used to.

Now think about your own view of yourself and the experiences that have fed into it, while you were growing up and perhaps also later in your life. What do you think your Bottom Line is? What do you say about yourself when you are being self-critical? What names do you call yourself when you are angry and frustrated? What were the words people in your life used to describe you when they were angry or disappointed in you? What messages about yourself did you pick up from your parents, other members of your family or your peers? If you could capture the essence of your doubts about yourself in a single sentence ('I am _____'), what would it be?

Remember, your Bottom Line will not have come from nowhere. You were not born thinking badly of yourself. This opinion is based on experience. What experiences exactly? What comes to mind when you ask yourself when you first felt as you now do about yourself? Was there a single event which crystallised your ideas for you? Do you have any specific memories? Or was there a sequence of events over time? Or perhaps a general climate, for example of coldness or disapproval? Make a note of your ideas. You will be able to use this information later on as a basis for changing your perspective on yourself.

Understanding the origins of low self-esteem is the first step towards change. You can probably see that the conclusions Briony and the others reached about themselves were based on misunderstandings about the meanings of their experiences – misunderstandings that make perfect sense, given that at the time they reached the conclusions they had no adult knowledge on which to base a broader, more realistic and compassionate view or were too distressed to think straight.

This is the key thing about the Bottom Line at the heart of low self-esteem. However powerful and convincing it may seem, however well rooted in experience, it is usually biased and inaccurate, because it is based on a child's-eye view. If your confidence in yourself has always been low, it is likely that when your Bottom Line was formed, you were too young and inexperienced to say 'hang on a minute', stand back, take a good look at it and question it; in short, to realise that it is an opinion, not a fact.

Think about your own Bottom Line. Is it possible that you have reached conclusions about yourself on the basis of similar misunderstandings? Blamed yourself for something that was not your fault? Taken responsibility for another person's behaviour? Seen specific problems as a sign that your worth as a person is low? Absorbed others' standards before you were experienced enough to know their limitations? In particular, if you imagine another person who had had your experiences, would you judge them as unkindly as you do yourself or would you come to different conclusions? How would you understand and explain what has happened to you, if it had happened to someone you respected and cared about?

You may find it hard at this stage to approach any sort of different view. Once the Bottom Line is in place, it becomes increasingly difficult to realise that in fact it is just an idea you picked up a long time ago, an old unhelpful habit of mind – something you could learn to detach yourself from, question and test. This is because it is maintained and, indeed, strengthened by systematic biases in thinking, which make it easy for you to notice and give weight to anything that is consistent with it, while encouraging you to screen out and discount anything that is not. It also leads to the development of Rules for Living: strategies for managing yourself, other people and the world, based on your assumption that the Bottom Line is true.

Biases in thinking

Two biases in thinking contribute to keeping your Bottom Line alive and active. These are:

1) a bias in how you perceive yourself (biased perception)

2) a bias in what you make of what you see (biased interpretation).

1. Biased perception

Low self-esteem sets you up to notice anything that is consistent with your negative ideas about yourself. You are swift to spot anything about yourself that you are unhappy about or do not like. This may mean aspects of your physical appearance (e.g. your eyes are too small), your character (e.g. you are not outgoing enough) or simply mistakes that you make ('Not again. How *could* I be so stupid?') or ways in which you fall short of some standard or ideal (e.g. not performing 110 per cent on an assignment). All your shortcomings, flaws and weaknesses jump out and hit you in the face.

In contrast, you automatically screen out anything that is *not* consistent with your prevailing view of yourself. It is difficult for you to get a clear view of your strengths, qualities, assets and skills. The end result is that your main focus as you move through life is on what you do wrong, not on what you do right.

2. Biased interpretation

Low self-esteem not only skews your perception of yourself, but also distorts the meanings you attach to what you see. If something does not go well, you are likely to use this as the basis for a global, overgeneralised judgement of yourself – typical, you always get it wrong, etc. So even quite trivial mistakes and failings may seem to you to reflect your worth as a person, and so have (in your eyes) major implications for the future. Neutral and even positive experiences may be distorted to fit the prevailing view of yourself. If, for example, someone compliments you on looking well, you may privately conclude that you must have been looking pretty bad up till now or discount the compliment altogether (the exception proves the rule, they were only being kind, etc.). Your thinking is consistently biased in favour of self-criticism, rather than encouragement, appreciation, acceptance or praise.

The end result

As you will see illustrated in Figure 4, these biases operate together to keep low self-esteem in place. Because your basic beliefs about yourself are negative, you anticipate that events will turn out badly (as we shall explore in further detail in Chapter 4). The anticipation makes you sensitive to any sign that things are indeed turning out as you predicted. In addition, no matter how things turn out, you are likely to put a negative spin on events. Consequently, your stored memories of what happened will also be biased in a negative direction. This will strengthen your negative beliefs about yourself, and make you more likely to predict the worst in future.

Figure 4. Low Self-esteem: Biases in Thinking

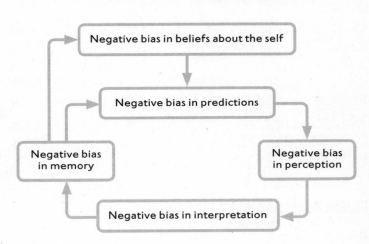

These consistent biases in thinking prevent you from realising that your beliefs about yourself are simply opinions – based on experience, true enough, and perhaps powerfully convincing – but opinions nonetheless. And opinions which are increasingly based on a biased perspective, and so further and further adrift from the real you. Christine Padesky, an American cognitive behavioural therapist, has suggested that holding negative beliefs of this kind is like having a prejudice against yourself. The key thing about prejudices is that they ignore anything that contradicts them, and rely entirely on evidence which seems to supports them. Prejudices can be powerful, out of all proportion to their real truth value. It's easy to see examples of such powerful beliefs all around us – prejudices against people of certain racial, cultural or religious groups, against those of particular age groups, gender or sexual orientation. Such strong opinions, with no real basis in evidence, can drive people to acts of rejection and cruelty, even to war.

So it is with low self-esteem. Biases in your thinking about yourself (prejudices against yourself) keep your negative views in place, make you anxious and unhappy, restrict your life and prevent you from searching out a kinder, more compassionate, more balanced, accepting and accurate view of the person you really are.

Rules for Living

Even if you believe yourself to be in some way incompetent or inadequate, unattractive or unlovable, or simply not good enough, you still have to function in the world. Rules for Living help you to do this. They allow you to feel reasonably comfortable with yourself, so long as you obey their terms. That is, they make it possible for people to operate more or less effectively in life, despite their belief in the Bottom Line.

Paradoxically, however, they also in fact help to keep the Bottom Line in place and so maintain low self-esteem. A look at the Rules for Living of the people described above may give you an idea of how they make sense in the context of the Bottom Line, and how they work in practice to protect self-esteem.

The Rules for Living each of these people developed (see pages 72–73) can be understood as an attempt to get by, an escape clause, based on the assumption that the Bottom Line is true. Rules tell you how you must act, who you must be, in order to feel OK about yourself. So long as you follow the Rules, all is well. But if you fall short, then up comes the Bottom Line. So obeying the Rules is not a matter of choice – it's something you have to do, no matter what.

In everyday situations, the Rules are reflected in specific policies or strategies. For example, Briony's rules about the dangers of exploitation and about hiding her true self led her to adopt the strategy of avoiding close relationships. She kept social contact to a minimum and, if forced to spend time with people, kept the conversation light and avoided questions about herself. She was always vigilant for any signs that people might push her into doing things she did not wish to do, and fiercely protective of her personal space.

And it is important to realise that, to some degree, such strategies work. For example, Rajiv's high standards and fear of failure and criticism motivated him to perform to a consistently high level, and allowed him to make a resounding success of his working life. But he paid a price for this. His Rules for Living created an increasing sense of strain, and made it impossible for him to relax and enjoy his achievements. In addition, his need to perform meant that work dominated his life, at the expense of personal relationships and leisure time.

Figure 5. Rules for Living

	Bottom Line	**Rules for Living**
Briony	I am bad	If I allow anyone close to me, they will hurt and exploit me
		I must never let anyone see my true self
Rajiv	I am not good enough	Unless I always get it right, I will never get anywhere in life
		If someone criticises me, it means I have failed
Evie	I am fat and ugly	My worth depends on how I look and what I weigh
Jack	I am unacceptable	I must always keep myself under tight control
Aaron	I am worthless	Survival depends on hitting back
		No matter what I do, no one will accept me
Kate	I am unlovable	Unless I do everything people expect of me, I will be rejected
		If I ask for what I need, I will be disappointed

Lin	I am unimportant I am inferior	If someone is not interested in me, it's because I am unworthy of interest Nothing I do is worthwhile unless it is recognised by others
Tom	I am stupid	Better not to try than to fail
Mike	I am strong and competent ↓ I am pathetic	I should be able to cope with anything life throws at me Letting my emotions get the better of me is a sign of weakness
Mary	I am kind and caring ↓ I am completely useless	Unless I am caring for others, I am completely useless

In Chapter 7, you will find more detail about Rules for Living, their impact on your thoughts and feelings and how you manage your life, and how to change them and liberate yourself from the demands they place upon you.

Chapter summary

1. *Your negative beliefs about yourself (your Bottom Line) are opinions, not facts.*

2. *They are conclusions about yourself based on experience (usually, but not necessarily, early experience). A broad range of experiences, including both the presence of negatives and the lack of positives, can contribute to them.*

3. *Once in place, the Bottom Line can be hard to change. This is because it is kept in place and strengthened by biases in thinking, which mean that experiences that are consistent with it are readily attended to and given weight, while experiences that contradict it are ignored or discounted.*

4. *The Bottom Line also leads to the development of Rules for Living, standards or guidelines which you must obey in order to feel comfortable with yourself. These are designed to help you to function in the world, given that you assume the Bottom Line is true. In fact, they serve to keep it in place and maintain low self-esteem.*

3

What keeps low self-esteem going

Introduction

Negative beliefs about yourself may have roots in the past, but their impact continues into the present day. Otherwise, you would not be reading this book! This chapter will help you to understand how everyday patterns of thinking and behaviour keep low self-esteem going and prevent you from relaxing into your experiences, accepting, valuing and appreciating yourself.

We shall be looking at the vicious circle that is triggered when you find yourself in a situation in which you might break your Rules for Living and so activate your Bottom Line. The circle is shown in the bottom half of the flow chart on page 42. This may look rather complicated, but don't worry. It is described in detail below, and this chapter will outline how it works in practice, showing step by step how anxious predictions and self-critical thinking affect how you feel and act in your daily life. The idea is to investigate how these ideas apply to *you*, to explore how they might fit *your* particular pattern of thoughts, feelings and behaviour. So, while you read the chapter, keep asking yourself: How does this fit? What are the situations that trigger anxious predictions in me? How do my predictions affect my emotions and my body state? What do I do (or not do) to stop them from coming true? What does confirmation of my beliefs about myself feel like? How do I know it is happening? What is the nature of my self-critical thoughts? What effect do they have on my feelings and what I do – and, most particularly, on my beliefs about myself?

You may find it helpful to draw up your own vicious circle as you go through the chapter, either on paper or electronically. Use the ideas described here as an opportunity to focus closely on your own experience, to reflect on yourself and to deepen your understanding of how low self-esteem influences you on a day-to-day basis.

Triggering the system: Breaking the Rules

In the last chapter, we introduced the idea that the Rules for Living that you have devised, and the day-to-day strategies in which they are reflected, can, in the short term, help to keep low self-esteem at bay. However, at the end of the day, they actually keep it going because they make demands which are impossible to meet – for example, perfection, universal love and approval, complete self-control or control over your world. This means that wellbeing is inevitably fragile.

Two kinds of situation activate your Bottom Line. The first kind is situations where you feel you *might* break your Rules – you are not sure, but it *could* happen. In this case, there is an element of uncertainty and an anxious sequence of reactions follows. The second kind is situations where you are absolutely certain that your Rules *have* been broken, there is no shadow of a doubt. In this case, what follows will have more of a low, depressed flavour. Let us consider each of these in turn.

Figure 6. The Vicious Circle That Keeps Low Self-esteem Going

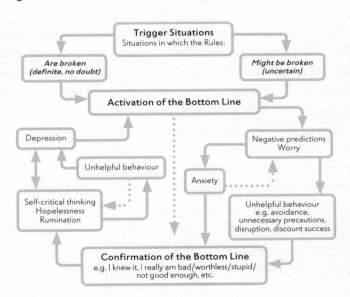

When your Rules might be broken: The anxious path

If you find yourself in a situation where you are in danger of breaking the Rules (e.g. operating below 100 per cent, being disliked or disapproved of, losing control of yourself or your world), the Bottom Line, which your Rules have protected you from, rears its ugly head. Self-doubt emerges from the shadows and begins to dominate the picture. You experience a sense of uncertainty – suddenly you feel insecure, anxious, and vulnerable. You begin to doubt yourself, and it feels as if your sense of your own worth is balanced on a knife-edge.

Trigger situations may be quite major events, e.g. a relationship beginning to break down, a job under threat, the possibility of serious illness or the approach of a child leaving home. But many of the situations which rouse self-doubt and uncertainty on a day-to-day basis are on a much smaller scale. Many are small ups and downs of a kind you may not even be fully aware of, or may brush aside with 'Don't be silly' or 'Come on, pull yourself together'. If you want to understand fully what keeps your poor opinion of yourself going, tuning into these small events is a vital step.

The exact nature of the situations that activate your Bottom Line will depend on the nature of the Bottom Line itself, and on the Rules you have adopted to cope with it. So, for example, if your Bottom Line concerns how acceptable you are to other people, and your Rules are designed to ensure that you will be accepted, then the situations which are likely to be problematic for you are those where you fear you might *not* be acceptable. If, on the other hand, your Bottom Line concerns achievement, success or competence, and your Rules focus on high standards and are designed to ensure that you always achieve these, then the situations in which you will feel threatened are those where you might fall below what you expect of yourself. And so on.

Think back to the people you met in the last chapter. As Figure 7 shows, the situations that triggered the Bottom Lines were a direct reflection of the nature of their beliefs about themselves, and of each person's Rules for Living:

Figure 7. Situations Triggering the Bottom Line

Briony	Situations where she felt her true (bad) self might be exposed, or had been exposed.
Rajiv	Fearing he might be unable to meet the high standards he had set himself, or actually failing to meet them. Encountering criticism.
Evie	Noticing that she had gained weight, or needing to buy clothes and fearing that she might attract stares or not fit into the size she thought she should be.
Jack	Feeling high levels of energy and emotion (including positive emotions); encountering any signs of disapproval.
Aaron	Situations where he felt vulnerable to attack or rejection, including close relationships.
Kate	Being unable to do what was expected of her; having to ask for help.
Lin	Exhibiting her work to public scrutiny.

Tom	Having to write, especially if he had to do it in front of other people; having to face any challenge (especially any intellectual challenge).
Mike	Noticing signs that he was still upset and not his normal self.
Mary	Situations where she was no longer able to care for others as she used to.

In the chapters to come, you will learn how to become more sensitive to the changes in mood that tell you that your Bottom Line is activated, and how to observe the thoughts, feelings and behaviour that follow. For now, just reflect for a moment. Think over the last week. Were there any moments when you felt anxious or ill at ease, uncomfortable with yourself, or doubtful about your ability to handle what was going on? Were there any times when you suspected that you were not coming over as you might wish, felt a bit useless or attracted worrying reactions from other people? Did you at any point feel that things were starting to get on top of you, or as if you were not operating at the level you expect of yourself?

Make a note of those situations. Do you notice any patterns? If so, what does this tell you about your own personal Rules for Living – what you require of yourself and what you need from other people, in order to feel good about yourself? What Rules were you in danger of breaking? What kind of ideas about yourself came into your mind in those situations? Were you aware of using any uncomplimentary words to describe yourself? What were they? They may reflect your central negative beliefs about yourself (your Bottom Line).

The response to threat: Anxious predictions

Once the Bottom Line is activated by the possibility that you *might* break your Rules for Living, a sense of uncertainty follows. This gives rise to specific negative predictions (fears about what might happen), whose content depends on the nature of your particular concerns. To illustrate this, let us take a situation which most people find somewhat intimidating, but which for a person with low self-esteem can be real torture. Suppose you had to stand up and give a talk to a group of people, i.e. to speak in front of an audience. Imagine having to do this in any situation with which you are familiar – work, perhaps, or your church, an evening class you have attended, the clinic you take your baby to, or your child's school assembly. What is your immediate reaction when you contemplate having to stand up and speak in public? What thoughts come to mind? 'I couldn't do it'? 'I'd make a total fool of myself'? 'No one would want to listen to me'? 'I'd get so anxious I would have to run out'?

Or perhaps an image of what might happen pops up in your mind's eye? Yourself red in the face and sweating and everyone staring, for example? The dreadful silence or muttering that will follow what you said? People gazing out of the window and looking bored and irritated? Or perhaps trying to look kindly on you, but in their heart of hearts thinking what a sad case you are? The thoughts and images that spring to mind when you contemplate giving a talk in public will probably be about what you fear might happen, and in particular what you imagine might go wrong. That is, they are your own personal view of the future – negative predictions which, as we shall see, have a powerful impact on your feelings and on your behaviour.

When a person with low self-esteem is confronted with speaking in public, what immediately springs to mind will be all the ways in which things could go wrong. He or she will probably assume that the worst will happen, and that there is little or nothing that can be done to prevent it. Just as the situations that activate the Bottom Line vary from person to person, depending on its focus of concern, so the exact nature of the negative predictions will vary from person to person, depending on what is most important to them. When Aaron imagined the public-speaking scenario, for example, he predicted that people would write him off before he even opened his mouth – no one would accept that someone like him could possibly have anything to say that was worth listening to. Kate's main concern, in contrast, was that she would fail to meet her audience's expectations. Lin's prediction was simply that people would be bored. Jack thought he would make a fool of himself by saying something inappropriate. People would consider he was showing off. Mike was concerned that he would be nervous – pathetic!

You can see here how each person's predictions stem from the beliefs they have about themselves, and from the Rules they have devised to compensate for those beliefs.

Once you know their stories, their fears make perfect sense. In Chapter 4 (pages 101–146), you will be learning how to tune in to your own anxious predictions by observing your reactions in situations which make you nervous and observing the thoughts, the words or images which come into your mind when you feel your self-esteem is at risk. This is important, because negative predictions, if unchallenged, have a powerful impact on your emotional state and on your behaviour, and so contribute to keeping low self-esteem going. And anxious predictions can easily shade into worry – over and over and over again running through all the dreadful things that might go wrong. Let's see how this works by continuing the public-speaking example.

The impact of negative predictions on your emotional state

Put yourself back into the public-speaking scenario. Imagine the worst that could happen. Make your anxious predictions as real as you can. What happens to your emotional state when you do this? What changes do you notice in how you feel?

Predicting that things will go wrong normally leads to anxiety. This may not be quite the word you would use – perhaps you feel scared, apprehensive, nervous, uptight, frightened, panicky or even terrified. You will recognise all these as varieties of fear. Now, notice what happens in your body when you are afraid. What changes do you observe? What happens to your heart rate? Your breathing? The level of tension in your muscles? Which muscles in particular have tightened up? Do you notice any sweating – perhaps on your forehead or the palms of your hands? Do you feel shaky? What about your digestive system? Do you notice any sensations in your stomach – fluttery feelings, perhaps, or a churning sensation?

All these are physical signs of anxiety, the body's wired-in response to threat.

To a person with low self-esteem, these normal reactions may seem to have a more sinister meaning. They could become a source of further anxious predictions (this mini-vicious circle is illustrated on the right-hand side of Figure 6, page 77). If your mouth had gone dry, for example, you might fear that you would be unable to speak. If your hands were feeling shaky, you might predict that your nervousness would be obvious to your audience, and that they would think you incompetent or weird. If, when you are anxious, your mind tends to go blank, you may worry that you will appear tongue-tied or incoherent, or as if you don't know what you are talking about. Such reactions to signs of anxiety naturally tend to intensify it and add to the stress of the situation.

The impact of anxious predictions on your behaviour

Anxious predictions can affect your behaviour in a number of unhelpful ways. To understand how this works, let's go back to the public-speaking scenario again.

Anxious predictions can lead to:

- Complete avoidance
- Unnecessary precautions
- Disrupted performance
- Discounting success

ANXIOUS PREDICTIONS CAN LEAD TO AVOIDANCE

If you believed your anxious predictions strongly enough, you might simply decide to avoid the situation altogether. You might phone the person who had asked you to speak and tell them you had flu and would not be able to make it. Or you might simply not turn up.

This would mean that you had no opportunity to discover whether or not your anxious predictions were in fact correct. It could be that things would actually have gone much better than you predicted – events are often much less intimidating in reality than they are in anticipation. Avoiding the situation stops you from finding this out for yourself. So avoidance, although it may help you feel better in the short term (what a relief – you got out of it), ultimately contributes to the continuation of low self-esteem.

What this means is that, in order to develop your confidence in yourself and your self-esteem, you will need to begin approaching situations that you have been avoiding. Otherwise, your life will continue to be restricted by your fears, and you will never gain the information you need to have a realistic, balanced, accepting perspective on yourself.

ANXIOUS PREDICTIONS CAN LEAD TO UNNECESSARY PRECAUTIONS

Rather than avoiding the situation altogether, you might decide to go and give your talk, but put in place a whole range of precautions designed to ensure that your worst fears do not come true and guarantee that you will obey your Rules and escape from the situation with your self-esteem intact. So, for example, Kate thought she would need to spend a great deal of time considering carefully what people might want to hear and trying to include all the possibilities in her talk. During the talk itself, she would be watching constantly for signs that people were not happy with what she was saying, and would smile a lot at her audience. Rajiv, on the other hand, believed that the crucial thing was to appear 100 per cent confident and competent, and thought he would rehearse and rehearse and rehearse what he was going to say in order to get the content and presentation style absolutely right in every detail. He would make sure his talk filled all the time available, so that there would be no time for questions that he might not be able to answer.

What would you do if you had to speak in public, in order to ensure that your worst fears were not realised?

The problem with self-protective manoeuvres like these is that however well things go you are left with the feeling that you had a 'near miss'. If you had *not* taken these precautions, then the worst would certainly have happened. In fact, precautions at best prevent you from learning and updating your view of yourself, and at worst can actually make the situation worse. For example, people who are socially anxious because they fear that others will think badly of them often use self-protective strategies which, unfortunately, backfire. For example, avoiding eye contact and speaking as little as possible so as to protect yourself from exposure can mistakenly come across as arrogance, standoffishness or a simple a lack of interest in the other person – who naturally then escapes as soon as possible and is probably not keen to meet you again.

Whatever precautions you adopt, you will have no opportunity to find out for yourself whether your fears were actually true or not, to discover whether your precautions were excessive, self-defeating or unnecessary. You will be left with the sense that your success (and so your feeling of self-worth) was entirely due to the precautions you took. In practice, this means that part of becoming more confident and content with yourself is to approach situations where you normally use precautions empty-handed, with none in place. This is the only way to discover that your precautions are unnecessary – that you can get what you want out of life without them.

ANXIOUS PREDICTIONS CAN DISRUPT PERFORMANCE

It is possible, on occasion, that your performance is quite genuinely disrupted by anxiety. You find yourself stammering, you can see your notes shaking in your hand or your mind genuinely does go blank. These things happen, even to accomplished speakers. Supposing something like this happened to you: what would your reaction be? What thoughts might come into your mind?

People with robust self-esteem might observe the signs of nervousness with interest or detachment rather than fear, and see them as an understandable reaction to being under pressure. They might believe that to be nervous under these circumstances is quite normal, and be pretty confident that their anxiety was much less evident to other people than it was to them, and that even if others noticed, they would not make much of it. In short, as far as confident people are concerned, being anxious does not matter particularly. Their personal Rules allow room for a less than perfect performance, and they would not see it as having any real significance for their worth.

If you have low self-esteem, however, then you are likely to see minor disruptions in your performance as evidence of your usual uselessness, incompetence or whatever. That is, they say something about you *as a person*. In effect, you are expecting yourself to be superhumanly perfect. Naturally enough, this also helps to keep low self-esteem going. Life being what it is, you will not always operate as you might wish to. An important part of overcoming low self-esteem is to begin to view your weaknesses and flaws – the things you do not do particularly well and the mistakes you make – as simply part of being a normal, imperfect human being, rather than a reason for condemning yourself as a total person.

ANXIOUS PREDICTIONS CAN LEAD TO SUCCESS BEING DISCOUNTED

Despite your anxieties, your presentation might in fact go just fine. You say what you wanted to say, people seem interested, your nervousness does not get out of hand, there are some interesting questions and you find good answers to them. Supposing this happened to you: what would your reaction be? Would you feel good about yourself – you did a good job, and you deserve a pat on the back? Or would you have a sneaking suspicion that you did it by the skin of your teeth: the audience were just being kind, you were lucky or the stars were on your side? But *next* time . . .

Even when things go well, low self-esteem can undercut your pleasure in what you achieve and make you likely to ignore, discount or disqualify anything that does not fit with your prevailing negative view of yourself. The 'prejudice' against yourself described in Chapter 2 (pages 39–74) prevents you from taking in and accepting evidence that contradicts it. So part of overcoming low self-esteem is to begin to notice and take pleasure in your achievements and in the good things in your life. Chapter 6 (pages 193–244) will focus in detail on how to go about this.

Confirmation of the Bottom Line

Whether you avoid challenging situations altogether, hedge them about with unnecessary precautions, condemn yourself as a person because they did not go well, or discount and deny how well they actually did go, the end result is a sense that your Bottom Line has indeed been confirmed. You were absolutely right – you *are* useless, inadequate, unlovable, or whatever it may be. You may actually say this to yourself in so many words – 'There you are, I always knew it, I am simply not good enough.' Or confirmation of the Bottom Line may take the form of an image in your mind's eye, or be reflected more in a feeling (sadness, despair) or a change in body state (a heaviness, a sinking in your stomach). Whatever the form confirmation takes, the essential message is that what you always knew about yourself has been proved true yet again – you are indeed the person you always thought you were. And the process may not stop there.

Self-critical thoughts

At this point on the vicious circle, the feel of things shifts from anxious to something heavier, gloomier (this is shown on the left-hand side of the vicious circle at the bottom of the flow chart).

Once you believe that your Bottom Line has been confirmed, you may well react with a spate of self-critical thoughts, often accompanied by a sense of hopelessness.

'Self-critical' here does not mean a calm observation that you have done something less well than you wanted or attracted a negative reaction from someone, followed by considering if there is anything constructive you might want to do to put things right. It means condemning yourself as a person. Self-critical thoughts may just flash briefly through your mind, before you turn your attention to something else. Or you may find yourself trapped in a spiralling sequence of attacks on yourself, perhaps in quite vicious terms. Just as anxious predictions can easily shade into worry, so self-critical thinking can easily shade into rumination – focusing relentlessly on how you fell short of your standards, over and over and over again judging yourself and writing yourself off. What else can you expect? You'll always be like this, and that's all there is to it.

Here is what Rajiv (the boy whose father quizzed him at the supper table) said to himself when his computer crashed and he lost an important document he was rushing to complete to deadline:

> Now look what you've done. You are a complete and total idiot. How could you be so stupid? You always mess things up – absolutely typical. You'll never amount to anything – you simply haven't got what it takes. Why are you always so useless? Why can't you get anything right? You're a waste of space. And look at the state of you now. Pull yourself together, man.

Something which was actually not at all his fault was taken by Rajiv to confirm his negative ideas about himself. Because he assumed the crash was all down to something integral to his personality, it also seemed to him to have major implications for his future – it would always be this way. You can probably imagine the mixture of anger, frustration and despair which Rajiv experienced at that point, and how difficult it was for him to set about putting the situation calmly to rights.

Self-critical thoughts, like anxious predictions, have a major impact on how we feel and how we deal with our lives. They contribute to keeping low self-esteem going.

Think about your own reactions when things go wrong or do not work out as you planned. What runs through your mind in these situations? Are you hard on yourself? Do you put yourself down and call yourself names, like Rajiv? Does your reaction make it easier or harder for you to put things right and learn from experience? Learning to detect and answer your self-critical thoughts, and to find a more realistic and compassionate perspective, is part of overcoming low self-esteem. Chapter 5 (pages 147–192) will focus in detail on how to do this.

The impact of self-critical thoughts on your emotional state and behaviour

When Rajiv's computer crashed, he completely abandoned his project. He felt really down, completely fed up with himself, and unable to see any possibility that things might change for the better. All this had an understandable (but unhelpful) effect on his behaviour too. He just wanted to shut himself away and lick his wounds. He simply couldn't make himself get started again. He had been due to go away at the weekend with some friends, but he couldn't face it. He told everyone he was ill, and sat around at home doing nothing in particular. He couldn't even be bothered to watch television. With nothing else to occupy his mind, he began to ruminate, to criticise himself even more for feeling so bad, and to brood about the future. He couldn't see any real prospect that things would change, so what was the point of carrying on?

As this example shows, self-critical thinking affects both mood and behaviour. Consider this for yourself. How do you feel when you are putting yourself down or being hard on yourself? What effect does it have on your motivation to problem-solve and tackle difficulties you may have in your life? What effect does it have on your willingness to engage in activities you normally enjoy, to face challenges, to spend time with people, and to look after yourself? And how do you then react when you notice what's going on? Are you compassionate and encouraging towards yourself or (like Rajiv) do you just become even more self-critical? This too will feed into low mood.

Being critical of yourself, especially if you believe that what you criticise in yourself is a permanent part of your make-up and cannot change, will pull you down into depression. This may be only a momentary sadness, swiftly banished by spending time with people you care about or by engaging in an absorbing activity. Or it may develop and snowball – as Rajiv's began to do – into a serious depression which may be quite hard to get out of. This is particularly likely if you have experienced serious depression in the past. If this is the case for you, you may need to address the depression in its own right before you begin to tackle low self-esteem (see Chapter 1, pages 15–17, for information on how to recognise depression that might need treatment).

Whether the dip in mood is short-lived or whether it is difficult to shift, depression closes the vicious circle. Depression in itself has a direct impact on thinking. Once you become depressed, whatever the reason for your dip in mood, the depression itself will make you more likely to indulge in self-critical thinking, and to view the future with gloom and pessimism. So depression feeds into more harsh and hopeless rumination, makes it difficult to take constructive action, keeps the Bottom Line activated, and sets you up to continue to predict the worst. Bingo! You have a self-maintaining process which is quite capable of continuing to cycle, if you do not interrupt it, for long periods of time.

When the Rules definitely *have* been broken: The depressed path

When people with low self-esteem believe they definitely *have* broken their Rules, rather than following the anxious path we have just mapped out, they immediately experience the sense that their Bottom Line has been confirmed – there is no doubt about it. They *did* fail, someone *did* disapprove of them, they *did* let their feelings get the better of them, or whatever. In this case they may take a short cut directly from activation to confirmation (this can happen in a fraction of a second), moving straight into self-criticism, hopelessness and depression without experiencing the uncertainty reflected in the anxious path. The long dotted line in the centre in the vicious circle in Figures 1 and 6 reflects this, forming a depressed vicious circle which can cycle on, trapping the person in low mood.

Mapping your own vicious circle

As you have made your way through this chapter, you have been asked from time to time to consider how you personally might react in particular situations, to reflect on your own anxious predictions and their impact on your emotional state and your behaviour, your own sense that your negative beliefs about yourself have been confirmed, your own typical self-critical thoughts, and the impact these have on how you feel and how easy it is to lead your life as you wish and to accept yourself just as you are. If you have not already done so, now is the time to bring your observations together by drawing up your own vicious circle. As an illustrative example, you will find the circle Rajiv drew up after his computer crashed in Figure 8, page 96.

Start by calling to mind a type of situation in which you reliably feel anxious and uncertain about yourself. Now look for a specific recent example. Make sure you select something that is still fresh in your mind, so that you will be able to recall accurately how you felt and thought in the situation. Follow the circle through, using the headings in the flow chart in Figure 6 on page 77, and noting your own personal experiences and reactions under each heading. If you wish, when you have completed one circle, start from a different anxiety-provoking situation and repeat the process.

Tracking more than one vicious circle will help you to begin to notice repeated patterns in your thoughts, your feelings and what you do. You could also look for an example of a time where the sense of confirmation of the Bottom Line occurred immediately because you were quite

Figure 8. The Vicious Circle That Keeps Low Self-esteem Going: Rajiv

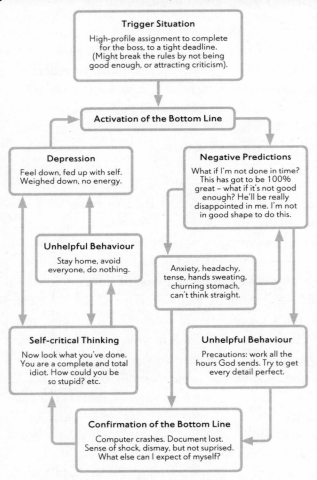

Trigger Situation

High-profile assignment to complete for the boss, to a tight deadline. (Might break the rules by not being good enough, or attracting criticism).

Activation of the Bottom Line

Depression

Feel down, fed up with self. Weighed down, no energy.

Negative Predictions

What if I'm not done in time? This has got to be 100% great – what if it's not good enough? He'll be really disappointed in me. I'm not in good shape to do this.

Unhelpful Behaviour

Stay home, avoid everyone, do nothing.

Anxiety, headachy, tense, hands sweating, churning stomach, can't think straight.

Self-critical Thinking

Now look what you've done. You are a complete and total idiot. How could you be so stupid? etc.

Unhelpful Behaviour

Precautions: work all the hours God sends. Try to get every detail perfect.

Confirmation of the Bottom Line

Computer crashes. Document lost. Sense of shock, dismay, but not suprised. What else can I expect of myself?

certain, beyond any shadow of doubt, that you *had* broken your Rule. This mapping process will allow you to become increasingly aware of how habits of anxious and self-critical thinking operate to keep low self-esteem going. Your task is to get curious about this sequence – to be a detective and ferret it all out. This is the first step to breaking the circle and moving on.

Breaking the circle

In the chapters that follow, you will discover ways of breaking the vicious circle that keeps low self-esteem going. You will learn how to become aware of your own anxious predictions as they arise, how to question them, and how to find out for yourself through direct experience whether they tell the truth. By approaching situations you normally avoid and dropping unnecessary precautions, you will discover what is really going on. You will learn how to notice self-critical thinking and rumination and nip them in the bud, short-circuiting the development of depression. You will learn how to counter the bias against yourself by focusing on your skills, qualities, assets and strengths, allowing yourself to take pleasure in the good things in your life, and beginning to treat yourself kindly and with respect. You will move on to changing the Rules that make you vulnerable to entering the vicious circle when you break their terms, and finally you will pull together all the changes you have made and tackle your Bottom Line. Your objectives throughout will be to overcome the low self-esteem that has been hampering your acceptance and appreciation of yourself, and sabotaging your ability to enjoy your life to the full. As you do so, a new, more kindly and helpful perspective will come into focus.

Chapter summary

1. *The Bottom Line at the heart of low self-esteem comes to life in situations where it appears your Rules for Living might be broken or have been broken. Once activated, it triggers the vicious circle which keeps low self-esteem going in the present day.*

2. *Uncertainty and self-doubt then lead to negative predictions – anticipating the worst and assuming there is little or nothing you can do to prevent it.*

3. *Negative predictions produce anxiety, with all its physical signs and symptoms (the body's normal response to threat).*

4. *They also affect behaviour, leading to complete avoidance, adopting unnecessary precautions, or genuine disruptions in performance. Even if things go well, the prejudice against yourself makes it difficult to recognise or accept this.*

5. *The end result is a sense that your Bottom Line has been confirmed.*

6. *Confirmation then triggers self-critical thinking, which may spiral into rumination.*

7. *Self-critical thinking in turn often leads to changes in behaviour and to a dip in mood, which may develop into a full-blown depression.*

8. *Low mood ensures the continued activation of the Bottom Line, thus completing the circle.*

PART THREE

OVERCOMING LOW SELF-ESTEEM

4

Checking out anxious predictions

Introduction

So far, we have focused on understanding how low self-esteem works — how it develops, and the thinking habits and unhelpful patterns of behaviour that keep it going (the vicious circle). Now you will be able to use this understanding as a basis for undermining old, negative beliefs about yourself and begin instead to cultivate healthy self-esteem.

The first step is to tackle the predictions that make you anxious in situations where you fear that your Rules for Living might be broken. This means exploring three core skills:

1. **Awareness** Closely observing and recording what is going on.
2. **Rethinking** Learning to step back and question unhelpful thoughts, instead of simply accepting them as an accurate reflection of the way things are.
3. **Experiments** Using direct experience as a way of testing out old perspectives and checking if new ones will genuinely be more helpful to you.

These core skills are central to your journey towards a new, kinder and more realistic sense of yourself. So this chapter lays a strong foundation on which you will be able to build as you move through the book. The same core skills will also come into play when it comes to dealing with self-critical thinking, learning to recognise your good qualities and to treat yourself with respect and consideration, developing less harshly demanding Rules for Living, and creating a new Bottom Line.

Anxious predictions and low self-esteem

In a manner of speaking, people are like scientists. We make predictions (e.g. 'If I press this switch, the light will come on', 'If I stand in the rain, I will get wet', 'If I have too much to drink, I will have a hangover') and we act on them. In fact, many of our predictions are so well rehearsed and so automatic that we do not even notice them or put them into words – we just act as if they were true. We use information from what happens to us, and from what we do, to confirm our predictions or to change them. Acting in line with predictions is generally a useful strategy – so long as we keep an open mind, are receptive to new information and remain willing to change our predictions in the light of experience and in response to variations in circumstances (e.g. sticking with the light-switch prediction could cause some frustration in the event of a power cut).

Low self-esteem makes it hard to make realistic predictions or to act on them with an open mind. When people with low self-esteem make predictions about themselves (e.g. 'I won't be able to cope', 'Everyone will think I'm an idiot', 'If I show my feelings, they will reject me'), they tend to treat them as facts, rather than as hunches which may or may not be correct. So it is difficult to stand back and look at the evidence objectively or to remain open to experiences that suggest the predictions do not fit the facts. What's the point? The result is a foregone conclusion.

In low self-esteem, anxious predictions arise in situations where the Bottom Line has been activated because there is a chance that personal Rules for Living *might* be broken. (If you are absolutely 100 per cent sure that your rule *has* been broken, then you will bypass anxiety and head straight for the sense that your Bottom Line has been confirmed, self-criticism and depression.) If it is not clear whether a rule will actually be broken or not and there is an element of uncertainty or doubt, the consequence will usually be anxiety.

Doubt and uncertainty lead a person to wonder what is going to happen next. Will I be able to cope? Will people like me? Will I make a hash of this? The answers to these questions – predictions about what is about to go wrong – spark anxiety, and lead to a whole range of strategies designed to prevent the worst from happening. Unfortunately, in the long run, these strategies rarely work. The end result, however things actually turn out, is a sense that the Bottom Line has been confirmed or, at best, that you have had a narrow escape.

In this chapter, you will learn how to break the vicious circle that keeps low self-esteem going and give yourself more freedom of movement by identifying your own anxious predictions (awareness), questioning their accuracy (rethinking), and checking them out for yourself by approaching situations you might normally avoid and dropping unnecessary precautions (experiments). This is the part of the vicious circle that we shall be addressing:

Figure 9. The Vicious Circle: The Role of Anxious Predictions in Keeping Low Self-esteem Going

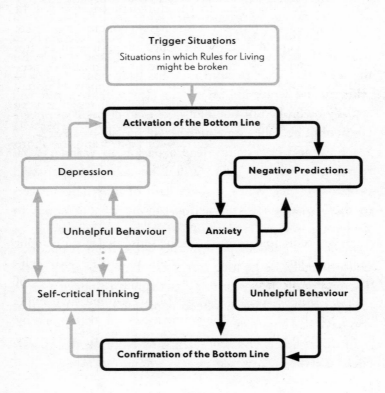

Situations that trigger anxiety

Think back to the people you met in Chapters 2 and 3. On page 79 was a list of the kind of situations that activated their Bottom Lines. You will see from these examples that, in each case, these are situations where self-protective rules might be broken. And, in each case, there is an element of uncertainty or doubt. Briony's true (bad) self *might* be exposed – but she is not sure. Rajiv *might* not be able to meet his high standards – but he is not certain. Evie *suspects* before she goes shopping that nothing she tries on will fit her or look good – but, as yet, she has no concrete evidence.

Doubt is central to the experience of anxiety. It creates a vacuum, which we fill with dreadful imaginings – predictions about what we most fear might happen. We may be aware with a part of our minds that the worst is very unlikely, or even that we would be able to deal with it, should it occur – but we are not convinced and the more anxious we feel, the less convinced we are.

How anxious thinking works

Anxious predictions result from the sense that we are about to break Rules which are important to our sense of self-esteem. Chapter 7 (pages 245–300) focuses on ways of changing and adapting Rules for Living in their own right. Here you begin to lay the foundations for that work by tackling the predictions that make you anxious in everyday situations.

Anxious predictions usually contain biases in thinking which feed into the sense of uncertainty and dread. These are:

Biases in anxious thinking:
- Overestimating the chances that something bad will happen
- Overestimating how bad it will be
- Underestimating your personal resources
- Underestimating resources outside yourself

Overestimating the chances that something bad will happen

When we find ourselves in situations where our ability to stick to our personal Rules is under threat, the likelihood that something will go wrong is much inflated in our minds. Let's take Kate as an example. You may remember that Kate's parents had difficulty in expressing their affection for her.

Her Bottom Line was that she was unlovable, and her Rules for Living were that if she failed to meet others' expectations she would be rejected, and that if she ever asked for her needs to be met she would be disappointed. Kate worked as a hairdresser. She and her workmates took it in turns to go out and buy the lunchtime sandwiches. One day, when it was her turn, her boss forgot to pay her back for his sandwich. Kate felt completely unable to ask for what she was owed. She was convinced that, if she did so, her boss would despise her and think she was mean. This was despite the fact that she knew from months of working for him that he was a kind, thoughtful man who was careful of his employees' welfare. She took no account of the evidence, which suggested that in fact he was likely to be embarrassed, apologise and immediately give her what she was entitled to.

Overestimating how bad it will be if something bad does happen

Anxious predictions assume that bad things will probably happen and that, when they do, they will be *very* bad. They rarely suppose that if something bad does happen, it will be a momentary hiccup, quickly over, after which life will go on. At the heart of anxious predictions is the notion that the worst possible thing is sure to happen and that, when it does, it will be a personal disaster.

So Kate, for example, when she looked ahead, could not see her boss being mildly inconvenienced by having to pay her back, and then quickly forgetting all about it. She assumed that asking for what was owed her would permanently change their relationship. He would never look at her in the same way again, and she would probably need to find another job – which would be difficult, because he would not want to give her a reference, and she might get a reputation as someone with a tendency to cause personality clashes and find it difficult to get work of any sort. Then she would not be able to live independently, but would have to go back to her parents and be stuck with taking whatever job she could find, no matter how menial and poorly paid. In her mind's eye, Kate could clearly see all this happening.

You can see here how what, to someone else who saw things differently, might seem no big deal (asking to be repaid for a single sandwich), for Kate leads into a whole saga unfolding, each step worse than the last. This kind of sequence (sometimes called 'catastrophising') is typical of anxious thinking.

Underestimating personal resources to deal with the worst, if it does happen

When people are anxious they are apt to think that if the worst should happen, there will be nothing they can do to prevent it or make it manageable. Kate assumed that, no matter what she did, her boss's reaction would be completely rejecting. It did not occur to her, for example, that she could stand up to him, if he did indeed respond as she predicted, and remind him assertively that she was entitled to get her money back. Nor did she take account of her professional skill and experience, which in fact made it very likely that she would find other employment quite easily.

Underestimating outside resources

In addition to underestimating their own personal resources, people making anxious predictions tend to underestimate things outside themselves that might improve the situation or even defuse it entirely. Kate, for example, forgot the support she would get from her workmates, friends and family if her boss reacted so unreasonably.

Taking precautions: Unnecessary self-protection

Put together, these biases in thinking constitute a perfect recipe for fear. They give you a strong sense that you are at risk – of failure, of rejection, of losing control, of making a fool of yourself. In short, of breaking your Rules. So, like any sensible person facing a threat, you take precautions to protect yourself, to stop the worst from happening. Your precautions may help you to feel better in the short term, but unfortunately, in the long run they stop you from discovering for real whether your anxious predictions have any true foundation and so prevent you from updating old, unhelpful ideas and keep low self-esteem going.

It will not be possible for you to discover whether or not your anxious predictions have any basis in reality, unless you drop the precautions you have been taking to ensure that they do not come true. Here is where experiments come in – learning through direct personal experience. This is the only way to discover if your ideas are correct – if you do not experiment with dropping your precautions, you will always have a sneaking feeling that you had a narrow escape, and will never really be certain whether your thinking was realistic or not.

An example may help to make this point. Imagine you go for a meal at the house of Vladimir, an old friend. As soon as you come in, you notice a powerful smell. Could it be something to do with the cooking? With your pre-dinner drinks, you have garlic croutons and a garlic dip. The first course is garlic soup, with garlic bread. This is followed by roast lamb with whole garlic cloves, and salad with a garlic dressing. For dessert, garlic ice cream (surprisingly interesting) and, to conclude, a creamy French cheese with herbs and – you've guessed it – garlic. As the evening progresses, you become gradually aware that the room is hung with wreaths and garlands of garlic. Finally, curiosity wins out over politeness.

'What's with all this garlic?' you ask.

'Ah!' replies Vladimir, 'I was hoping you wouldn't notice. I didn't want you worrying.'

'Worrying?'

'Well, yes. It's the vampires, you see. I didn't want you worrying about the vampires.'

'The vampires?'

'Yes. I think we've got enough garlic to keep them away, though,' says Vladimir reassuringly.

'But there aren't any vampires,' you protest.

'Exactly!' says Vladimir smugly.

The strategies people employ to prevent their worst fears from coming true are like Vladimir's garlic. It seems to him that the only reason the house is not overrun with vampires is that it is full of garlic. He could, of course, be right: though a review of available evidence might suggest that his fears are exaggerated. In order to discover that the danger is more apparent than real, he would have to abandon this self-protective strategy and get rid of all the garlic. Given the strength of his belief in vampires, this would probably be quite difficult for him to do. He might need to do it one step (or clove) at a time. Or, if he were able to consider the evidence coolly, he might be prepared to go the whole hog and rid the house of garlic entirely. Only then could he discover that his fears are unfounded – he is actually quite safe.

How to identify anxious predictions and spot unnecessary precautions (Core skill 1: Awareness)

You will only be able to change things for the better if you can see clearly what is going on in situations where you have the feeling that your Rules for Living might be broken. So, first of all, you need to become aware of exactly what you are predicting when you become anxious. Secondly, you need to notice the precautions you take to stop your predictions from coming true. This means learning how to tune in to anxiety or apprehension as soon as it happens, noticing what is running through your mind when the feeling starts and as it grows, and spotting what you do to protect yourself. This information will provide you with a sound basis for rethinking your predictions, and then checking out their accuracy by doing what you are afraid of without taking unnecessary precautions (experiments).

It is worth being structured and systematic as you begin to fine-tune your observational skills, and the best way to do this is to keep a record for a time. An advantage of this is that later you can look back over what happened and review it, see for yourself how things are progressing. In addition, seeing your anxious predictions written down, having them out in the open instead of trapped in your head, can help you to step back and rethink them. Once recorded, they may not feel quite so convincing.

You can keep your record on paper if you wish – some people find there is something down-to-earth about writing by hand, a feeling they are getting a grip on things. Or you can do it electronically if you prefer. On page 114, you will find a blank record sheet, which you can use to make your own record of anxious predictions and the steps you take to avert disaster (the 'Predictions and Precautions' worksheet; further blank copies are provided in the Appendix, and can also be downloaded from the 'Overcoming' website). Kate's dilemma is illustrated as an example on page 115, to give you a sense of what you are aiming at.

The main benefit of creating a structured record like this, rather than simply keeping a day-to-day diary of things that come up, is that it will encourage you to follow things through in a systematic way. The headings will remind you of what you should be looking out for, and later on what steps you need to take to change things for the better. In contrast, simply keeping a narrative diary may result in you getting lost in your fears, especially if your low self-esteem has been in place for some time and anxious predictions have become a habit that is hard to break. If you *do* prefer to use your own form of record, whether paper or electronic, you will probably still find it most helpful to shape your investigations by following the headings suggested here.

See if you can bring a spirit of interest and curiosity to your observations – just exactly how *does* this intriguing mind of yours work? Day by day, as you observe and record, you will begin to notice patterns emerging – old, habitual, automatic reactions coming up again and again. Once you can see them clearly, you are in a good position to start to do things differently.

If at all possible, make your record at the time you actually experience the anxiety. If this is not possible (e.g. you are with people who would find it odd if they saw you doing it), carefully observe your reactions, make a mental note of what happens, and complete your record as soon as you can. This is because it is often difficult to tune in to anxious predictions when you are not actually in the situation and feeling anxious. Even if you can work out what they are, with hindsight and from a safe distance they may seem ridiculous or exaggerated. So it will be difficult to accept how convincing they were at the time and how anxious you felt. These are the things you need to record:

Figure 10. Predictions and Precautions Worksheet

Date/Time	Situation What were you doing when you began to feel anxious?	Emotions and body sensations (e.g. anxious, panicky, tense, heart racing) Rate 0–100 for intensity	Anxious predictions What exactly was going through your mind when you began to feel anxious? (e.g. thoughts in words, images) Rate 0–100% for how strongly you believed each one	Precautions What did you do to stop your predictions coming true? (e.g. avoid the situation, safety-seeking behaviours)

Figure 11. Predictions and Precautions Worksheet – Kate

| Date/Time | Situation
What were you doing when you began to feel anxious? | Emotions and body sensations (e.g. anxious, panicky, tense, heart racing) Rate 0–100 for intensity | Anxious predictions
What exactly was going through your mind when you began to feel anxious? (e.g. thoughts in words, images) Rate 0–100% for how strongly you believed each one | Precautions
What did you do to stop your predictions coming true? (e.g. avoid the situation, safety-seeking behaviours) |
|---|---|---|---|---|
| 6th January 2pm | Bought sandwich for Ian for lunch. He forgot to pay me back. | Anxious 85
Embarrassed 80
Heart racing 90
Sweaty 70
Hot 90 | If I ask for the money, he will think I'm really mean 90%
It will spoil our relationship for ever 80%
I will have to find another job 70%
I won't be able to 70%
I'll be stuck at home with no money 70% | Avoid him altogether
If I did ask, I would:
Make myself small
Be very apologetic
Not look at him directly
Keep my voice down
Tell him it didn't really matter
Get it over and done with as fast as possible and then run away |

Date and time

When exactly did you begin to feel anxious? This information may help you to spot patterns from day to day. If, for example, your Rules relate to competence and achievement, then you may notice peaks in anxiety as you arrive at work. If, on the other hand, your doubts relate to how acceptable you are to others, then you may find your worst time is weekends, when you are expected to socialise.

The situation

What was going on when you started to feel anxious? What were you doing? Who were you with? What was happening? Was the situation that activated your Bottom Line something that happened (for example, having to answer a difficult question in front of colleagues or receiving a bill through the post)? Or was it something inside yourself (for example, remembering a time in the past when you felt embarrassed and humiliated, thinking about a task that you have been putting off, or noticing that your palms are sweating when you are about to shake hands)?

Your emotions

Anxiety is a signal telling you that you are making anxious predictions. What exactly was the emotion – or emotions – you experienced? Apprehension? Fear? Anxiety? Panic? Look out for other emotions, too – for example, feeling pressurised, worried, frustrated, irritable or impatient. Rate each emotion between 0 and 100, according to how strong it is. One hundred would mean it was as strong as it could possibly be, 50 would mean it was moderately strong, 5 would mean there was just a hint of emotion, and so on. You could be anywhere between 0 and 100. The idea of rating the intensity of your emotions, rather than just noting that they were present, is that when you come to work on changing your anxious predictions, you will be able to pick up small changes in your emotional state which you might otherwise miss.

Your body sensations

Anxiety normally goes along with a whole range of body sensations. These are vital clues to our emotional state, a valuable source of information about how we are feeling. So it is worth fine-tuning your awareness of them. What exactly is your personal bodily anxiety signature? What sensations do you experience, and where? Bodily anxiety signatures vary to some extent from person to person, and are reflected in the sayings we commonly use to describe anxiety – 'uptight', 'shaking like a leaf', 'on edge', 'white as a sheet', 'sick with fear', and so on. They include:

- Increases in muscle tension (for example, in your jaw, forehead, shoulders or hands). Many people have a 'favourite' tension site in the body. Where is yours?

- Changes in heart rate (for example, your heart speeds up, pounds heavily or seems to miss a beat).

- Changes in breathing (you may notice you are holding your breath, breathing faster, breathing unevenly, or feeling as if you cannot get enough air).

- Mental changes (for example, it may become hard to focus on what is going on, your mind may go blank or you may feel muddled and confused).

- Changes in the gastric system (for example, churning stomach, 'butterflies', needing to go to the toilet repeatedly).

- Other physical symptoms like shakiness, sweating, a sense of weakness, feeling dizzy or faint, numbness or tingling sensations, changes in vision (for example, blurring or tunnel vision).

All of these are in fact part of the body's normal built-in response to threat. To some extent, they are actually helpful. For performers such as musicians or athletes, for example, being keyed up gives an edge to their performance. The physical symptoms of anxiety are signs that glands near the kidneys are releasing adrenalin, a hormone that prepares the body for 'fight or flight' – that is, to confront and tackle the danger that threatens, or to run away from it. Your anxious predictions are telling your body that it needs to go on red alert. Once you become skilled at defusing the predictions, your body will stop responding in this way. In the meantime, it will be helpful to notice your own particular bodily reactions to anxiety, not least because (as we said in Chapter 3) these reactions can in themselves give rise to further anxious predictions – for example, 'Everyone will notice how nervous I am and think I'm weird', 'If this goes on, I'm going to crack up' or 'I can't possibly cope with this situation, feeling as I do'. Naturally enough, these extra predictions are likely to intensify the anxiety, forming a mini-vicious circle that contributes to keeping the problem going.

So make a note of your body sensations, and rate them between 0 and 100, according to how strong they are, just as you rated the intensity of your emotions. Watch out for any extra predictions you make, based on how you are feeling, and record them too.

Your anxious predictions

What was going through your mind just before you began to feel anxious? And as your anxiety built up? The thoughts you are looking for will be concerned with the future – with what is about to happen. They will, in effect, be your predictions about what is going to go wrong, or is already going wrong. Record them, word for word, just as they occur to you. Then rate each one between 0 and 100 per cent, according to how strongly you believe it. One hundred per cent means you are fully convinced, with no shadow of doubt; 50 means you are in two minds; 5 means you think there is a remote possibility; and so on. Again, you could be anywhere between 0 and 100 per cent. Generally speaking, you are likely to find that the more strongly you believe your predictions, the more anxious you feel. And, of course, the reverse is also true – the more anxious you feel, the more likely you are to be convinced by your predictions and to behave accordingly, taking steps to protect yourself that are in fact unnecessary and unhelpful.

You may find that your thoughts do not take the form of identifiable predictions. You may experience images in your mind's eye instead. These may be snapshots or freeze frames, or they may take the form of movies – a stream of events following on from one another – like Kate's fears about her boss's reaction and what would follow from that. These images and sequences may be very vivid and therefore highly convincing. They usually illustrate what a person fears may happen. That is, they are like a visual version of your worst fears – your anxious predictions. Describe them as clearly as you can, identify the predictions they contain, and rate how strongly you believe each one (0–100 per cent).

Alternatively, you may find that your thoughts do not take the form of explicit predictions, but rather of short exclamations like 'Oh my god!' or 'Here I go again!'. If this is the case, write the exclamation down, and then spend some time considering what it may mean. What is the prediction concealed in the exclamation? If you unpack the meaning behind the exclamation, the level of anxiety you are experiencing will make sense. Ask yourself: What might be about to happen? What is the worst that could happen? And then what? And then what? 'Here I go again' – well, where? Again, write the hidden predictions down, and rate how strongly you believe each one (0–100 per cent).

Finally, your prediction may be concealed in questions such as 'Will they like me?' or 'Supposing I can't cope?' or 'What if everything goes wrong?' Many anxious thoughts take the form of questions, which makes sense when we consider that they are a response to uncertainty or doubt. To find the hidden prediction, ask yourself: What is the answer to this question that would account for the anxiety I am experiencing? For example, if your question is, 'Will they like me?', then 'Yes, they will' is not likely to make you anxious. The hidden negative prediction is probably, 'They won't like me'. You could believe this fairly strongly, or hardly at all, or somewhere in the middle.

The precautions you take to prevent your predictions from becoming true

When one is faced with a genuine threat, it makes perfect sense to take steps to prevent it from causing harm. The threat you are facing may be more apparent than real once you stand back and take a good look at it, but for the moment it seems real enough. So what do you do to protect yourself from it? What steps do you take to ensure that it does not come to pass? Complete your record by writing down the precautions you take, in as much detail as you can.

In particular, look out for:

- Complete avoidance (for example, Kate said nothing to her boss for several days and avoided spending any time with him at all).
- Entering the situation you fear, but setting things up so as to protect yourself from what you think might happen.

In cognitive behavioural therapy, such precautions are called 'safety-seeking behaviours', precisely because they are things we feel we have to do in order to keep ourselves safe and protect ourselves from breaking our Rules. Complete avoidance is usually relatively easy to spot. Safety-seeking behaviours may be less obvious. In fact, sometimes they are quite subtle – you may not be fully aware of them at all. Here again, a spirit of interest and curiosity is a great help in encouraging close self-observation. If it is hard to identify your precautions, a really effective method of finding out more is to experiment with entering situations you fear and watching out for how you keep yourself safe in those situations. If this feels too difficult and threatening, you can start by practising it in your imagination. Kate, for example, did not at first feel ready to approach her boss at all. But, as she wrote on her record, she could imagine how she *would* operate if she was able to screw up her courage to the point of asking for her money back. She could see how she would make herself small, avoid eye contact, apologise profusely, tell him it wasn't really important, speak quietly and hesitantly, and rush to get it over with as quickly as possible. Before speaking at all, she would rehearse numerous times exactly what to say, trying to make sure she made her request in the most inoffensive way.

Keep your record for a few days or a week, making a note of as many examples as you can. By the end of that time, you should have a pretty good idea of the situations in which you feel anxious, the predictions that spark off your anxiety, and the precautions you take to prevent the worst from happening. This is your basis for beginning to question and rethink your anxious predictions, and to check them out by dropping unnecessary precautions and finding out for yourself whether or not what you fear is really likely to happen.

Tackling anxious predictions

Anxious predictions are unhelpful. Far from preparing you to deal effectively with daily life, they make you feel bad and lead you to waste energy on taking precautions that only serve to keep the vicious circle of low self-esteem going. So changing them has a number of benefits: it makes you feel better, gives you an improved chance of approaching life with confidence and enjoying your experiences, and encourages you to experiment with being your true self.

Here is where you get to practise the second and third of the core skills we identified in the introduction: rethinking (questioning your predictions so as to arrive at more realistic alternatives) and experiments (testing out new perspectives in practice by approaching – instead of avoiding – the situations you fear, and dropping your safety-seeking behaviours).

This may seem a rather daunting prospect. However, you will find that rethinking your predictions and discovering possible alternatives to them will help you to feel less fearful about going into what now seem like risky situations and dropping your self-protective strategies. This is important: if you do not change how you operate when you feel yourself to be under threat, you will never feel fully confident that the new perspectives you discover are genuinely reality-based, rather than rationalisations with no real truth. Let experience be your teacher.

Finding alternatives to anxious predictions (Core skill 2: Rethinking)

The best way to construct a more helpful and realistic perspective on situations that make you anxious is to learn to stand back and question your predictions, rather than accepting them as fact. You can use the questions listed on page 126, to help you to discover more helpful and realistic perspectives and to tackle the catastrophising biases that contribute to anxiety. Each time you find an answer or alternative to your anxious predictions, write it down and rate how strongly you believe it (0–100 per cent). You may well not believe your alternatives very strongly at first, but you should at least be prepared to accept that they might theoretically be true. Once you have a chance to test them out in practice, you will find your degree of belief will increase. You may find it helpful to record your alternatives on the worksheet you will find on page 127 ('Checking Out Anxious Predictions' worksheet; additional blank copies are provided in the Appendix and on the 'Overcoming' website). A completed record, using Kate as an example, is on pages 128–9. Again, a structured record (whether paper or electronic) may be more helpful than a simple diary because it will help you to follow things through in a systematic way rather than getting stuck in your fears.

**Figure 12. Key Questions to Help You Find
Alternatives to Anxious Predictions**

- What evidence supports what I am predicting?

- What is the evidence against what I am predicting?

- What alternative views are there? What evidence supports
  them?

- What is the worst that can happen?

- What is the best that can happen?

- Realistically, what is most likely to happen?

- If the worst happens, what can I do about it?

Key questions to help you find alternatives to anxious predictions

What evidence supports what I am predicting?

What is the basis for your fears? What makes you think the
worst will happen? Are there experiences in the past (maybe
even very early in your life) that have led you to expect
disaster in the present day? Or perhaps things you have been
told, or read about, or seen happen to other people? Or is
your main evidence simply your own feelings? Or the fact
that in this sort of situation, you always expect things to go
wrong – it's a habit?

Figure 13. Checking Out Anxious Predictions Worksheet

Date/ Time	Situation	Emotions and body sensations Rate intensity 0–100	Anxious predictions Rate 0–100% for how strongly you believed each one	Alternative perspectives Use the key questions to find other views of the situation Rate belief 0–100%	Experiment 1 What did you do instead of taking your usual precautions? 2 What were the results? 3 What did you learn?

Figure 14. Checking Out Anxious Predictions Worksheet – Example: Kate

Date/Time	Situation	Emotions and body sensations Rate intensity 0–100	Anxious predictions Rate 0–100% for how strongly you believed each one	Alternative perspectives Use the key questions to find other views of the situation Rate belief 0–100%	Experiment 1 What did you do instead of taking your usual precautions? 2 What were the results? 3 What did you learn?
20th February	Ask Ian for money	Anxious 95 Embarrassed 95 Heart pounding 95 Feeling hot and red 100	He will shout at me 90% He'll think I'm really mean 90% It will spoil our relationship 80% I will have to find another job 80% I won't be able to 70% I'll be stuck at home with no money 70%	There's no evidence he'll react like that. What I know of him shows he's not that kind of person 100% He might be a bit annoyed but it would pass and he'd be thinking of something else two minutes later 95%	1 Ask him. Don't apologise or say it doesn't matter. Be polite and pleasant, but firm. Take your time. 2 He gave it to me right away! He said he was sorry, he'd just forgotten. No sign afterwards that he thought anything of it.

		3 I learned that it's OK to take the risk of asking for what I want, and I CAN do it, and get results – even if it does make me nervous.
	Even if he did react like that, everyone would support me. I would if it was someone else. I would think they're entitled to what they were owed 100% Maybe I'm entitled too 30% Even if I did lose my job I'm a good enough hairdresser to find another 60% I could be making a mountain out of a molehill here 50%	

What is the evidence against what I am predicting?

Stand back and take a broader view. What are the actual facts of the current situation? Do they support what you think or do they contradict it? In particular, can you find any evidence which does *not* fit your predictions? Is there anything you have not been paying attention to which would suggest that your fears may be exaggerated? Are there any resources in yourself that you have been ignoring? Any indications from past or current experience that would suggest things may not go as badly as you fear?

The temptation with anxious predictions is to assume the worst – to jump to conclusions. Instead, stick to the facts.

What alternative views are there? What evidence supports them?

Are you falling into the trap of assuming that your view of things is the only one possible? There are always many ways of thinking about an experience. A mistake, for example, may seem to a person with low self-esteem to be a disaster or a sign of failure. But to another person, making mistakes might simply be part of being a normal imperfect human being, or a result of temporary conditions like tiredness or stress, a moment's inattention – in short, understandable, allowable, probably repairable, and not a reflection of fundamental identity or worth.

These more accepting attitudes mean that mistakes can even be seen as valuable opportunities to learn, grow and extend knowledge and skill.

Consider the situation you are facing at the moment. What would your view of it be, for example, if you were feeling less anxious and more confident? What might another person make of it? What would you say to a friend of yours who came to you with the same concern – would your predictions be different? Are you exaggerating the importance of the event? Assuming it will have lasting repercussions if things do not work out as you wish they would? What will your perspective be on this event after a week? A month? A year? Ten years? Will anyone even remember what happened? Will you? If so, will you still feel the same about it? Probably not.

Record the alternative perspectives you have found, and then make sure you review the evidence for and against them, just as you reviewed the evidence for and against your original predictions. An alternative which does not fit the facts will not be helpful to you, so make sure your alternatives have at least some basis in reality.

What is the worst that can happen?

This question is particularly useful in dealing with anxious predictions. Making your predicted 'worst' explicit allows you to get a clear take on it, and can be helpful in a number of ways. Once you have put the worst into words, or perhaps imagined it in vivid high-definition detail, you may immediately see that what you fear is so exaggerated as to be impossible. Kate, for example, had a flash in her mind's eye of her boss having a major tantrum in the middle of the salon and throwing her out. In reality, there was no way that he would behave so unprofessionally in front of all his clients and staff, however he felt about her request.

Look for whatever information you need to obtain a more realistic estimate of the true likelihood of what you fear occurring. Even if it is not impossible, it may be much less likely to happen than you predict. Additionally, there may be things you can do to reduce the likelihood of the worst happening, in just the same way that you might have the wiring checked and buy smoke alarms and a fire extinguisher when you move into a new house.

What is the best that can happen?

This is a counterbalance to the previous question. Try to think of an answer which is just as positive as your worst is negative. You may notice, incidentally, that you are less inclined to believe in the best than you were to believe in the worst. Why? Could it be that your thinking is biased in some way? Again, you could perhaps imagine the best outcome in vivid detail, just as you did the worst.

Kate called up an image of her boss congratulating her in front of everyone for standing up for herself, rushing out to buy her flowers and chocolates, and insisting on giving her an immediate pay rise and a promotion. Creating this unlikely vision made her smile, and helped her to see how exaggerated her fears were, too.

Realistically, what is most likely to happen?

Look at the best and worst you have identified. Realistically, what is most likely to happen is probably somewhere in between. See if you can work out what it might be.

If the worst happens, what can I do about it?

Once you have worked out what the worst is, you can plan how best to deal with it. And once you have worked out how to deal with the worst, anything else is a piece of cake. Remember, anxious predictions underestimate the resources likely to be available to you in difficult situations. Even if what you fear is quite likely, it is possible that you would in fact be better able to cope with it than you have automatically assumed, and that there would be resources available (including the good will, qualities and skills of other people) to help you to do so. Consider:

- What personal strengths and skills do you have that would help you to deal with the worst if it arose?
- What past experience do you have of successfully dealing with other, similar threats?
- What help, advice and support are available to you from other people?

- What information could you get that would help you to gain a full picture of what is going on and deal more effectively with the situation? Who could you ask? What other sources of information are open to you (e.g. the internet, social media, books, people you know)?
- What can you do to change the situation itself? If the situation that makes you anxious is genuinely unsatisfactory in some way, what changes do you need to make? Perhaps someone's unreasonable expectations of you need to change, or you need to begin doing more for yourself or organise extra help and support. You may well find that such changes are blocked by further negative predictions (e.g. 'But they'll be angry with me') or by self-critical thoughts (e.g. 'But I should be able to cope alone'). If so, make a note of these thoughts and search for alternatives to them. They, too, can be questioned and tested out. And even if the situation cannot be changed, or is not really the source of the problem, then you can still learn to change your thoughts and feelings about it – and, indeed, that is what you are doing right now.

Checking out anxious predictions in practice (Core skill 3: Experiments)

Discovering alternatives to anxious predictions is often helpful in itself. It is rather like clearing the undergrowth that is blocking a path you want to travel. Now the way is clear, and you can begin to see the way forward. You may well find that, as the view opens out and you start to see the bigger picture, so too you realise that your usual perspective is not the only one possible, and perhaps begin to feel less fearful of the catastrophic consequences of breaking your rules.

However, rethinking alone may not be enough to convince you that things are not as bad as they seem. You need to act differently, too, to learn how things really are through direct experience. Experimenting with new ways of doing things (for example, being more outgoing and assertive, taking the risk of being yourself with other people or accepting challenges and opportunities you would previously have avoided) allows you to build up a body of experience that contradicts your original predictions and supports new perspectives.

Experiments provide a direct test of what you think, a chance to fine-tune your answers in the real world, to break old habits of thinking and strengthen new ones. They give you an opportunity to find out for yourself whether the alternatives you have thought up are in line with the facts, and therefore helpful to you, or whether you need to think again. But this will only happen if you take the risk of entering situations you have been avoiding, and drop the precautions you have been taking to keep yourself safe.

Experiments will help you to weed out alternative ways of thinking that do not work for you, and to strengthen and cultivate those that do. Without them, your new ideas are largely theoretical. With them, you will know on a gut level what the reality is.

How to conduct experiments: Taking action to check out anxious predictions

You have learned to identify your anxious predictions, their impact on your feelings and body state, and the precautions you take to ensure that they do not come true. You have moved on to begin to rethink your predictions, examining the evidence and searching for alternative perspectives that may be more realistic and helpful. You can use these skills as a basis for setting up experiments which will allow you to check out for yourself whether your predictions are accurate. You can do this intentionally (for example, planning and carrying out one experiment every day), and you can also use situations that arise without you planning them (e.g. an unexpected phone call or an invitation) to practise acting differently and observing the outcome, using the final column of the record on page 127.

Designing, carrying out and learning from an experiment involves six key steps. These are:

Six key steps to successful experiments:
1. State your predictions clearly

2. What will you do instead of taking precautions?
3. Carry out your experiment
4. What was the outcome?
5. What have you learned? What next?
6. Give yourself credit for what you have done

1. State your predictions clearly

Make sure that what you fear might happen is very clearly and explicitly stated (you have already learned to tune in to anxious predictions). Experiments are most useful when they are designed to test out specific troublesome predictions. Vague predictions produce vague results – it is difficult to be sure whether they have come true or not. So, as you learned earlier in the chapter, write down exactly what you think will happen, including if relevant how you think you and other people will react, and rate each prediction according to how strongly you believe it (0–100 per cent). For example, if you are predicting that you will feel bad, rate in advance how bad you think you will feel (0–100), and in what way. Many people find that, to their surprise, they do indeed feel anxious (for example), but not as much as they expected, especially once they get over the initial hurdle of entering the feared situation. Your advance rating will give you a chance to find out if this is true for you.

Similarly, your predictions may involve others' reactions. Perhaps you think that if you behave in a given way, people will lose interest in you or disapprove of you. If so, work out how you would know this was happening. What would they say or do that would be a signal that they were indeed losing interest or disapproving? Include small signs like changes of facial expression, and shifts in direction of gaze. Once you have defined how you would know that what you fear is happening, you will know exactly what to look for when you go into the situation.

2. What will you do instead of taking precautions to ensure that the predictions do not come true?

Again, you will be aware from your record-keeping what precautions you normally take to keep yourself safe. If you continue to do so, you will not be able to find out if your predictions are true or not. Even if your experiment seems to turn out well, you will be left with the sense that you have had a 'near miss'. So be as clear as you can here. Think of all the things you might be tempted to do to protect yourself, no matter how small. Work out in advance what you will do instead ('I will …', not 'I will not …'). For example, if your normal pattern when you talk to someone is to avoid eye contact and say as little as possible about yourself, in case people discover how boring you are, your new pattern might be to look at people (how else, apart from anything, will you have the remotest idea what they think?) and talk as much about yourself as they do about themselves. If your normal pattern at work is to have an answer to every question and never admit to ignorance, in case people think you are not up to the job, you could practise sometimes saying 'I don't know' and 'I have no opinion on that'. If your normal pattern is to hide your feelings, because to show them at all could lead you to lose control, you might experiment with being a little more open with someone you trust about something that has annoyed or upset you, or with showing affection more openly than you normally would.

3. Carry out your experiment

What exactly do you plan to do to test your predictions? Where will you do it, and when? If it involves others, who would be the best person with whom to act differently to start with? And what exactly will you do differently – are you planning to approach something you have always avoided? Or is it more a case of dropping precautions you have always taken to protect yourself? Whatever you decide on, make sure that you are closely observing what happens as the experiment proceeds – the thoughts running through your mind (especially noticing if anxious biases in thinking are operating), the emotions you experience, what is happening in your body, what you do (including being alert for sneaky safety-seeking behaviours), and what follows from that. It would also be helpful to be clear in advance about what outcome would support your anxious predictions, and what outcome would contradict them – that is, exactly how you will know if they were correct or not.

The idea is to find a situation which takes you out of your comfort zone, but not something that demands too much of you. If you aim too high, anxiety may get in the way of new learning and you may end up disappointed and demoralised. If you aim too low, nothing will change. So don't try to run before you can walk – go at the pace that best allows you to learn and grow. Your experiments need to be challenging, but also manageable.

When you are clear about your plans, and have perhaps rehearsed in imagination what you will do, it's time to do the experiment for real, closely observing what happens.

4. What was the outcome of your experiment?

Whatever the nature of your experiment, it will be crucial to observe the consequences of acting differently so that, if your worst fears do turn out to be incorrect, you will be in a position to come up with more accurate predictions in similar situations in the future. To make sure you always make the most of any experiment you carry out, always review your results afterwards. What did you discover? What impact did acting differently have on how you felt? To what extent was what happened consistent with your original predictions, and with the alternatives you found? What implications does what actually happened have for your negative view of yourself? And your Rules for Living? Does it fit? Or does it suggest that you could afford to think more kindly of yourself?

In terms of outcome, there are two broad possibilities. Both are useful to you as sources of information about what is keeping your low self-esteem going. On the one hand, experience may show that your anxious predictions were *not* correct, and that the alternatives you found were indeed more realistic and helpful. So much the better. On the other hand, sometimes experience shows anxious predictions to be absolutely spot on. If so, do not despair. This is invaluable information. How did it come about? Was it in fact anything to do with you or something else about the situation? What other explanations might there be for what went wrong, besides you? If you did contribute in some way to what happened, how so? Was there some information you didn't have or some skill you need to practise? See if you can work out how to handle the situation differently in future, so as to bring about a different result. Especially important: are you sure you dropped *all* your safety-seeking behaviours?

Safety-seeking behaviours can be very sneaky, so be alert for signs they might still be hanging around, especially that 'Phew, just made it!' feeling. Be honest! Look back over what happened and scrutinise yourself carefully. If some precautions were still in place, what do you think might have happened if you *had* dropped them (anxious predictions)? How could you check this out? Exactly what changes do you still need to make to your behaviour? How will you ensure that you drop your safety-seeking behaviours completely, next time?

5. What have you learned?

What does the outcome of your experiment mean? What does it tell you about yourself, other people and how the world works? Does it support your Bottom Line and your

Rules or does it in fact suggest they may not be entirely accurate or helpful?

And what are the implications for where to go next? Given what has happened, what predictions would make better sense next time you tackle this type of situation? How could you use what happened in this *specific* situation as a basis for more *general* strategies that will help you to deal even more effectively with similar situations in future?

It is rare for a single experiment to completely wipe out an anxious way of thinking. More usually, over time, experiments gradually open up new perspectives. So when you have carefully thought through what happened, work out what experiments you need to carry out next, and plan them using the exact same steps. How could you build on your experiment, apply what you learned in other situations? What further action do you need to take? Should you repeat the same experiment to build your confidence in the results? Or should you move on to try similar changes in a new and perhaps more challenging situation? What's your next step?

Planning ahead like this means that each experiment does the groundwork for the next. Each discovery, rather than being a one-off, becomes a step on your road to real change.

6. Give yourself credit for what you have done

Whatever the outcome of your experiment, congratulate yourself on the courage and determination it took to do what you did. Giving yourself credit for facing challenges and things that involve an effort is part of learning to accept and value yourself – part of enhancing healthy self-esteem and discovering the freedom to be confidently yourself.

An example: Kate goes shopping

Kate needed to buy a new washing machine. She had successfully experimented with asking her boss for the money he owed her, and discovered that her predictions were not accurate. But she was still doubtful about her ability to ask effectively for what she needed, and her usual shopping strategy was to avoid the whole issue by using the internet. She predicted that if she went into a real store and took the time to enquire fully about the options available, and if she did not immediately understand the technological detail, the sales assistant would be impatient and would not respect her. She would know this because the assistant would use a snappy tone of voice, leave her for another customer, and make faces at other assistants. She would have to pretend to understand, only look at one or two models, and be effusively apologetic about taking the assistant's time.

Kate decided instead to ask as many questions as she needed in order to be clear about what her options were, to look at models right across the price range, and to be pleasant and friendly but not apologetic at all. After rethinking her prediction in advance, she came to the conclusion that although the reaction she feared might happen, it was unlikely, and might say more about the assistant than about her. This gave her the courage to have a go.

To her dismay, in the first store she tried, the assistant

behaved almost exactly as she had predicted. He was dismissive, kept turning to talk to other people, and did not seem to care whether she bought a machine or not. Fortunately, she had an opportunity that evening to talk over what had happened with a friend. The friend said that she had had much the same experience in the same store, and recommended trying another with a better record of customer service. This allowed Kate to understand what had happened in a new way, rather than simply assuming that her original predictions must be correct. It restored her morale enough to have another go.

She discovered that it was possible to follow through her new, more assertive strategy without penalty. She asked lots of questions, asked the assistant to repeat himself a number of times, looked at a whole range of models, and in the end did not buy anything. The assistant treated her with courtesy, invited her to telephone if she had any further queries, and gave her his card. Further experiments on the same lines in other stores confirmed this new experience. Kate's conclusion was: 'I am entitled to take as long as I want to make a decision to spend my money. Asking questions and showing ignorance is OK – how else am I to find out what I need to know? If people are rude, that's their problem – it doesn't say anything about me.'

Naturally, she could still shop on the internet if she chose – but it was a choice, not something she was forced to do out of fear. She had taken an important step towards freeing herself from her old anxieties, and by doing so had opened up a wealth of new opportunities.

Chapter Summary

1. *In this chapter, we introduced the three core skills you will be using to tackle low self-esteem: awareness, rethinking and experiments. Here we focused on these in relation to anxious predictions.*

2. *In situations where your Rules for Living might be broken, your Bottom Line is activated and triggers predictions about what could go wrong.*

3. *These are coloured by biases in thinking: overestimating the chances that something will go wrong; overestimating how bad it will be if it does go wrong; and underestimating your personal resources and the resources outside yourself which could help to make the situation manageable.*

4. *To prevent predictions from coming true, people take precautions. In fact, these are unnecessary and indeed they make it impossible to discover if your predictions are correct or not.*

5. *In order to tackle anxious predictions, you need first to learn to spot them as they occur, to observe their impact on emotion and on body state, and to identify the unnecessary precautions they lead to (awareness).*

6. *The next step is to open up the way forward by questioning the predictions, examining the evidence that supports and contradicts them, and searching for alternative, more realistic perspectives (rethinking).*

7. *The most powerful way to build confidence is to do things differently and discover you can. So the final step is to discover through direct personal experience how accurate your predictions and your new alternatives are. You do this by setting up experiments — facing situations you would normally avoid, and taking the risk of dropping unnecessary precautions.*

5

Questioning self-critical thoughts

Introduction

In low self-esteem, self-critical thinking follows the sense that negative beliefs about yourself (your Bottom Line) have been confirmed by experience. It feeds into low self-esteem because it triggers feelings like guilt, shame and depression, and so keeps the Bottom Line active. In this chapter you will explore the impact of self-critical thinking on your feelings and how you lead your life, investigate why self-criticism does more harm than good, and learn how to catch yourself thinking self-critical thoughts, to question them, and (with the help of record sheets and a list of helpful questions) to seek a more compassionate and balanced view.

The impact of self-criticism

People with low self-esteem are hard on themselves. For them, self-criticism may be more or less a way of life. They call themselves names, tell themselves they should do better and put themselves down whenever things go wrong. They are on the lookout for every little weakness and mistake. These are not a part of normal frailty or natural human error – they are evidence of inadequacy or failure, a sign that they are simply not good enough. People with low self-esteem criticise themselves for all the things they should be doing and aren't – and for all the things they should not be doing and are. They may even criticise themselves for being so critical.

People with low self-esteem notice some difficulty, or something wrong about themselves, and on that basis make judgements about themselves as whole people ('stupid', 'incompetent', 'unattractive', 'rotten mother', etc.). These judgements completely ignore the other side of the picture, aspects of themselves which are not consistent with the judgement. The end result is a biased point of view, rather than a balanced perspective. And the bias expresses itself in self-critical thoughts.

Self-critical thoughts result in painful feelings (sadness, disappointment, anger, guilt), and keep low self-esteem going. Take Mike, for example, the man who accidentally knocked down and killed a woman who stepped off the pavement in front of his car (page 59). At one point, after several months of being troubled by what happened, Mike felt considerably better for a few days. The accident seemed to be playing on his mind rather less, and he had been feeling more relaxed, more on top of things and like his normal self.

Then, one day, his daughter was very late home from school. Mike was terrified. He was certain something terrible had happened to her. In fact, he had forgotten that she was going to a friend's house. When she came in, he went ballistic. Afterwards, he felt thoroughly ashamed of himself. What a way to behave! 'This proves it,' he thought. 'I am really losing it. I'm a total mess.' He felt more and more upset. 'Pull yourself together,' he said to himself. 'This is pathetic. Get a grip.' The episode confirmed his worst suspicions about himself: he *was* a pathetic wreck; there was no doubt about it. And there seemed little chance of change. Mike was just about ready to give up.

You can get some sense of the emotional impact of self-critical thoughts by carrying out the following experiment. Read the list of words printed below, carefully, allowing each to sink in. Imagine they apply to you, and notice their impact on your confidence, and on your mood:

Useless	Unattractive	Incompetent
Weak	Unlikeable	Ugly
Pathetic	Unwanted	Stupid
Worthless	Inferior	Inadequate

Self-critical thinking undermines any positive sense of yourself and pulls you down. Some of the words on the list may even be familiar to you, from your own self-critical thoughts. If so, highlight them. What other words do you use to describe yourself when you are being self-critical? Make a note of them. These are words you will need to watch out for.

In this chapter you will have an opportunity to use the core skills you have already practised in relation to anxious predictions to help you move towards a more balanced and accepting view of yourself. This is the part of the vicious circle we shall be working on:

Figure 15. The Vicious Circle: The Role of Self-criticism in Keeping Low Self-esteem Going

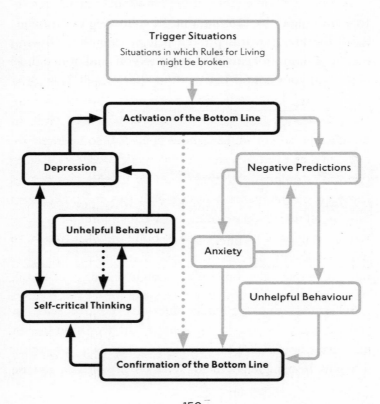

In the next chapter, we shall address the other side of the equation: learning to become more aware of positive aspects of yourself, to pay more attention to your strengths, assets, qualities and talents, and learning to give yourself the same consideration you would give to another person you cared about.

Why self-criticism does more harm than good

In many cultures, self-criticism is viewed as a good and useful thing. This idea is captured in sayings like 'spare the rod and spoil the child', which suggests that the road to growth is through correction and punishment. People sometimes fear that thinking well of yourself will lead to boasting and big-headedness (we will return to this idea later, in the chapter on enhancing self-acceptance). So children are often taught to behave better and work harder by having their faults emphasised, rather than by having their virtues and successes highlighted and praised. Parents and teachers may spend their time pointing out what children have done wrong, instead of helping them to build on what they have done right. This may breed a sense that self-criticism is the only thing that keeps one on the straight and narrow – stop, and you could sink into a swamp of smug self-indulgence and never do anything worthwhile, ever again.

So self-critical thinking is often learned early in life. It becomes a habit, a knee-jerk reaction, of which you may not be fully aware. You may even see it as helpful and constructive – the royal road to self-improvement. This idea is worth exploring in some detail. You will discover that, in fact, self-criticism has a number of serious drawbacks.

Self-criticism paralyses you and makes you feel bad

Imagine someone you know who is quite self-confident. Imagine following them around, pointing out every little mistake they make, telling them what they have done is all very well but could have been done better/faster/ more effectively, calling them names and telling them to ignore or discount anything that went well, any successes or achievements. As the days and weeks went by, what impact would you expect this constant drip, drip, drip of criticism to have? How would they feel? How would it affect their confidence in their ability to cope and succeed in life? How would it influence their ability to make decisions and take initiatives? Would it make life easier for them or more difficult? Would you even consider doing this to a friend of yours? If not, why not?

If you have the habit of self-critical thinking, then this is probably what you are doing to yourself, perhaps without even being particularly aware of it. Self-critical thoughts are like a parrot on your shoulder, constantly squawking disapproval in your ear. Take a moment to consider how this may be discouraging and demoralising you, paralysing your efforts to change and grow.

Self-criticism is unfair

Sydney Smith, once Dean of St Paul's Cathedral in London, suffered from depression. In 1820, he advised a lady friend, who had experienced similar difficulties: 'Don't be too severe upon yourself, or underrate yourself, but *do yourself justice.'* In other words, be fair to yourself. This is not what self-critical thinking does.

Being self-critical means that you react to even small mistakes, failures or errors of judgement as if they tell the whole story about you. Your radar for faults and weaknesses is highly sensitive and, when you detect one, you use it as a cue to write yourself off. You tell yourself you are bad, pathetic or stupid *as a person.* Is this fair?

In fact, you are made up of millions of actions, feelings and thoughts – some good, some bad and some indifferent. When you condemn yourself as a person on the basis of an error or something you regret, you are drawing a general conclusion about yourself on the basis of biased evidence, taking only negative aspects of yourself into account. Be realistic: give yourself credit for your assets and strengths as well as acknowledging that, like the rest of the human race, you have weaknesses and flaws.

Self-criticism blocks learning and growth

Self-criticism undermines your confidence and makes you feel down, discouraged, demoralised and bad about yourself. Far from helping you to overcome problems, it prevents you from thinking clearly about yourself and your life and altering those aspects of yourself you genuinely want to change. Generally speaking, people learn more when their successes are rewarded, praised and encouraged than when they are criticised and punished for their failures. Self-criticism simply points you in the direction of what you did wrong and makes you feel bad – it does not give you any clues as to how to do better next time. If you only pay attention to what you do wrong, you lose the opportunity to learn from and repeat what you do right. Similarly, if you write yourself off every time you make an error, you lose the opportunity to learn from your mistakes and to work constructively on aspects of yourself that you wish to change.

Self-criticism ignores the realities

When things go wrong, in addition to criticising yourself for what you did, you probably tell yourself you *should* have acted differently. Perhaps you are right in thinking that acting differently would have been in your best interests. With hindsight, it is often easy to see how one could have handled things better. But how did things appear to you *at the time*? In reality, the chances are that you had good reasons for acting as you did, even if in the end your course of action turned out to be mistaken, misguided or regrettable. Given all the circumstances (you were tired, you were not thinking clearly, you did not have all the information you needed to deal with the situation in the best possible way), you *should* have acted exactly as you did.

This does not mean letting yourself off the hook if you genuinely did do something worthy of regret or remorse, or ignoring genuine mistakes you have made. If you can see things more clearly in retrospect, use your new insight to learn from the experience. Then, if a similar situation arises again, you will have a different perspective on how to deal with it. But brooding on the past and using things you regret as a stick to beat your back with will only make you feel bad and paralyse you. It will not help you to think more clearly and do better next time.

Self-criticism kicks you when you are down

People sometimes demoralise themselves and reduce their confidence still further by criticising themselves for being unconfident, unassertive, anxious or depressed. But these are common problems, and could probably affect most (or indeed, all) of us, given the right circumstances.

As we have seen, personal difficulties are often a natural reaction to stressful events, and, generally speaking, are an understandable product of early learning. They do not mean there is anything fundamentally wrong with you. Very likely, anyone who had had the experiences you have had would see themselves as you do, and with the same impact on daily living. With the help of this book, and other resources if need be, you will be able to find ways to manage self-doubt and its consequences more successfully. What is certain is that criticising yourself for having difficulties will not help you to resolve them.

Questioning self-critical thoughts

Now that we have established how harmful self-critical thoughts can be, how can you set about dealing with them? The skills involved are the same core skills as those used when you were learning how to question and test anxious predictions (Chapter 4, pages 101–146). They are:

1. Awareness: Learning to catch self-critical thoughts as they happen
2. Rethinking: Questioning self-critical thoughts
3. Experiments: Practising treating yourself more kindly and behaving in accordance with your new perspective. (We shall focus on this in more detail in Chapter 6)

Let us consider each of these steps in turn.

1. Awareness: Learning to catch self-critical thoughts as they happen

What are the signs that alert you to the fact that you are being self-critical? Thought patterns (e.g. making sweeping self-judgements, 'shoulds')? Mood changes (e.g. a drop in confidence, feeling guilty)? Body sensations (e.g. a sinking feeling, your jaw tightening)? Or maybe something you habitually do (avoiding people, working harder than ever)? See if you can identify your own 'self-criticism signature'.

Becoming more aware of your own self-critical thoughts is not always as easy as it sounds. If you have felt bad about yourself for a long time, self-criticism may have become an automatic habit of which you are hardly aware – a routine part of how you think about yourself. So the first step is to learn to notice when you put yourself down, and to observe the impact it has on how you feel and how you go about the business of living.

When you are self-critical, your feelings will be affected. Changes in your emotional state can be your most obvious clue that self-critical thinking is going on. The emotions you experience when you are hard on yourself are probably different from the anxiety, apprehension, fear or panic that are triggered when you are predicting that things are about to go wrong. You are more likely to feel:

Guilty	Ashamed
Sad	Embarrassed
Disappointed in yourself	Angry with yourself
Frustrated	Depressed
Hopeless	Despairing

As you know from working with anxious predictions, the first step towards changing old habits of thinking is to be able to spot them when they occur. Instead of being swept away by the feelings that go with self-criticism, you can learn to approach them with a spirit of curiosity, and use them as a cue for rethinking and for action. Again, keeping a record of your investigations is likely to be helpful to you. You may find it helpful to use the worksheet, 'Spotting Self-Critical Thoughts' on page 160. The worksheet will prompt you to notice what is running through your mind when you feel bad about yourself, and to understand more clearly how these thoughts affect your life and how they keep the vicious circle of low self-esteem going. You may well find that the same thoughts (or very similar ones) occur again and again.

Over the course of a few days, you will become more sensitive to changes in your feelings, and to the self-critical thoughts that spark them off. Make sure you bear in mind that these thoughts are a matter of opinion, an old habit, not a reflection of the person you really are. In this way, you can begin to distance yourself from them – 'Aha! There's another one of those!' – even before you begin the process of questioning them systematically.

How to use 'Spotting self-critical thoughts'

The worksheet is designed to encourage self-awareness, to help you to tune in to self-critical thoughts, as a first step to questioning them and searching for more helpful and realistic alternatives. You will see a blank example on page 160, and a completed example on page 161; additional blank copies are provided in the Appendix and can also be downloaded from the 'Overcoming' website.

As with anxious predictions, a structured record sheet with headings may be more helpful to you than a daily narrative diary. It will help you to start thinking clearly about what is going on, instead of getting lost in telling the story or in being upset. This is particularly important now that you are working on self-criticism, because self-critical thoughts are often quite close reflections of the Bottom Line and so may appear especially convincing to you. Even if you decide to make your own paper or electronic record, you may find it helpful to use the headings on the worksheet as a guide.

The best way to become more aware of self-critical thoughts is to make a note of them as soon as they occur. You will see that the headings on the worksheet are very similar to the headings on the 'Predictions and Precautions' worksheet (page 114). You will need to record:

Date and time

When did you feel bad about yourself? Use this information to pick up patterns over time, as you did with your anxious predictions.

The situation

What was happening at the moment you began to feel bad about yourself? Where were you? Who were you with? What were you doing? Briefly describe what was going on (e.g. 'asked a girl out – she turned me down' or 'boss asked

Figure 16. Spotting Self-critical Thoughts Worksheet

Date/Time	Situation What were you doing when you began to feel bad about yourself?	Emotions and body sensations (e.g. sad, angry, guilty) Rate each 0–100 for intensity	Self-critical thoughts What exactly was going through your mind when you began to feel bad about yourself? (e.g. thoughts in words, images, meanings) Rate 0–100% for degree of belief	Unhelpful behaviour What did you do as a consequence of your self-critical thoughts?

Figure 17. Spotting Self-critical Thoughts Worksheet – Example: Mike

Date/Time	Situation What were you doing when you began to feel bad about yourself?	Emotions and body sensations (e.g. sad, angry, guilty) Rate each 0–100 for intensity	Self-critical thoughts What exactly was going through your mind when you began to feel bad about yourself? (e.g. thoughts in words, images, meanings) Rate 0–100% for degree of belief	Unhelpful behaviour What did you do as a consequence of your self-critical thoughts?
5th March	Got in a rage with Kelly when she came home late. Had completely forgotten she was going to Lucy's house.	Guilty 80 Fed up with myself 100 Hopeless 95	This proves it – I'm really losing it 100% I'm a total mess 95% I should pull myself together 100% This is pathetic 100% What's the matter with me? I just don't think I'll ever get back to how I was 95%	Stomped out of the house and went to the pub. Came back late and shut myself in the basement alone to watch TV. Didn't talk to anyone.

me to rewrite a report'). It may be that you were not doing anything in particular (e.g. washing up, watching television) and that what triggered self-critical thinking was not what was going on around you but rather something in your own general train of thought. In this case, write down the general topic you were focusing on (e.g. 'thinking about my ex-husband taking the children for the weekend' or 'remembering being bullied at school'). Your exact thoughts, word for word, belong in the 'Self-critical Thoughts' column.

Emotions and body sensations

You may have felt only one main emotion (e.g. sadness). Or you may have experienced a mixture of emotions (e.g. not only sadness, but also guilt and anger). As with anxiety, you may also have experienced changes in your body state (e.g. a sinking feeling, a churning stomach or a weight on your shoulders). Record each emotion and body sensation, and give it a rating between 0 and 100 according to how strong it was. Remember: a rating of 5 would mean just a very faint emotional reaction or physical change; a rating of 50 would mean a moderate emotion or sensation; and a rating of 100 would mean the emotion or sensation was as strong as it could possibly be. You could score anywhere between 0 and 100.

Self-critical thoughts

What exactly was running through your mind when you began to feel bad about yourself? Just as with anxiety, your thoughts may have been in words, like a conversation or commentary in your mind. You may have been calling your- self names, for example, or telling yourself you should have done better. Write your thoughts down, as far as possible, word for word. On the other hand, some of your thoughts may take the form of images in your mind's eye. Jack, for example, the boy whose energy and curiosity got him into trouble as a child, saw his father's angry, disapproving face and felt his body shrinking in on itself. Briefly describe the image, just as you saw it. If you can, note down the message the image is giving you (for Jack, the message was that he had got it wrong yet again).

There may be times when you find yourself feeling upset but cannot identify any thoughts or images as such. If so, ask yourself what the *meaning* of the situation is. What does it tell you about yourself? What kind of person would find him- or herself in that situation or would act that way? What implications does it have for what others think of you? What does it say about your future? This may give you a clue as to why the situation is upsetting you. A disagree- ment, for example, might mean that another person does not like you. A friend telling you about a new love affair might mean that, unlike other more worthy people, you will not find someone to love you. Reflect on the situation in which you began to feel bad about yourself, explore its meaning and, when you have found it, write it down. You will be able to question images and meanings and find alter- natives to them, just as you can question and find alterna- tives to thoughts in words.

As with anxious predictions, give each self-critical thought, image or meaning a rating between 0 per cent and 100 per cent, according to how strongly you believed it when it occurred. One hundred per cent would mean you believed it completely, with no shadow of doubt; 50 per cent would mean you were in two minds; 5 per cent would mean you only believed it slightly. Again, you could score anywhere between 0 per cent and 100 per cent.

Self-defeating behaviour

What impact did your self-critical thoughts have on your behaviour? Self-critical thoughts not only affect how people feel; they also affect how they act. They can lead you to behave in ways that are not in your best interests, and that will tend to keep your low self-esteem going.

In the last column of the diary sheet, make a note of anything you did or did not do, as a result of the thoughts. For example, did you apologise for yourself? Or withdraw into your shell? Or avoid asking for something you needed? Did you allow yourself to be treated like a doormat or discounted? Did you avoid an opportunity that you might otherwise have taken?

Making the most of 'spotting self-critical thoughts'

Why bother to write it down?

Why not just make a mental note of what happens when

you experience self-critical thoughts? Because, as we noted before, our memories are unreliable – they change and fade over time. Having a written record can help you to stay in close touch with what actually happened. You have something concrete to think about and reflect on, and the detail of incidents has less chance of being forgotten. You can notice repeating patterns, consider how thoughts affect your behaviour in different situations, and become aware of the exact words you use to yourself when you are being self-critical.

Equally, people often find that writing the thoughts down encourages distance from them. It takes them out of your head (so to speak), where it is difficult to question their truth because they seem so much a part of you, and puts them 'out there' on paper or on-screen, where you can start to stand back, take a good look at them and gain a different perspective. As we said earlier, this will help you to move towards the point where you can begin to say, 'Aha, there's another one of those!' and to see them as simply something you do, rather than a true reflection of yourself.

How long should I keep the record for? How many thoughts do I need to record?

Continue for as long as it takes to gain a clear understanding of your self-critical thinking and its impact on your emotional state and your behaviour. You could start by noting one or two examples a day. Over time, try to collect a sample of self-critical thoughts that is a good reflection of the unkind things you commonly say to yourself. When you feel you have reached the point where noticing them and observing their impact has become fairly automatic, you are ready to move on to finding alternatives to your thoughts. This may take you just a few days. But if your habit of self-critical thinking is well entrenched and for the most part out of your awareness, it may take you longer.

When should I make the record?

As with anxious predictions, the ideal is to record your self-critical thoughts as soon as they occur. This means keeping your record with you for a few days. The reason for this is that, although self-critical thoughts can have a very power-ful effect when they actually occur, it may be hard after-wards to remember exactly what ran through your mind. It is especially easy to lose the exact detail and flavour of thoughts and feelings that may have been present only for moments and at times when you felt powerfully distressed. This will make life difficult for you when you come to question the thoughts and look for alternatives to them.

But, of course, the ideal is not always possible. You may be in a meeting, or at a party, or changing the baby, or driving down a busy motorway. If you cannot record what happened at the time, make sure that at least you make a mental note of what upset you, or jot down a reminder on anything that comes to hand (such as the back of an envelope, your diary, your shopping list, your phone or tablet). Then set aside time later to make a proper, detailed record. Run through an 'action replay' in your mind – remember as vividly as you can where you were and what you were doing the moment when you started to feel bad about yourself, what was running through your mind at that moment, and what you did in response to your thoughts.

Won't focusing on my thoughts just upset me?

Meeting your thoughts face to face may seem like a daunting prospect, especially if they closely reflect your Bottom Line and seem very convincing to you, and if the habit of self-criticism has been with you for a long time. You may be tempted to avoid looking at them too closely. Perhaps you are afraid they will upset you. And what if they turn out to be true? Or perhaps part of you already knows that they are biased or exaggerated, and you feel you should be able to dismiss them rather than continuing to be distressed and restricted by them.

It is natural to want to avoid focusing on upsetting ideas, especially if one suspects they may be true. You may feel understandably reluctant to record these damning judgements of yourself in black and white. But if you want to tackle your self-critical thoughts effectively, it is necessary first to look them straight in the eye. You need to know the nature of the enemy. So beware of excuses ('I'll do it later', 'It doesn't do to dwell on things'). If you act on these, you will deprive yourself of a chance to develop a more kindly perspective. And ignoring the thoughts will not make them go away.

2. Rethinking: Questioning self-critical thoughts

Developing awareness of your self-critical thoughts is the first step towards questioning and rethinking them, instead of simply accepting them as a reflection of how things really are. You have already practised this skill when you were learning to check out your anxious predictions (remember the questions on page 126). The aim here is to stop taking your self-critical thoughts as statements of the truth about yourself, and to begin to find alternative perspectives which will provide you with a more balanced view.

On page 170 you will find a blank worksheet called 'Questioning Self-critical Thoughts'; additional blank copies are provided in the Appendix and can also be downloaded from the 'Overcoming' website. A completed example is on page 172. You will see that the first four columns of this sheet are identical to 'Spotting Self-critical Thoughts' (date/time; situation; emotions/body state; self-critical thoughts). But the new sheet does not stop there. It also asks you to record 'Alternative Perspectives' (rethinking), and to assess the impact these have on what you originally thought and felt. Finally, it asks you to decide on a plan of action to test out how helpful the alternative perspectives are (experiments).

In addition to continuing to collect the information you have been noting on 'Spotting Self-critical Thoughts', you will need to record:

Alternative perspectives

You will not have to snatch alternatives to your self-critical thoughts out of thin air. You can use the series of questions listed on page 177 and discussed in detail later in the chapter, to help you generate alternatives and look at your thoughts from fresh angles. Rate each alternative according to how strongly you believe it, just as you rated the original self-critical thoughts (100 per cent if you believe it completely, 0 per cent if you do not believe it at all, and so on). You do not have to believe all your answers 100 per cent. They should, however, be sufficiently convincing to make at least some difference to how you feel.

Outcome

Go back to your original emotions and body sensations. How strong are they now? Rate each one out of 100. Then go back to your original self-critical thoughts. Now that you have found alternatives to them, how strongly do you believe them? Give each one a new rating out of 100. If your answers have been effective, you should find that your belief in the self-critical thoughts, together with the painful emotions that go with them, have lessened to some extent.

Key questions to help you find alternatives to self-critical thoughts

People rarely manage to come up with alternatives to self-critical thoughts right away.

Figure 18. Questioning Self-critical Thoughts Worksheet

Date/ Time	Situation	Emotions and body sensations Rate each 0–100	Self-critical thoughts Rate belief in each 1–100%	Alternative perspectives Use the key questions to find other perspectives on yourself. Rate belief in each 0–100%	Outcome 1 Now that you have found alternatives to your self-critical thoughts, how do you feel (0–100)? 2 How strongly do you now believe your self-critical thoughts (0–100%)? 3 What can you do now (action plan, experiments)?

Figure 19. Questioning Self-critical Thoughts Worksheet – Example: Mike

Date/ Time	Situation	Emotions and body sensations Rate each 0–100	Self-critical thoughts Rate belief in each 1–100%	Alternative perspectives Use the key questions to find other perspectives on yourself. Rate belief in each 0–100%	Outcome 1 Now that you have found alternatives to your self-critical thoughts, how do you feel (0–100)? 2 How strongly do you now believe your self-critical thoughts (0–100%)? 3 What can you do now (action plan, experiments)?
8 March	Had a row with Kelly again. She wanted to go out on a friend's motorbike.	Guilty 80 Angry with myself 100 Hopeless 90	Here I go again, losing my temper about nothing. I'm a wreck 100%	It's true that I was angrier than the situation warranted. But it's because I get frightened for her.	1 Guilty 40% Angry with self 30% Hopeless 40%

Tense & uptight 100%	I've got to get a grip on myself, or I'll ruin everything 100% There's no end to this 90%	Bikes are quite dangerous, and I'm afraid of losing her. So it wasn't really about nothing. 100% I do need to do something about all this, it's true. I have changed a lot. But then, I went through something really bad, so maybe it's not surprising I'm not my usual self. 90% Rows are not good for any of us. But in fact we usually get over it. She's a good girl, even if a bit of a cranky teenager at the moment. We have some good times together 95% I don't know how to answer that it's been going on a while. I don't like doing it, but maybe it's time to get help 50%	2 30% 20% 50% 3 Tell Kelly I'm sorry about shouting at her and explain why Talk to Viv (my wife) and tell her how I feel instead of shutting her out Get help?

Here are some questions designed to help you explore fresh perspectives and recognise how your self-critical thoughts are not only biased and one-sided, but also unhelpful and unkind (you will find them listed together on page 177). You may find it helpful initially to use the list as a whole to help you get into the swing of questioning your self-critical thoughts. As you go along, notice which questions seem particularly helpful in tackling your own personal style of self-critical thinking. For example, you may find that you have a habit of taking the blame for things that are not your responsibility. Or you may discover that considering what you would say to another person in your situation opens up new ideas for you. As a reminder, you could write down these especially helpful questions on a card small enough to carry in your wallet or purse, or on the electronic equivalent, and use them to free up your thinking when self-critical thoughts strike. With practice, useful questions will become part of your mental furniture. At this point, you will no longer need a written prompt.

What is the evidence?

AM I CONFUSING A THOUGHT WITH A FACT?

Just because you believe something to be true, it does not follow that it is. I could believe that I was a giraffe. But would that make me one? Your self-critical thoughts may be opinions based on unfortunate learning experiences you have had, not a reflection of your true self.

WHAT IS THE EVIDENCE IN FAVOUR OF WHAT I THINK ABOUT MYSELF?

What are you going on, when you judge yourself critically? What actual evidence do you have to support what you think of yourself? What facts or observations (rather than ideas or opinions) back up your self-critical thoughts?

WHAT IS THE EVIDENCE AGAINST WHAT I THINK ABOUT MYSELF?

Can you think of anything that suggests your poor opinion of yourself is not completely true? Or indeed contradicts it? For example, if you have criticised yourself for being stupid, can you think of anything about you, past and present, that does not fit the idea you are stupid? Finding counter-evidence may not be easy, because you will tend to screen it out or discount it. This does mean it does not exist. It may be help-ful to discuss this with a trusted friend or supporter – they may have a clearer view of you than you have of yourself.

What alternative perspectives are there?

AM I ASSUMING THAT MY PERSPECTIVE ON MYSELF IS THE ONLY ONE POSSIBLE?

Any situation can be viewed from many different angles. How would you see this particular situation on a day when you were feeling more confident and on top of things? How do you think you will view it in ten years' time? What would you say if a friend of yours came to you with this problem? And what would your friend say if they knew what you were thinking? Would they agree? If your loss of confidence has been relatively recent, how would you have viewed the situation before the difficulty began? Remember to check out alternative perspectives against available evidence. An alternative with absolutely no basis in reality will not be helpful to you.

What is the effect of thinking the way I do about myself?

ARE THESE SELF-CRITICAL THOUGHTS HELPFUL TO ME OR ARE THEY GETTING IN MY WAY?

In this specific situation, what do you want? What are your goals or intentions? How do you *want* things to turn out? Remember the pros and cons of self-critical thinking we explored earlier. Right now, do its disadvantages outweigh its advantages? Is it the best way to get what you want out of the situation, or would a more balanced, compassionate, encouraging perspective be more helpful? Are your self-critical thoughts helping you to handle things constructively or are they encouraging self-defeating behaviour?

What are the biases in my thinking about myself?

AM I JUMPING TO CONCLUSIONS?

This means deciding how things are without proper evidence to support your point of view – for example, concluding that the fact someone didn't call you means that you *must* have done something to offend them, when actually you have no idea what might be behind their behaviour. People with low self-esteem typically jump to whatever conclusion reflects badly on themselves. Is this a habit of yours? If so, remember to review the evidence, the facts. When you look at the bigger picture, you may discover your critical conclusion about yourself is incorrect.

Figure 20. Key Questions to Help You Find Alternatives to Self-critical Thoughts

- What is the evidence?

  Am I confusing a thought with a fact?

  What is the evidence in favour of what I think about myself?

  What is the evidence against what I think about myself?

- What alternative perspectives are there?

  Am I assuming my perspective is the only one possible?

  What evidence do I have to support alternative perspectives?

- What is the effect of thinking the way I do about myself?

  Are these self-critical thoughts helpful to me, or are they getting in my way?

  What perspective might be more helpful to me?

- What are the biases in my thinking about myself?

  Am I jumping to conclusions?

  Am I using a double standard?

  Am I thinking in all-or-nothing terms?

  Am I being fair to myself, or am I condemning myself as a total person on the basis of a single event?

  Am I concentrating on my weaknesses and forgetting my strengths?

  Am I blaming myself for things that are not really my fault?

  Am I expecting myself to be perfect?

AM I USING A DOUBLE STANDARD?

People with low self-esteem are often much harder on themselves than they would be on anyone else. Their standards for themselves are much higher, more rigid and more out of reach than the standards they expect other people to meet. Are you expecting more of yourself than you would of other people? Would you be so hard on them?

To find out if you are using a double standard, ask yourself what your reaction would be if someone you cared about came to you with a problem. Would you tell them that they were weak or stupid or pathetic, or that they should know better? Or would you be encouraging and sympathetic and try to help them to get the problem into perspective and look for constructive ways of dealing with it? People with low self-esteem sometimes fear that if they become kinder to themselves, they will cease to make anything of their lives. In fact, the reverse is probably true. Think of a child learning to walk and talk. If the child's parents shouted at it, and criticised it and called it names every time it fell over or said a word wrong, what impact would you expect that to have? Would you treat a child that way? If not, how come you are doing it to yourself?

How about trying out a different policy? Take a step back from your usual critical and disapproving stance and experiment with being kind, sympathetic and encouraging to yourself, just as you would to another person. You may find that if you treat yourself more kindly you will feel better and be better able to think clearly and act constructively.

AM I THINKING IN ALL-OR-NOTHING TERMS?

All-or-nothing, 'either/or' thinking oversimplifies things. Nearly everything is relative (sometimes, not always or never; somewhat, not completely or not at all; some, not all or none; some people, not everyone). So, for example, people are not usually either all good or all bad, but a mixture of the two. Events are not usually either complete disasters or total bliss, but somewhere in the middle. Are you thinking about yourself in all-or-nothing terms? The words you use may be a clue here. Watch out for extreme words (always/ never, everyone/no one, everything/nothing). They may reflect all-or-nothing thinking. In fact, things are probably less clear-cut than that. So look for the shades of grey.

AM I CONDEMNING MYSELF AS A TOTAL PERSON ON THE BASIS OF A SINGLE EVENT?

People with low self-esteem commonly make global judgements about themselves on the basis of one thing they said or did, one problem they have, one sole aspect of themselves. They take difficulties to mean that they have no worth or value at all as a person. Are you making this kind of blanket judgement of yourself? If one person dislikes you, it must mean there is something wrong with you? One mistake, and you are a failure? One missed phone call, and you are irresponsible and selfish? Judging yourself as a total person on the basis of any one single thing you do does not make sense. Supposing you did one thing really well – would that make you totally wonderful as a person? Probably you would not even dream of thinking so. But when it comes to your weaknesses, failures and mistakes, you may be only too ready to write yourself off. You need to look at the bigger picture. And remember especially that when you are feeling bad about yourself, or down, you will be homing in on anything that fits with your poor opinion of yourself and screening out anything that does not fit. This skews your judgement even more. So hold back from making global judgements, unless you are sure that you are taking *all* the evidence into account.

AM I BEING FAIR TO MYSELF OR AM I CONCENTRATING ON MY WEAKNESSES AND FORGETTING MY STRENGTHS?

Low self-esteem makes you focus on your weaknesses and ignore your strengths. People with low self-esteem commonly overlook problems they have successfully handled in the past, forget resources that could help them to overcome current difficulties and screen out their good qualities. Instead, they focus on failures and weaknesses. On a day-to-day basis, this may mean noting and remembering everything that goes wrong during the day, and forgetting or discounting things you have enjoyed or achieved. It may be difficult at bad times to think of a single good quality or talent.

It is important to try to keep a balanced view of yourself. Of course, there are things you are not very good at, things you have done that you regret, and things about yourself that you would prefer to change. This is true for everyone. But what about the other side of the equation? What are the things you *are* good at? What do other people appreciate about you? What do you like about yourself?

How have you coped with difficulties and stresses in your life? What are your strengths, qualities and resources? (We will return to this point in more detail in Chapter 6.)

The automatic tendency to focus on the bad and ignore the good in you is like having an extremely vigilant, powerful and effective inner prosecutor who is alert for every flaw and weakness and ready to condemn at the drop of a hat. What you need is an equally strong 'inner advocate', who will convincingly present the evidence for the defence. And, most importantly, you need to discover an 'inner judge' who, like a real judge, will have no axe to grind, but will take *all* the evidence into account and come to a fair and balanced view, rather than condemning you solely on the basis of evidence presented by the prosecution. Remember Sydney Smith: 'Do yourself justice.'

AM I BLAMING MYSELF FOR THINGS THAT ARE NOT REALLY MY FAULT?

When things go wrong, do you consider all the possible reasons why this might be so, or do you tend immediately to assume that it must be due to some lack in yourself? If a friend stands you up, for example, do you automatically assume that you must have done something to annoy them or that they do not want to know you any more?

There are all kinds of reasons why things do not work out. Sometimes, of course, it will indeed be a result of something you did. But often, other factors are involved. For example, your friend might have forgotten, or been exceptionally busy, or have misunderstood your arrangements.

If you automatically assume responsibility when things go wrong, you will not be in the best position to discover the real reasons for what happened. If a friend of yours was in this situation, how would you explain what had happened? How many possible reasons can you think of? If you remain open-minded and ask yourself what other explanations there might be, you may discover that you are less to blame than you thought – in fact, what happened may have had absolutely nothing to do with you.

AM I EXPECTING MYSELF TO BE PERFECT?

As we have said, people with low self-esteem often set very high standards for themselves which are reflected in their Rules for Living (we shall return to these in Chapter 7). For example, they may think they should be able to deal calmly and competently with everything life throws at them. Or they may believe that everything they do should be done to the highest standard, regardless of circumstances and personal cost. This is simply not realistic, and opens the floodgates to self-criticism and painful feelings of guilt, depression and inadequacy. Unless you are some sort of superhuman being, it is just not possible to get everything 100 per cent right all the time. If you expect to do so, you are setting yourself up to fail.

Accepting that you cannot be perfect does not mean you have to give up even attempting to do things well. But it does allow you to set realistic targets for yourself, and to give yourself credit when you reach them, even if they were less than perfect. This will encourage you to feel better about yourself, and so motivate you to keep going and try again. It also means you can learn from your difficulties and mistakes, rather than being upset and even paralysed by them. As G.K. Chesterton, the English writer, said: 'If a thing is worth doing, it is worth doing badly.'

3. Experiments: Practising treating yourself more kindly and behaving in accordance with your new perspective

The question here is: What can I do to put my new, kinder perspective into practice and treat myself more compassionately? Here we return to the idea of experiments that you learned about in Chapter 4. Work out what you need to do in order to test out your new perspectives in the real world, rather than just leaving them in writing or in your mind. As we said before, direct personal experience is the best teacher: you will find your alternatives most convincing if you have discovered for yourself what impact they have, and how they change your feelings and the possibilities open to you.

Here again we come to the importance of taking action, experimenting with doing things differently. What can you do to put your new perspective into practice? How could you find out for yourself if it works better for you? Is there anything you can do to change the situation that sparked the self-critical thoughts (for example, changing or leaving a job where you are not valued, or ending a relationship with a person who feeds into your negative view of yourself)?

Or is there something about your own reactions you could change? Old habits die hard – what will you do if in future you find yourself thinking, feeling and acting in the same old way? How would you like to handle the situation differently, next time it occurs? This will include spotting and dealing with self-critical thoughts. It may also involve experimenting with behaving in new ways that are less self-defeating and more compassionate (accepting compliments gracefully, not apologising for yourself, taking opportunities, asserting your own needs, etc.). Write down your ideas on the worksheet, and then take every opportunity to try them out, to develop and strengthen new perspectives on yourself.

You will find an example on Mike's 'Questioning Self-critical Thoughts' worksheet on page 161.

Making the most of 'Questioning self-critical thoughts'

How long will it take to find good alternatives to my self-critical thoughts?

Questioning your self-critical thoughts and searching for alternative perspectives is probably not something you are in the habit of doing. At first, you may find the same old thoughts cropping up again and again. It may be difficult at first to step back from them far enough to see them clearly for what they are – the unkind voice of low self-esteem speaking. As you learn to do so, you will be able to free up your thinking and find alternatives that make a real difference to how you see yourself and how you feel (though some people find it makes a noticeable difference right away). Don't rush things – give yourself plenty of opportunity to practise, learn from your mistakes and develop your skill.

The habit of self-criticism takes time to break. Changing your thinking is rather like taking up a form of exercise you have never tried before. You are being asked to develop mental muscles you do not normally use. They will complain and feel awkward and uncomfortable. But, with regular practice, they will become strong, flexible and able to do what you require of them. And the exercise itself will feel good, let alone its results.

The objective of this stage is to reach the point where you automatically notice, answer and dismiss self-critical thoughts so that they no longer influence your feelings or how you act. Regular daily practice (one or two thoughtfully recorded examples a day) is the best way to achieve this. Later, you will be able to find answers to self-critical thoughts in your head without needing to write anything down. Eventually, you may find that most of the time you do not even need to answer thoughts in your head – they no longer occur very much. Even so, you may still find the worksheet helpful to deal with particularly tough thoughts, or at times when for some reason they pop up again (for example, something happens that takes you back to past experiences, or you are simply feeling tired or stressed or unhappy). The worksheet is something you will always have in your 'tool kit' to deal with future difficulties and tough situations. But regular daily recordings need go on only until you achieve the objective of dealing with self-critical thoughts without a written prompt.

How can I expect to think differently when I'm feeling really upset?

Self-critical thoughts are the voice of your Bottom Line speaking in the present moment. This means that they can be loud, compelling and highly charged with emotion. It does not follow that they are true, and now you are learning to distance yourself from them, to stop buying into them and taking them seriously.

Still, if something happens that upsets you deeply, you will probably find it very difficult indeed to see any alternatives to your self-critical thoughts. Instead of grasping that this is a common, natural difficulty, you may fall into the trap of seeing it as yet another reason to criticise yourself. The most helpful thing to do is simply to make a note of what happened to upset you, and your feelings and thoughts, but then to leave the search for alternatives until you are feeling calmer. You will be in a better position to see things clearly after you have weathered the storm.

Watch out for 'It-should-be-different' thinking

Self-criticism often reflects what psychologists call 'discrepancy-based processing'. This rather dry technical term actually means something you may begin to recognise as you bring self-critical thinking into focus: a relentless focus on the gap (discrepancy) between things as they *are* and things as you *want* them to be or think they *should* be. In other words, your mind fastens on all the ways in which you fall short, and this is a terrific recipe for feeling bad about yourself. Examples might include: 'I wish I were more confident [but I'm not]', 'If only I was smarter [but I'm not]', 'I should be stronger [but I'm not]'. This it-should-be-different thinking feels bad in itself and, what is more, it opens the door to rumination.

Beware the rumination trap

Sometimes self-criticism consists of a simple judgement – 'You idiot', 'Done it again', 'Why do I never get anything right?' But it can easily shade into rumination, brooding – going over and over the same thing, round and round, again and again, like a cow chewing the cud (in fact, this is what 'rumination' means). Streams of 'whys', 'if onlys', unfair self-judgements, harping on about the gap between who you are and who you want to be or think you ought to be. This is not constructive problem-solving though, as psychologist Adrian Wells showed by simply inviting people who ruminate to think about why they did it, it may feel as though it is. It turned out they had the feeling that if they just thought it all through one more time, they would finally understand their difficulties and how to resolve them. In fact, rumination is a dead end; it goes nowhere.

Occasionally when we ruminate answers do pop up, but generally speaking (like any kind of self-critical thinking) rumination just leads to more rumination and makes you miserable, especially if you are already feeling low. So if you notice the same old thing coming round the block yet again, pause for a moment and ask yourself: Am I ruminating? And if I am, how is it actually affecting me? My mood? My motivation? My feelings about myself?

If you observe closely, you may recognise that you are caught in an endless loop, with no exit in sight. If so, it's time to make a choice. We cannot stop thoughts from coming into our minds, but we *can* do something about what happens next. We can learn to be aware that rumination is present, and to respond differently to its presence.

For example, you can choose to continue to listen to your self-critical ruminations, to give them weight, in the distant hope of ending up somewhere useful. Or you can decide this is futile and upsetting, however seductive it may seem, and choose to experiment with deliberately directing your attention elsewhere. This is not the same as trying to run away from your own mind, to outdistance or suppress it. It is a conscious and kind decision to stop doing something that is not in your best interests. For example, you could experiment with opening all your senses (sight, hearing, touch, taste and smell) to your current environment. Or you could choose to engage in an absorbing activity or turn intentionally to other, more fruitful trains of thought. When you make these changes, observe the effects on how you feel.

It is not easy to distance yourself from rumination. But you will improve with practice. Self-critical ruminations may not disappear, but perhaps you can learn to let them be like a radio programme in the background that you're not really listening to. You can still tune in if you want to, but most of the time you have better things to do.

How good does the record have to be?

Many people with low self-esteem are perfectionists who expect the highest possible standard in everything they do. 'Good enough' is not good enough. We shall be returning to perfectionist rules in Chapter 7. For the time being, however, it is important to bear in mind the purpose of making a record: increasing self-awareness and increasing flexibility in your thinking. Approaching the record with a perfectionist stance will not help you to achieve this – it will create pressure to perform, and stifle creativity. Your record does not have to be a literary masterpiece, or a perfect piece of writing with every 'i' dotted and 't' crossed. You do not have to find the one *right* answer or the answer you think you *should* put. The 'right' answer is the answer that works for you – the answer that makes sense to you, changes your feelings for the better, and opens up avenues for constructive action. No one answer, however sensible it may seem, will work for everyone. You need to find the one that works best for *you*. And if by chance you are a perfectionist, then your 'fit for purpose' record is a great opportunity to experiment with doing it differently.

What if my alternatives don't work?

Sometimes people find that the answers they come up with do not have the desired effect – they make little difference to how they feel, and they do not help them to operate differently. If this is the case for you, it may be that you are disqualifying the answer in some way – telling yourself it is just a rationalisation, perhaps, or that it might apply to other people, but not to you. If you have 'yes, buts' like this, write them down in the 'Self-critical Thoughts' column and question them.

Do not expect your belief in the old thoughts and your painful feelings to shrink to zero right away, especially if they reflect beliefs about yourself which have been in place for many years. Self-critical thinking may be like a pair of old shoes – not very pleasant, but you are used to them and they are moulded to your shape. New perspectives, in contrast, are like new shoes – unfamiliar and stiff, and not at first a comfortable fit. You will need time and practice to strengthen the kinder view, and you will also need to experiment repeatedly with acting differently so that you learn on a gut level that compassion and kindly self-acceptance work better for you than self-criticism.

What if I'm no good at this?

Don't let yourself get caught in the trap of self-criticism while you are recording your self-critical thoughts. Changing how you think about yourself is no easy task. It takes time and practice to build the skill. So beware of being hard on yourself when you find the going tough. If you had a friend who was trying to tackle something difficult, what would you consider would be more helpful to them? Criticism and punishment? Or encouragement and praise? You may catch yourself thinking, 'I must be really stupid to think this way' or 'I'm not doing enough of this' or 'I will never get the hang of this'. If you do spot thoughts like these – write them down, answer them, and experiment with consciously treating yourself as you would treat your friend. Give yourself the respect and encouragement your work on this difficult task deserves.

Chapter Summary

1. *Self-critical thinking arises when you have the sense that an event or experience has confirmed your Bottom Line. This chapter has focused on the steps that will help you to question self-criticism and search for fairer and more helpful ways of thinking about yourself.*

2. *Self-critical thinking is a learned habit. It does not necessarily reflect the truth about yourself.*

3. *Self-criticism does more harm than good. Believing your self-critical thoughts makes you feel bad and encourages you to act in self-defeating ways.*

4. *You can learn to stand back from self-critical thoughts, and see them as the voice of low self-esteem speaking, something you do rather than a mirror image of your true self.*

5. *Self-critical thoughts, like anxious predictions, are open to question. You can learn to observe and record them and their impact on your feelings, body state and behaviour, and to rethink them and search for more balanced and kindly perspectives on yourself.*

6. *The final step is to experiment with treating yourself more fairly and kindly, valuing your strengths, qualities and assets as you would those of another person. We shall look at this is more detail in the next chapter.*

6

Enhancing
self-acceptance

Introduction

In Chapter 2 (pages 39–74), we identified two comple-
mentary thinking biases which contribute to keeping low
self-esteem going. First, a negative bias in *perception,* which
keeps your attention firmly fixed on what you feel is wrong
with you, and screens out your strengths and good points.
Second, an equally negative bias in *interpretation* which
inclines you to see yourself in a negative light, whatever the
circumstances. Both of these biases make it hard for you to
accept and value yourself, just as you are.

In Chapter 5 (pages 147–192), we focused on the bias
in interpretation: the way negative beliefs about yourself
lure you into the trap of self-critical thinking. You learned
how to spot and rethink self-critical thoughts, and began
to experiment with treating yourself more kindly. In this
chapter, we shall investigate the other side of the equation:
the bias in perception that makes it hard for you to see
positive aspects of yourself clearly or to treat yourself well.

Each of these two shifts in perspective is equally important. Rethinking self-criticism helps you to weaken old, unhelpful patterns of thought, and forms a sound foundation for later work on your Bottom Line. Learning to recognise and value your good points and to treat yourself with respect and consideration adds an extra dimension. It opens up new possibilities in how you relate to yourself, a new feeling of warmth and acceptance towards yourself – a new sense that it is OK to be exactly who you are.

Naturally, learning to boost everyday awareness of your good qualities and to treat yourself as someone worthy of respect and kindness may not be as easy in practice as it sounds in theory. Just as the habit of self-criticism is often learned early in life, so a taboo on thinking well of yourself may also have been drummed in from an early age. Unless you are alert to it and prepared to counter its effects, this taboo may make it hard for you to use the methods described in this chapter to enhance self-acceptance and self-esteem.

The taboo against thinking well of yourself

I'm beautiful
I'm clever
I'm a really good cook
I have a terrific sense of humour
I am a gifted musician
I'm lovable
I'm great

If you heard someone saying these things, what would your immediate reaction be? Would you be delighted to meet someone so gifted? Or would you feel uncomfortable and disapproving? Would you find yourself muttering 'Bighead' or 'Talk about blowing your own trumpet!' or 'Who on earth does s/he think s/he is?'? Would you instantly take it for granted these things must be true? Or would you see such self-enhancing statements as boasting, getting above oneself? Would you feel this person was ripe for a fall, and it was about time they were cut down to size?

If you have low self-esteem, the chances are that you view the idea of making statements like these about yourself (however accurate) as uncomfortable, risky, abhorrent or plain wrong-headed. Thinking well of yourself, allowing yourself to acknowledge your good points, may seem to you just like boasting. The very thought may make you squirm with embarrassment. You may also fear that, if you admit anything good about yourself, someone else will be sure to step in and say, 'Oh, no, you aren't' or 'Oh yeah, you reckon?' or 'Really? Where'd you get *that* idea from?' Thinking well of yourself in private may feel as extreme as hiring a sound system and standing in the town centre or going on social media, and shouting your virtues to the whole world. Naturally enough, these ideas and feelings stand in the way of enhancing self-acceptance and self-esteem.

Like the habit of self-critical thinking, seeing self-acceptance as equivalent to smug self-congratulation is often learned early in life. Just as children are taught to focus on their mistakes and wrongdoings, so they may encounter disapproval and ridicule if they show any sign of appreciating their own successes. This can happen, for example, to intelligent, academically gifted children, who do well at school and receive public praise from teachers. Schoolmates may ridicule and reject them. In some families, academic excellence may be regarded as nothing to celebrate, but rather as irrelevant to the real business of living. So they may learn to underperform, or to hide and downgrade their successes, putting them down to luck rather than their own gifts. They stop valuing their talents and achievements, and come to believe that anything they do well is a fluke, not a reflection of inherent qualities and hard work. In the end, they may not even feel fully able to pursue their real interests, to enjoy learning or to fulfil their true potential. It can take time and persistence to recover from these experiences.

Hans Christian Andersen wrote a story called *The Snow Queen*. At the beginning of the story, the devil makes a mirror. No one who looks in the mirror sees a reflection of his or her true self, but rather a distorted image, twisted and ugly. If you have low self-esteem, you see yourself in this distorted way without the benefit of the devil's mirror. What jumps out at you is what you dislike about yourself – the weaknesses and faults that are an inevitable part of being human. Your qualities, assets, resources, strengths and skills are much harder to recognise and accept.

Like self-criticism, ignoring or undervaluing positive aspects of yourself is unfair. The idea that self-acceptance – noticing and taking pleasure in your strengths and qualities, treating yourself with kindness and consideration, and allowing yourself to enjoy and savour the good things in your life – will lead to complacency does not make sense. Self-acceptance (that is, a realistic appraisal of your strong points, just for yourself) is part of healthy self-esteem, not self-inflation. In fact, ignoring your positive qualities contributes to keeping low self-esteem going, because it stops you from having a balanced view that takes account of the good things about you as well as your genuine shortcomings and things you might prefer to change.

In this chapter, you will have an opportunity to try out two main strategies for enhancing self-acceptance using the three core skills you have already practised (awareness, rethinking and experiments). The first strategy is to bring your positive qualities into focus, to learn to accept the good things about yourself. The second is to learn to feel worthy of treating yourself with the same respect and kindness that you would give to another person you cared for, allowing yourself to fully experience life's pleasures and to give yourself credit for what you do.

As you move through the chapter, notice the impact of each of these things on how you feel about yourself and how you go about your daily life. As you do so, you will also be chipping away at your Bottom Line and building the foundations for a new, more accepting and appreciative perspective on yourself.

In essence, you are learning to be a good friend to yourself, someone who values and appreciates you and, most importantly, accepts you for who you are. You are discovering how to treat yourself as you would treat a good friend whom you had known for a long time. You know that they are by no means perfect – like every fallible human being, they have weaknesses and faults, and you are not blind to those. But you do not spend all your time focusing on them. Instead you see them as part of a bigger picture, which also includes a warm appreciation of your friend's strengths and good qualities. When things go wrong for them, you are sensitive to how they are feeling and treat them with compassion. You want them to enjoy life, and you encourage them to celebrate their achievements and successes, however small. This is exactly how you are learning to relate to yourself: as your own good friend.

Bringing good qualities into focus

Learning to acknowledge and value your good qualities involves three steps:

1. Recognising
2. Reliving
3. Recording

We shall look at each of these in turn.

Step 1: Recognising (awareness)

It is impossible to value your good points if you have no idea what they are. So the first step to a balanced view is simply to learn to recognise them and bring them into focus rather than letting them pass you by. A helpful starting point is to make a list of your qualities, talents, skills and strengths. This task kills two birds with one stone. It will help you to build and strengthen a new, more balanced view of yourself. It is also a marvellous opportunity to spot what keeps you stuck in low self-esteem, *as it actually happens*, in front of your very eyes – to become increasingly aware of how screening out and discounting positives shuts out experiences that might encourage you to think more kindly of yourself.

So while you are working on bringing your good qualities into focus, be alert to self-critical thoughts that try to disqualify them and stand in the way of developing a more balanced, kindly and accepting perspective. You will probably (at least at first) not be able to stop self-critical thoughts from automatically popping into your mind, but you can learn to treat them with less respect. After all, they are just old learned habits, out-of-date ideas which you no longer need to believe, feel bad about or act on. They will weaken and decay, so long as you see them for what they are and refuse to allow them to get in your way. Your aim is to reach the point where you can calmly notice these automatic 'yes, buts' ('Oh look, there's another one') and move on, instead of taking them seriously and being knocked sideways by them. If you can, simply put them to one side and continue with your task. If they are too persistent or seem too convincing to let go in this way, then you could use a 'Questioning Self-critical Thoughts' worksheet (page 170) to rethink them them before moving on.

Some people find making a list of their good qualities quite easy. Their doubts about themselves may be relatively weak, or may only surface in particularly challenging situations. As well as a negative view of themselves, they may have more positive, helpful views they can call on when it comes to identifying pluses. Other people, with very powerful and convincing Bottom Lines, can find listing their positive qualities an almost impossible task. The habit of screening them out and discounting them may be so strong that it is difficult initially to accept any good points at all.

Consider for a moment: What if I were to ask you instead to make a list of your weaknesses and failings? You might well get going right away, and be scribbling busily for some time! If you have been discouraged from thinking well of yourself and told not to get above yourself, if your achievements have been ignored, and your needs regarded as unimportant, then it will be hard for you to begin to see yourself in a kindly, appreciative way. This does not mean that, with time and patience, you will not be able to see good things about yourself and value them. However, it may be that you will need some help, perhaps from a close friend or someone else you care about and trust. It is worth investing your time in this task. Even if it takes a while to come up with a good list, making awareness of your good qualities part of day-to-day living will have a considerable impact, over time, on how you feel about yourself.

In order to get started, select a time where you can be sure you will not be interrupted and settle down to make your list. You may feel most comfortable doing this with a sheet of paper and a pen or pencil, or you may prefer to use electronic means. It's up to you – use whatever means work best for you. Make sure you sit somewhere comfortable, where you can feel peaceful and relaxed. You could perhaps put on some music you enjoy. Now make a list of as many good things about yourself as you can think of.

You may at once be able to list several. Or you may be hard put to think of even one or two. Give yourself plenty of time, and don't worry if the task is hard at first. You are trying something new, a fresh perspective on yourself, a shift of emphasis. Take your list as far as you can, and when you feel you have come up with as many items as possible for the time being, stop. Put the list somewhere easily accessible – it may even be helpful to carry it with you. Over the next few days, even if you are not actually working on it, hold it at the back of your mind and add to it as things occur to you. Be pleased even if you can only find one or two things to begin with. You have made a good start in freeing up your thinking and taken the first crucial step towards acknowledging and accepting good things about yourself.

Helpful questions to get you going

If your self-esteem has been low for some time, you will very probably have difficulty in identifying your strong points and qualities. This does not mean that you do not have any – it means that you are out of the habit of noticing and giving weight to them. There are some questions to help you get the ball rolling (see Figure 20). Notice that each question is picking up on a possible 'yes, but', for example, 'Yes, but it's only small', 'Yes, but I'm not always like that', 'Yes, but other people are more like that than I am', and so on.

Figure 21. Questions to Help You Identify Your Good Points

- What do you like about yourself, however small and fleeting?
- What positive qualities do you possess?
- What have you achieved in your life, however small?
- What challenges have you faced?
- What gifts or talents do you have, however modest?
- What skills have you acquired?
- What do other people like or value in you?
- What qualities and actions that you value in others do you share?
- What aspects of yourself would you appreciate if they were aspects of another person?
- What small positives are you discounting?
- What are the bad things you are not?
- How might another person who cared about you describe you?

What do you like about yourself, however small and fleeting?

Look out for anything about yourself that you have ever felt able to appreciate, even if only for a moment.

What positive qualities do you possess?

Include qualities that you feel you do not possess 100 per cent or that you do not show all the time. No one is totally, utterly, completely kind/honest/punctual/thoughtful/ competent/whatever all the time. Give yourself credit for having the quality at all, rather than discounting it because it is less than perfect.

What have you achieved in your life, however small?

You are not looking for anything earth-shattering here (winning the Olympics, being the first to cross the Antarctic on a donkey). Take account of small difficulties you have mastered and steps you have successfully achieved. My list, for example, would start with learning to ride a tricycle by pushing the pedals all the way round, rather than pumping them up and down.

What challenges have you faced in your life?

What anxieties and problems have you tried to conquer? What difficulties have you dealt with? What qualities in you do these efforts reflect? Facing challenges and anxieties takes courage and persistence, whether or not you resolve them successfully. And what about the fact that you are now taking on the challenge of overcoming your low self-esteem? Give yourself credit for all these things.

What gifts or talents do you have, however modest?

What do you do well? Take note: '*well*', not 'perfectly'! Again, remember to include the small things. You do not need to be Michelangelo or Beethoven. If you can boil a mean egg, or whistle a tune, or make farting noises by blowing on your baby's tummy, then add it to the list.

What skills have you acquired?

What do you know how to do? Include work skills, domestic skills, people skills, academic skills, sporting skills and leisure skills. These do not have to be exceptional, something only you can do or that you do to a very high standard. A skill is a skill. For example, do you know how to use a smartphone, social media, a microwave or a saw? Can you catch a ball? Can you drive a car or ride a bicycle? Do you know how to swim, how to sew or how to clean a bathroom? Are you good at listening to people or appreciating their jokes? Can you read in a thoughtful way? Have you learned any languages? Think about all the different areas of your life and note down skills you have in all of them, however partial or basic.

What do other people like or value in you?

What do they thank you for, ask you to do, or compliment you on? What do they praise or appreciate? You may not have been paying much attention to this. Now is the time to start.

What qualities and actions that you value in other people do you share?

It may be easier for you to see other people's strong points than your own. Which of the positive qualities you appreciate in others do you share? Beware of unfavourable comparisons here. You do not have to be or do whatever it is as completely or well or to the same degree as the other person, but simply to acknowledge that you share the quality, even if only to a more limited extent.

What aspects of yourself would you appreciate if they were aspects of another person?

Remember the double standard we discussed in the chapter on self-criticism. You may well be readier to acknowledge and accept qualities or strengths that you can see in other people than the same qualities and strengths in yourself. Be fair. If there are aspects of yourself that you would appreciate if they were another person's, write them on your list. Think also about things that you do that you would appreciate and value if another person did them. Write down anything that would count as a positive if it was done by someone else.

What small positives are you discounting?

You may feel that you should only include major positives on your list. Would you discount small negatives in the same way? If not, write the small positives down. Otherwise it will be impossible to achieve a balanced view.

What are the bad things you are not?

Sometimes people find it easier to think of positive qualities if they start by calling actively negative qualities to mind. The comparison highlights positives and strong points that might otherwise fade into the background and be taken for granted. So think of some bad qualities (e.g. irresponsible, cruel, dishonest or mean). Are you these things? If your answer is 'no', then by definition you must be something else. What are you (e.g. responsible, kind, honest or generous)? Write down the mirror images of the bad qualities you identify. Again, do not discount them because they seem to you to be less than perfect.

How might another person who cared about you describe you?

Think about someone you know who cares about you, respects you and is on your side. What sort of person would *they* say you were? What words would they use to describe you? How would they see you as a friend, a parent, a colleague or a member of your community? People who know you and wish you well may have a kinder, more balanced perspective on you than you do on yourself.

In fact, if there is someone close to you, whom you respect and trust, it could be very helpful to you to ask them to make a list of the things they like and value in you. Make sure you approach someone who will complete this task in the spirit in which it is intended. Otherwise it may backfire on you. Do *not* ask anyone who has contributed to the development of your poor opinion of yourself or whose behaviour is currently feeding into it. Equally, do not ask anyone who believes strongly in the taboo against thinking well of yourself – the task may be too hard for them. Choose someone you have good reason to believe cares about you and wishes you well (e.g. a parent, a brother or sister, a partner, a child, a friend or a colleague with whom you have a close relationship). You may find their list a revelation, and it will strengthen your relationship. But again, watch out for thoughts which lead you to discount and devalue what you read (for example, that they are only doing it to be kind and can't possibly mean what they say). If you have thoughts like these, rethink them on a 'Questioning Self-critical Thoughts' worksheet.

Lin, the artist whose parents had never been able to appreciate her talent, had some difficulty with her list, as you might imagine. Experience had taught her to place very little value on herself, and in particular to devalue what to other people appeared a striking gift. Initially, she could not think of anything to put on it except 'good-natured' and 'hard-working'. She found that, at first, trying to add other items roused all sorts of reservations (e.g. 'Yes, but other people are better at that than me' and 'Yes, but that isn't really important'). After a couple of tries, she used the questions on pages 202 to free up her thinking. She still got stuck and abandoned her list for the time being two or three times, but eventually added 'thoughtful', 'practical', 'good colour sense', 'persistent', 'creative', 'kind', 'good taste', 'adventurous cook' and 'open to new ideas'. In addition, she screwed up her courage and asked an old and trusted friend if he would make a list of her good points, too. He said it was about time she gave her confidence a boost, and set to with a will. Lin was moved and delighted by the affection that shone through his list. He echoed some of the items on her own list, and added 'makes me laugh', 'good listener', 'good drinking companion', 'has created a welcoming home', 'intelligent', 'sensitive' and 'warm'.

Step 2: Reliving

Once you have begun recognising your good qualities, the next step is to help them to sink in, to make them real. On its own, a list is a good first step – but it is not enough. You could put it in a 'safe place' – or, indeed, delete it or put it in the bin – and forget all about it. Your list will be most helpful to you if you use it as a basis for raising your awareness of your good qualities, aiming for the point where recognising, acknowledging and valuing them has become second nature. Of course this will not happen overnight. You will need to practise, to take time to get into the habit of quite deliberately directing attention to them. One way of doing this is to use your memory for experiences of acting in line with them as a resource.

Give yourself a few days to notice more items to add to your list and then, when you feel you have taken it as far as you can for the time being, once again find yourself a comfortable, relaxing spot and read the list to yourself.

Don't skip through it at top speed. Pause and dwell on each quality you have recorded. Let it sink in.

When you have read slowly and carefully through the list, go back to the top again. Now, as you consider each item, bring to mind a particular time when you showed that quality in how you behaved. See if you can find a relatively recent time, so that the memory is still clear in your mind. As you do this, you may find it helpful to close your eyes. Take time to recall the experience as vividly as you possibly can – almost as if you were reliving it, right now. When was this experience? Where were you, and who with? What exactly was it you did that expressed this good quality in action? What were the consequences? See with your mind's eye what you saw at the time, hear with your mind's ear what you heard. What sensations were you aware of in your body (taste, smell, touch, a sense of your body position)? See too if you can call up the emotions you experienced at that moment. Take all the time you need to allow the memory to develop fully in your imagination.

Lin, for example, recalled a time when she had been home by herself and a friend had telephoned, apparently for a casual chat. Lin picked up something in her friend's voice which prompted her to ask gently, *Are you OK?* Her friend burst into tears and confided that she had had an argument with her boyfriend and was feeling really depressed. She was pleased to have an opportunity to talk. Lin was able to accept this as an example of her own sensitivity. In remembering it, she recalled the soft light in her living room and the shapes and colours in the painting opposite where she sat, the sound of her friend's voice, the softness of her sofa cushions, the smell and taste of the coffee she had poured just before the call, the combination of affection and concern she had felt for her friend, and the pleasure of helping and supporting her.

Notice what effect this exercise has on your mood and how you feel about yourself. If you can absorb yourself in it fully, you will find that the items on your list become much more vivid and meaningful to you. You should find your mood lifting, and a sense of self-acceptance and confidence creeping in.

If this does not happen, it could be that in some way you are disqualifying what you have written. Throughout the exercise, keep a watchful eye for feelings of shame, embarrassment or disbelief. These feelings may be a cue that self-critical thoughts are going through your mind. Are you, for example, telling yourself that it's wrong to be so smug? Do you feel as if you are showing off? Are you thinking that what you did was trivial – anyone could have done it? Are you telling yourself it was only what would be expected of any decent human being? Or that you could have done it better? Or faster? Or more effectively? Or that you may be kind/supportive/competent or whatever some of the time, but not all of the time, and if it's not 100 per cent then it doesn't count? Are you devaluing qualities because other people have them too – they are too ordinary to be worth considering?

When 'yes, buts' like these intrude, simply notice their presence and put them to one side. Remember: old habits die hard, so it is hardly surprising if they turn up once again. Then return your attention fully to focusing on your list of positive qualities. And if the disclaimers are too strong to be easily put aside, you can use the skills you have already learned for dealing with self-critical thoughts to rethink them.

Step 3: Recording: Your 'Positives Portfolio'

Making a list of your positive qualities is a first step towards enhancing self-acceptance and self-esteem. Vividly re-experiencing specific examples of those qualities in action takes you a step further, beginning the process of making them real to you, something you can feel on a gut level, instead of something rather theoretical which you can easily ignore or forget.

The next step is to make this awareness into an everyday event, rather than something you cultivate for short periods from time to time, when you remember. What you need to do here is to begin recording examples of your good points every day, as they occur, just as you have been recording examples of anxious predictions and self-critical thoughts. Your objective is to reach the point where you automatic-ally notice examples of your good qualities, without need-ing a reminder. You may reach this point in a few weeks, or it may take longer. Once you get there, there is no further need to record them, though you may like to continue, and it may also be helpful to return to doing so if something happens to give your confidence a knock.

One particularly helpful way of enhancing awareness of your good points is by using a 'Positives Portfolio'. You could open a special electronic file for this. Or, if you prefer paper records, you could buy yourself a special notebook with an attractive cover, small enough to carry in a pocket, wallet or handbag. Creating a special space for your Portfolio is a statement: it shows you are determined to notice and value aspects of yourself you have been ignoring, denying and taking for granted.

As best you can, record examples of your good points *as they occur*. The idea is to correct the bias against yourself by focusing on and highlighting your positive qualities, bringing them forward to centre stage instead of leaving them lurking in the wings. Use your list of qualities, skills, strengths and talents as a prompt to help you get started. Make sure you keep your Portfolio with you, so that you can write things down as soon as they happen. Otherwise, examples may be missed, forgotten or retrospectively discounted. Each day, decide in advance how many examples of positive qualities you wish to record. Many people find that three is about right to start with. But if this feels like too many, don't be afraid to start with two, or even one. Wherever you start, as you get into the swing of it, you will be able to add more. When recording three incidents is easy, increase the number to four. When four is easy, go up to five, and so on. By then, noticing pluses should be pretty automatic.

For each entry in the notebook, record what you did, and what quality it exemplifies. Here, as an example, are some of the items from Lin's first week of using a Positives Portfolio:

- Spent several hours completing a large landscape painting (hard-working)
- Went out for the evening with Simon – haven't laughed so much in ages (good drinking companion, funny)
- Bought flowers (creating a welcoming home)
- Tried cooking a Thai curry for the first time – tasted odd, but was edible (adventurous cook)
- Called Mother as it was her birthday (kind)
- Fixed shelving in workroom (practical)

Notice that Lin did not just write 'hard-working', 'funny', 'kind' and so on in her record. She put in enough detail to be able to remember later what had happened. This is important, because your record can then become a resource for you, a store of reminders of your strengths and good qualities. You can use it regularly to reinforce your new, kinder perspective on yourself. And you can call on these pleasurable and confidence-building memories any time you are feeling stressed, low or bad about yourself.

So, at the end of each day, perhaps just before you go to bed, make time to relax and be comfortable and review what you have recorded. Look over your Portfolio and recreate the memory of what you did in vivid detail, reliving each example. Let it sink in, so that it affects your feelings and your sense of yourself. You can also review the Portfolio weekly, to get the bigger picture, and to decide how many examples of good points to look out for next week. As you do this, step by step, you are learning to appreciate and accept yourself, just as you are.

Treating yourself with respect, consideration and kindness

As well as failing to notice or value their good points, people with low self-esteem often miss out on the richness of everyday experience in two major ways. They do not put any effort into making life pleasurable and satisfying, and they do not give themselves credit for what they do. Behind these patterns, there often lies a sense of being fundamentally unworthy of either of these things. This part of the chapter describes ways of learning to treat yourself with respect and kindness by enriching your life with pleasures, and by giving yourself credit for your day-to-day successes and achievements, however small. These ideas will be particularly useful if your mood is low; in fact, they were originally devised as part of CBT for depression. One of the major side-effects of focusing on your good qualities, increasing the pleasure in your life and giving yourself credit for what you do is to lift mood. And a lift in mood makes it easier to rethink self-critical thoughts and thus break the vicious circle that keeps low self-esteem going.

Increasing pleasure and satisfaction: The 'Daily Activity Diary' (DAD)

Enriching your experience of everyday life with pleasures and with a sense of achievement involves two key steps. The first step is to get a clear picture of how you spend your time, how satisfying your pattern of daily activities is to you, and how good you are at acknowledging your achievements and successes (awareness). This self-observation is the jumping-off point for any changes you would like to introduce – and that is the second step (experiments). Once again, you may well encounter anxious and self-critical thoughts as you go about this, and you can use your rethinking skills to tackle them.

The 'Daily Activity Diary' (DAD) is one way of getting the information you need. You will find a blank example on pages 216–217 and an additional copy is provided in the Appendix. You can also download copies from the 'Overcoming' website. The example, partly completed, on pages 222–223, will give you a sense of how the diary might be used in practice. You will see that it looks something like a school timetable, with the days across the top and the time down the left-hand side. Each day is divided into hourly timeslots, in which you can record what you do and what you gain from what you do, specifically how much you enjoy your activities and how much credit you give yourself for your achievements.

The diary can help you to identify changes you would like to make in how you spend your time, to focus your

Figure 22. Daily Activity Diary

		Mon	Tue	Wed
M O R N I N G	6-7			
	7-8			
	8-9			
	9-10			
	10-11			
	11-12			
A F T E R N O O N	12-1			
	1-2			
	2-3			
	3-4			
	4-5			
	5-6			
E V E N I N G	6-7			
	7-8			
	8-9			
	9-10			
	10-11			
	11-12			

ENHANCING SELF-ACCEPTANCE

Thurs	Fri	Sat	Sun

attention on the positive aspects of your experience (just as you have been focusing on positive aspects of yourself), and to tune in to 'killjoy' thoughts that get in the way of enjoyment and self-critical thoughts that lead you to discount and disqualify your successes. If you do not wish to use the DAD, you could instead use some other form of record (your actual diary, for example, whether paper or electronic). The benefit of an hour-by-hour diary like the DAD is that it prompts you to notice what is going on in close detail and readily offers an overview of your day. At the end of the day, you have an accurate record with lots of useful information, rather than a vague impression of how things have gone. So, however you choose to record your day, following an hour-by-hour format is likely to be most useful to you, at least until you have a clear sense of how you are spending your time.

The first step: Self-observation (Awareness)

Over the course of a week or so, keep a detailed daily record of your activities, hour by hour. You will gather most useful information if the week you record is typical of your life at the moment. This is the information which will be most helpful when you come to consider changes you wish to make. If you record your activities over an exceptional week (e.g. you were on holiday, you were off sick or your mother had come to stay), the information you gather will only really be directly relevant to similar times in the future, not to your everyday life.

What you did

Simply note the activity (or activities) you were engaged in. Anything you do counts as an activity, including sleeping and doing nothing in particular. Even 'doing nothing' is actually doing something. What does it mean exactly? Sitting, staring into space? Pottering around, doing minor domestic tasks? Sitting slumped on the couch, channel-surfing?

Ratings of pleasure (P) and achievement (A)

PLEASURE (P)

How much did you enjoy what you did? Give each activity a rating between 0 and 10 for Pleasure (P). 'P10' would mean you enjoyed it very, very much. On the partially completed Diary on pages 226–227, for example, Lin gave 'P10' to an evening at the theatre with friends. She felt she had thoroughly enjoyed herself. The play was excellent, funny and thought-provoking, and she had had a really good time with people she knew very well and felt completely relaxed with. 'P5' would mean moderate enjoyment. So, for example, Lin gave 'P5' to a walk in the country by herself. She had enjoyed the warmth of the sunny day, but had miscalculated the distance, so that she was very tired by the time she got back to her car. 'P0' would mean you did not enjoy an activity at all. Lin gave 'P0' to a meeting with her agent, who was hassling her to exhibit her recent paintings – even though normally she would have enjoyed his company as she liked and respected him.

You could, of course, use any number between 0 and 10

to show how much you enjoyed a particular activity. Like Lin, you will probably find that your pleasure level varies, according to what you do. This variation will be a useful source of information to you. It shows you what works for you, and what does not work. It may also give you clues about thoughts that get in the way of satisfaction and enjoyment (for example, Lin was aware that she could not enjoy talking to her agent because she was preoccupied with apprehension about exposing her work to public view).

ACHIEVEMENT (A)

To what extent was each activity an experience of mastering something effortful, and thus an achievement? These activities may not in themselves be wildly pleasurable, but they give you a sense of taking care of business, acting in your own best interests, doing things that need to be done – in short, taking control of your life rather than allowing it to take control of you.

'A10' would mean a very considerable achievement. Lin gave herself 'A10' for the phone call she made to her agent a couple of days after their conversation. This was because she called to agree that she would submit work to an exhibition, despite her anxieties. She gave herself a high 'A' rating as recognition that this was a difficult thing to do, and she had to push herself, but she did it. 'A5' would mean a moderate achievement. Lin gave herself 'A5' the morning after her walk when she got up in time to complete a picture she was working on, despite feeling tired. Her first reaction was that getting up was nothing special, but she realised on reflection that given how tired she felt it was quite an achievement. 'A0' would mean no sort of achievement at all. Lin gave herself 'A0' for an evening at home watching television. This was pure self-indulgence, and she enjoyed it, but it did not involve any sort of achievement and so she felt happy to give it a 0 for 'A'.

Again, like Lin, you could use any number between 0 and 10 to judge how much achievement was involved in carrying out a particular activity.

It is important to realise that 'achievement' as we use it here does not only refer to exceptional achievements like getting a promotion, hosting a party for 100 guests, or spring-cleaning the whole house from top to bottom. Nor does it only mean things you have done really, really well. As you may have realised from Lin's ratings, everyday activities can be real achievements, for which you deserve to give yourself credit. This is especially the case if you are feeling stressed, tired, unwell or depressed. When you are not in a good state emotionally or physically, even relatively minor routine activities (taking the children to school, answering the telephone, making a snack, getting to work on time – even getting out of bed) may take a lot of effort. That means that, routine or not, they represent real achievements. Not recognising this often leads people with low self-esteem to devalue what they do, and of course this helps to keep low self-esteem going.

So when you rate 'A', make sure you take into account how you felt at the time. Ask yourself: 'How much of an achievement was this activity, *given how I felt at the time?*' If

Figure 23. Daily Activity Diary – example: Lin				
		Mon	Tue	Wed
M O R N I N G	6-7			
	7-8			
	8-9			
	9-10			
	10-11			
	11-12			
A F T E R N O O N	12-1			
	1-2			Met agent for I wants me to exhibit A5 P0
	2-3			" A4 P1
	3-4			Went round to see F A0 P1
	4-5			" A0 P5
	5-6			Worked A6 P3
E V E N I N G	6-7			" A4 P6
	7-8			Supper A1 P4
	8-9			P came round depressed A4 P2
	9-10			" A4 P4
	10-11			Read A0 P6
	11-12			Bed A0 P4
	12-1			

Thurs	Fri	Sat	Sun
Sleep	Sleep	Sleep	Sleep
Sleep	Sleep A0 P3	"	"
Sleep A0 P5	Got up, coffee, shower. A3 P2	"	"
Got up, breakfast, radio. A1 P4	Out to buy art materials	" A0 P5	" A0 P5
Worked A2 P4	" A3 P4	Got up, breakfast A2 P4	Got up–tired, b'fast, shower A5 P2
" A2 P6	Coffee with M A0 P6	Drove out to Henley A3 P4	Worked A5 P2
" A1 P6	Worked A6 P5	Lunch with cousins A1 P6	" A4 P5
Lunch in park A0 P6	" A6 P5	"	Lunch with J A0 P8
Cleaned up mess in apartment A7 P0	" A4 P7	"	" A0 P8
" A8 P0	Called agent & agreed to exhibit A10 P2	Walked along the river by myself A2 P5	Went to the zoo with J A0 P8
Sat and read A1 P4	Worked A4 P6	" A3 P5	"
Shopping A2 P3	" A4 P6	" A8 P3	Home A0 P2
Met J. & F for drinks & eats A1 P6	Worked A3 P7	Drove home A3 P2	Worked A2 P4
Theatre A0 P10	Supper A1 P4	Phoned Mum A4 P1	" A5 P2
"	TV A0 P6	Listened to music, thinking about work	" A3 P4
"	" A0 P8	" A0 P6	" A2 P6
Pub again A0 P8	" A0 P7	Met P for late drink A1 P1	Bed A0 P5
Back to J's apartment A0 P8	Bed A0 P4	"	
"		Bed A0 P8!	

carrying out the activity represents a triumph over feeling bad, a real effort, a difficulty confronted, then you deserve to give yourself credit for it, even if it was routine, not done to your usual standard or not completed.

FINDING THE BALANCE OF P & A THAT WORKS FOR YOU

Make sure that you rate all your activities for both P and A. Some activities (e.g. duties, obligations, tasks) are mainly A activities. Others are mainly P (relaxing and pleasurable things that we do just for ourselves). Many activities are a mixture of the two. For example, going to a party might warrant a high A rating if socialising makes you nervous, because it represents a victory over your anxious predictions. But once you arrive and begin to relax and have a good time, the party could become enjoyable too. In the long run, you are aiming for a balance of A and P. Giving both ratings to all your activities will help you to find this balance.

Review

At the end of each day, take a few minutes to look back over your diary. A brief daily review will encourage you to reflect on what you have done, rather than simply recording it and leaving it. What do you notice about your day? What does the record tell you about how you are spending your time, how much pleasure you experience, and how easy you find it to give yourself credit for your achievements? What worked for you? What did not work? What were the high spots, both in terms of pleasure and of achievement?

What were the low spots? What would you like more of? Less of? Different? More broadly, what was the 'feel' of it? Did your pattern of activity lift your mood, energise and refresh you, leave you feeling relaxed, confident and calm? Or did it leave you feeling discouraged, drained, tense and ill at ease with yourself?

Here is Lin's review of her DAD (pp. 221).

Review (What do you notice about your day? What worked for you? What did not work? What would you like to change?)

Mon:

Tues:

Wed: Didn't enjoy lunch at all. He was hassling me. As usual, couldn't believe anyone would really like my work.

Thurs: Some good work, which I enjoyed. Great evening – worth planning more of this.

Fri: Hard to get started on work, but sticking with it paid off. Called agent and said yes – terrifying but I need to do it. Treated myself to relaxed, mindless evening at home.

Sat: Walk a good idea but too long. Should have paced myself.

Sun: Planned lunch with J a great success. Lot of fun watching street theatre in Covent Garden.

Making the most of self-observation

How long should I carry on keeping the record?

The objective of the record sheet is to give you a clear idea of how you are spending your time, and how pleasurable and satisfying your daily activities are to you. The record sheet is also an opportunity to start noticing how negative thinking patterns (anxious predictions, self-critical thoughts) may prevent you from making the most of your activities. So continue to keep it until you feel you have enough information for these objectives to be met. For many people, a week or two is enough. But if you feel you need more time to hone your awareness, then there is no need to stop at that point.

When should I complete the record sheet?

Just as with the other worksheets you have encountered, it is important to record what you did, and your ratings, *at the time*, whenever possible. Even if it's not possible to use the DAD itself, make a quick note on anything that comes to hand. It is worth doing this, because in the course of a busy day, things are easily forgotten. In addition, the biases against yourself that are present in low self-esteem are likely to give a clear memory of things that did not go well, and to screen out or minimise pleasures, successes and achievements. This will be all the more so if you are feeling generally low and bad about yourself. Noting your activities and ratings *at the time* will help to counter this bias.

226

Immediate ratings also help you to tune in to even small degrees of pleasure and mastery which may otherwise go unnoticed. Finally, if you put off recording what you do, you are more likely to completely forget to do it, put it off until tomorrow, or perhaps give up altogether before you have collected the information you need.

What if I discover that I am not enjoying anything very much?

This could be because you are not making space in your day for enjoyable activities. Perhaps you are genuinely very busy dealing with a range of responsibilities (e.g. work or study pressures, the needs of your family, looking after elderly parents, your commitment to a neighbourhood network or charity), and giving yourself pleasurable and relaxing 'me time' simply falls off the bottom of your 'to do' list. You can use the DAD to check out if this is so, and work out ways of ensuring that your day includes activities that will relax you and replenish your resources. Even small pauses and moments of pleasure (an extra couple of minutes in the shower, lingering over a coffee, pausing to notice what is around you as you walk to work) will make a difference, if you approach them as precious breathing spaces, opportunities to refresh and energise yourself.

Or perhaps you have a Rule that makes you uncomfortable about putting yourself first or taking time out to do things you enjoy? It feels selfish — even self-indulgent — to prioritise your own needs in this way. If you suspect that this may be the case, look carefully at the pattern of your day. What proportion of time is given over to activities which are pleasurable, relaxing, fun and just for you? Remember the old saying: 'All work and no play makes Jack a dull boy.' If your day is filled with tasks, obligations, duties and things you do for other people, you may end up feeling drained and resentful – exactly the opposite of your generous intentions. If this is your pattern, then experimenting with introducing more enjoyable activities into your day may be one of your objectives at the next stage.

Or perhaps your Rule says you do not deserve to enjoy yourself – you are not good enough. Lin, for example, became aware by keeping the record that, once she had committed herself to a particular piece of work, she did not feel entitled to make time for pleasurable activities until she had completed it and it had been approved.

On the other hand, it could be that you are engaging in potentially pleasurable activities, but that 'killjoy thoughts' are preventing you from enjoying them fully. You can also use the record to begin to become aware of these thoughts. Look for examples of activities which look intuitively as though they should be enjoyable, but in fact were not. What was going on? Were you fully absorbed in what you were doing? Or were you actually preoccupied with other things (like Lin with her agent)? Or stuck in 'it-should-be-different' thinking, making comparisons with other people, who seem to be enjoying themselves more than you? Or comparisons with how things used to be at some time in the past? Or with how you wish things were or think they *should* be?

If, when you engage in potentially pleasurable activities, your mind is actually elsewhere, then you will not enjoy them. So watch out for 'killjoy thoughts' and practise putting them to one side and absorbing yourself in what you are doing, engaging all your senses to the full. If the thoughts are too strong to put to one side, then write them down and look for answers to them (rethinking). This is the beauty of the core skills you have learned for dealing with anxious and self-critical thoughts. You can apply exactly the same core skills to killjoy thoughts – and, indeed, to any other thoughts that upset you and get in the way of leading the life you long to lead.

There is one other possibility, if you find that you are not really enjoying anything at all as you used to. This is one of the classic signs of depression. So if your capacity to experience pleasure seems impaired right across the board, check back to the signs of depression described in Chapter 1 (page 16). If this picture fits you, you may need to seek treatment for depression in its own right. A good starting point might be to read Paul Gilbert's book in this series, *Overcoming Depression,* or you could perhaps consult *The Complete CBT Guide for Depression and Low Mood* (also an 'Overcoming' publication). If these do not help, and your mood remains low, then it may be wise for you to seek professional help.

What if I'm not achieving anything?

If this appears to be the case, use your record and your observation of your thoughts about what you do to find out more about what is going on. It could be that low self-esteem is leading you to restrict your field of activities. Do you miss opportunities, for example, out of anxiety that you will not be able to cope with them? Do you avoid social contacts, lest you make a fool of yourself or people reject you? Do you shun challenges, convinced that you will not be able to meet them? If this is the case, then continuing to work on your anxious and self-critical thoughts can be used as a first step to extending your range or experimenting with a wider range of activities, which will allow you to gain a more positive view of your capabilities and enhance your sense of achievement.

Alternatively, it could be that you already engage in a wide range of activities, including some that are quite difficult or challenging or need a lot of effort, but that self-critical thinking undermines your sense of achievement. As we have discovered, self-critical thinking drains energy and motivation and gives a false impression that you are achieving nothing. It may well be based on very high standards you have for yourself – your Rules for Living. Watch out for 'shoulds', 'musts' and 'oughts' in your thinking – they may be a useful clue that your demanding Rules are active, preventing you from acknowledging and accepting small successes and achievements because they are not special enough or should have been done better or faster or more completely.

The kinds of thoughts that stop you recognising and

valuing your good qualities can also prevent you from giving yourself credit for day-to-day achievements. Watch what runs through your mind when you complete a task. Do your thoughts make you feel good and motivate you to do more? Or do they demoralise and discourage you and leave you feeling you did not do very well and there's little point in continuing? If so, you need to write them down and rethink them, using the skills you have already acquired.

Lin certainly found this to be the case when she first started recording what she did on the DAD. Here are some examples of her self-critical thoughts and how she answered them:

Figure 24. Lin's Self-critical Thoughts

Self-critical thoughts	Alternatives
I'm never going to finish this.	Take things one thing at a time. You're doing fine. Focus on what you have accomplished, not on what you've still got to do. And give yourself credit for what you have done, even if you don't achieve everything.
This is not worth doing.	You always think that, until someone tells you what you've done is OK. Never mind what other people think – those colours are great. And this painting is a real voyage of discovery for you – whether other people think it was worthwhile or not.

So I got out of bed. So what?	So good for me. I was really exhausted. I could have slobbed around all day, and I didn't.
I shouldn't be taking the evening off. I haven't done enough.	Doing things I enjoy helps me feel better about myself and then I relax and think more creatively. If I drive myself non-stop and rush at things like a bull in a china shop, I'll grind to a halt in the end. I know from experience that I get more done when I give myself time off than when I plough on regardless.

This links back to what was said in Chapter 5 (pages 183–4) about experimenting with acting more kindly and encouragingly towards yourself, instead of putting yourself down and ending up engaging in self-defeating behaviour. You can see how the thoughts that prevent Lin from making the most of her experiences are offshoots of her Bottom Line ('I am unimportant, inferior') and of one of her Rules for Living ('Nothing I do is worthwhile unless it is recognised by others'). You can see Lin learning to be more encouraging and appreciative towards herself, to notice and build on her successes, and to treat herself like someone who deserves praise, relaxation and pleasure. Doing these things will chip away at her Bottom Line and help her to act against her Rules, before she is ready to begin to tackle them head on.

The second step: Introducing changes (Experiments)

Now that you can see how you are spending your time, the next step is to use your observations as a basis for introducing changes that will increase your enjoyment and your sense of mastery and achievement. Your daily review of your diary should already have given you a good sense of some of the changes you would like to make. You can now move on to use the observations you have made and the conclusions you have reached to begin planning ahead, so as to ensure a balance between Achievement activities (duties, challenges, obligations, tasks) and Pleasure activities (relaxation, enjoyment). Taking the time to plan ahead is like a statement that you intend to take this seriously, that you value your time and want to make the most of each day.

Initially, it may be worthwhile to do this quite systematically, planning each day in advance using the DAD. This may be particularly important if, at the moment, you are feeling rather low and finding it difficult to motivate yourself. It may also be helpful if self-observation has shown you (for example) that you have strong perfectionist standards that make it difficult for you to give yourself credit for what you do, or that you have problems in putting yourself first or in getting down to things you need to do but have been putting off. If planning a whole day seems like too big a task, then you could break the day down into chunks (e.g. morning, afternoon, evening) and plan each one in turn. Or simply making a list every day of two or three particular things you wish to do (tasks you have been avoiding, perhaps, or things you will enjoy) may be enough to change the balance of your activities in a way that works for you, especially if you decide in advance exactly when you will do whatever it is. However you choose to go about this, once you get the hang of planning ahead, you may well find that you are automatically looking after yourself by balancing out Achievement and Pleasure without needing to record anything. Nonetheless, returning to a full written plan may well be helpful at times in the future, for example when you are particularly busy or under pressure. Then it becomes simply an aspect of effective time management, and a reminder that being busy need not necessarily exclude pleasure and relaxation. Remember: this is not about efficiency, it is about respecting yourself and being sensitive to your needs, making your life a rich and rewarding experience.

If you have decided to experiment systematically with planning ahead, you will need to write down:

Your plan for the day

You may prefer to do this first thing in the morning or in the evening. Choose whichever time is likely to be most helpful to you. For example, if your morning is usually madly busy getting children off to school and yourself off to work, you could do without the extra task. Use the evening (perhaps when you are relaxing just before going to bed) instead. If, on the other hand, you are normally too tired in the evening to think straight, but usually wake feeling refreshed, then use the morning. You can record your plan in draft on the DAD itself, if you wish, or somewhere completely separate. The key thing is to record your plan and what you actually do in such a way that you can easily compare the two at the end of the day. Some people, for example, record both their plan and their actual activity in the same place, but use different colours or typefaces to make it clear which is which.

Each day, aim for a balance between pleasure and achievement. If you fill your time with duties and chores, and allow no time for enjoyment or relaxation, you may end up tired and resentful. On the other hand, if you completely ignore things you have to do, you may find your enjoyment soured by a sense that nothing has been achieved, and the list of tasks you are putting off will hang about at the back of your mind, making it difficult to absorb yourself fully in your pleasures.

Record what you actually do

Use your plan as a guide for the day, and record what you actually do on the DAD. Rate each activity out of ten for Pleasure and Achievement, just as you did at the self-observation stage.

Review your day

At the end of each day, take a few minutes to sit down comfortably, relax and review what you have done.

Thoughtfully examine how you spent your time. To what extent did you stick to your plan? If you did not, why was that? Did you get sidetracked? Did something come up that you had not predicted? Had you planned too much to start with? If so, what prompted you to do that – could there be a perfectionist Rule lurking around here? How much enjoyment and satisfaction did you get from what you did? How good was your balance between P and A? What would you like more of? Less of? Different? What was the impact of your new pattern of activities on your mood, and on your feelings about yourself? This information will help you to get an increasingly clear idea of changes you might like to make in the pattern of your day.

Making the most of planning ahead

What if my plan is a success?

Success means devising a realistic plan, with a good balance of pleasurable activities and achievements, accomplishing what you set out to do, and getting the enjoyment and sense of achievement you wanted. If your plan works for you in this way, you have something really positive to build on. You have clearly found a pattern to the day which works well for you, and which you will want to repeat.

At the same time, you may still find it helpful to carry out some fine-tuning and perhaps use the plan as a way of encouraging yourself to continue to explore fresh pos-sibilities. For example, you might want to add in regular exercise or quality time with your family. You might decide to contact someone you have lost touch with, or to tackle a particular task you have been putting off. You might finally make the time to try something you have always wanted to do, or take the first steps towards new challenges or lifestyle changes you have been considering.

What if my plan doesn't work?

Plans can fall down for many reasons. Although you may feel disappointed that things did not work out as you had hoped, your plan's 'failure' is, in fact, likely to give you very useful information about what keeps you stuck in a pattern of activity which does not give you the pleasure and sense of achievement you seek.

Perhaps you failed to stick to your plan for some reason that you are unhappy about. Supposing, for example, you planned to spend an evening at the cinema with a friend, but then a colleague persuaded you to work late instead. Or supposing you planned to spend a whole morning sorting out your financial affairs, but somehow you never got round to it. Here is a chance to find out more about what might be preventing you from making the most of your experiences. What exactly was the problem? Did you overestimate what you could do in a particular chunk of time? Did you plan too much and exhaust yourself? Did you spend the day doing things you felt you *ought* to do, rather than things that you would enjoy? Did you forget to include breaks: time for yourself or relaxation? Or did you

237

fritter away your time on nothing in particular and end up feeling your day had been wasted? Did you end up doing what everyone else wanted, rather than what would have been good for you? If you notice patterns like these, ask yourself: Are these patterns familiar to me? Are there other situations in which I operate in the same way? Could what went wrong with my plan be a reflection of a more general Rule or strategy of mine?

Once you understand the nature of the problem, you will be in a position to begin tackling it, by making practical changes and by identifying and rethinking the self-defeating thoughts (like Lin's on pages 231–2) that are keeping you stuck. You may well find that what kept you from fulfilling your plan also gets in your way in other areas of your life.

What if I can't think of anything pleasurable to do?

Particularly if low self-esteem has prevented you from looking after yourself and taking pleasure in life, you may well find it hard to think of things to do that you might enjoy. It may be helpful to treat this difficulty as a special project: how many ways to enjoy yourself can you think of? Don't censor yourself as you do this – just let the ideas come and note them, however unlikely they seem.

You could start by noticing what other people do for pleasure. What about your friends and other people you know? What about what you see on the television or social media? Does your town have a 'What's On' website? What about all the activities on the noticeboard in your local library, university and college of further education? What do you notice people enjoying when you are out and about? Make a list. Then turn your attention to yourself. Even if you are not doing much for pleasure right now, have there been times in the past when you did things you enjoyed? What were they? Is there anything you have always fancied doing, but never got around to? What are all the possible things you could do, even if you have never tried them? Add these things to your list.

It's good to think of all the different kinds of pleasures that might work for you under different circumstances. What could you do alone (e.g. reading, watching TV or going for walks)? What could you do with other people (e.g. going to the pub, joining an evening class or going to an art gallery)? What can you do that takes time (e.g. holidays, day trips or going to stay with people)? What can you do that can be easily fitted into the corners of your day (e.g. having a cup of special tea or a glass of special beer, soaking in a hot scented bath or pausing to glance out of the window)? What can you do that costs money (e.g. buying some flowers, going to the cinema or having a meal out)? What can you do that is free (e.g. looking at a sunset, window-shopping or looking through old photographs)? What physical pleasures can you think of (e.g. going swimming, flying a kite or having a massage)? What pleasures can you think of that use your mind (e.g. listening to a debate, doing a jigsaw or a crossword)? What can you do out of doors (e.g. taking care of your garden, going to the beach or going for a drive)? And what can you do at home (e.g. choosing clothes from a catalogue, listening to music or playing computer games)? Add all these things to your list.

Once you have a list of potential pleasures, plan them into your day. You may still have doubts about whether they will work for you. There is only one way to find out: experiments! Remember to watch out for killjoy thoughts. Put them to one side, if you can, and record and rethink them if they persist in getting in your way. When you give yourself pleasures like these, you are treating yourself like someone you love and care about. This is exactly the approach you need to take to enhance your self-esteem. It is OK to look after yourself just as you would look after another loved and respected person – to be your own good friend.

How can I deal with the fact that my day is genuinely full of obligations?

If your day is genuinely busy with things you have to do, it can be difficult to make time for pleasure and relaxation. How can you possibly fit in even one more thing? People with many responsibilities – in fact, probably all of us at one time or another – find it hard to achieve a balance between obligations and pleasures. It is very important to realise, however, that failing to make time just for yourself can backfire on you. If you keep draining the water from a well, sooner or later it will run dry. You may find that you become increasingly tired and stressed so that, in the end, you are no longer able to do all the things you have to do as well as you would like to. Your health may even be affected. So finding time for relaxation is crucially important to your wellbeing and that of people around you.

If you accept that relaxation and pleasure are an essential part of caring for yourself, replenishing your resources and ensuring your health and wellbeing, you will be better able to make room for small pleasures, even on very busy days. Think of them as rewards for all your efforts, to which you are fully entitled. Take five minutes for a cup of coffee and a short walk round your building. Take ten minutes for a shower with special soap. Choose something to eat for supper that you really like. Buy a small bunch of flowers that does not cost much. Listen to a favourite radio programme or podcast while you do the ironing or fix the car. Take advantage of your baby falling asleep to sit and read a magazine instead of feeling obliged to catch up with the housework. Be ingenious and creative, and don't allow yourself to be ground down by a relentless round of tasks and obligations. In the long run, you will not do yourself or anyone else any good.

How can I tackle all the things I have been putting off?

If you have been putting things off for a while, the prospect of facing them may seem rather daunting. However, tackling practical problems enhances a person's feeling of competency and so contributes to self-esteem. Conversely, avoiding problems and tasks is likely further to undermine your sense that you are in charge of your life, and contribute to feeling bad about yourself.

You can begin to get a grip on problems you have been putting off by following these steps:

1. Make a list of the tasks you have been putting off and problems you have been avoiding, in whatever order they occur to you.

2. If you can, number the items on the list in order of importance. Which needs to be done first? And then what? And then what? If you cannot decide, or it genuinely does not matter, simply number them in alphabetical order or in whatever order they first occurred to you.

3. Take the first task or problem on the list. Break it down into small manageable steps. Rehearse the steps in your mind. As you do so, write down any practical problems you might encounter at each step and work out what to do about them. This may involve asking for help or advice, or getting more information.

4. As you rehearse what you plan to do, watch out for thoughts that make it difficult for you to problem-solve or tackle the task. You may find anxious predictions coming up (for example, you won't be able to find a solution, you'll never get everything done). Or you may find yourself being self-critical (e.g. you should have dealt with this weeks ago, you are a lazy slob). If this happens, write your thoughts down and

look for more helpful alternatives to them, as you have already learned to do.

5. Once you have a step-by-step plan you feel reasonably confident of, imagine following the steps through successfully as vividly as you can, just as an athlete imagines clearing the high jump or executing the perfect kick before actually doing it – and by doing so increases the chances that they will execute the manoeuvre successfully in real life.

6. Then tackle the task or problem one step at a time, dealing with any practical difficulties and anxious or self-critical thoughts as they occur – just as you did when you rehearsed doing it in your imagination.

7. Write down the end result in your Daily Activity Diary, and give yourself ratings for P and A. Remember that even a small task completed or a minor problem solved deserves a pat on the back if you have been putting it off! Acknowledge what you have achieved, rather than harping on about everything you have still to do.

8. Take the next task on the list and tackle it in the same way.

Chapter summary

1. *Ignoring your strong points, not allowing yourself to experience life's pleasures to the full, and discounting or denying your achievements are part of the bias against yourself that helps to keep low self-esteem going.*

2. *Enhancing self-acceptance (and thus self-esteem) involves recognising your good qualities (rather than simply focusing on your weaknesses) and developing a balanced and kindly view of yourself. This complements the work you have already done to tackle self-critical thoughts.*

3. *In order to do this, you can step by step learn to recognise, relive and (in your Positives Portfolio) record examples of your good qualities. As you do so, accepting and valuing them — and then accepting and valuing yourself — becomes second nature.*

4. *Paying close attention to how you spend your time, and to how much pleasure and sense of achievement you get from what you do, gives you the information you need to start offering yourself a rich and satisfying life.*

5. *These changes are not always straightforward. Unhelpful old thought patterns and strict Rules for Living can get in the way. You can use the same core skills you have already learned in previous chapters to tackle these.*

6. *The ultimate intention of these changes is to learn to accept yourself for who you are, and to feel worthy of treating yourself with the same kindness and consideration you would give to any other person you cared for — to be your own good friend.*

7

Changing the Rules

Introduction

Anxious predictions and self-critical thoughts do not come out of the blue. As you learned in Chapter 3 (pages 75–98), they are usually the end result of underlying Rules for Living, often formed early in life and designed to help a person get by in the world, given that the Bottom Line appears to be true. The purpose of Rules is to make life more manageable. But in fact, in the long run, they stand in the way of you getting what you want out of life, and prevent you from accepting yourself as you are.

Rules for Living are reflected on a day-to-day basis in strategies or policies, ways of acting which ensure their terms are met. When you have low self-esteem, your personal Rules determine the standards you expect of yourself, what you should do in order to be loved and accepted, and how you should behave in order to feel that you are a good and worthwhile person. Thus personal Rules define the boundary between what is acceptable and what is not. They leave little room for choice: this is the way things must be. They may also detail the consequences if you fail to meet their terms.

Briony's Rule about relationships would be an example of this: 'If I allow anyone close to me, they will hurt and exploit me.' Since the consequences of breaking the Rules are generally painful, you may have become exquisitely sensitive to situations where their terms might not be met. These are the situations that are likely to activate your Bottom Line, leading to the vicious circle of anxious predictions and self-critical thinking described in Chapter 3.

By now, you have discovered how helpful it is to check out anxious predictions and to question and rethink self-critical thoughts. However, stopping at the level of day-to-day thoughts, feelings and actions and leaving your Rules for Living and your Bottom Line untouched might be equivalent to dealing with weeds in your garden by chopping their heads off rather than digging up their roots. This chapter will tell you how to go about identifying your own personal Rules. It will help you to see how they contribute to low self-esteem, and suggest how to go about changing them and formulating new Rules, which will allow you more freedom of movement and encourage you to accept yourself just as you are. You will see that once again the core skills you learned when tackling anxious predictions and self-critical thinking come into play: awareness, rethinking and experiments.

As you work through the chapter, it is worth summarising either on paper or electronically what you discover about your Rules, your line of argument when you question them, your new Rule and your action plan for putting it into practice. You will find some suggested headings on page 248, and an example of a summary on pages 297–9. The headings echo the questions you will find later on in the chapter, and will help you to organise your thoughts in a form that you can come back to and use to ensure that new understanding has a practical impact on your life. This is important because unhelpful Rules for Living can be difficult to change. A line of argument which seems crystal clear to you when you work through the chapter may become hazy and difficult to grasp next time you are in a problem situation and have real need of it. Old Rules that you have acted on again and again in many different situations can be very powerful and compelling, especially if you are upset and it is difficult to think straight. A written summary will help you to keep your new Rule in view and make it easier for you to act on it, even when the going gets tough.

Where do Rules for Living come from?

Rules can be helpful. They help us to make sense of what happens to us, to recognise repeating patterns and to respond to new experiences without bewilderment. They can even help us to survive (e.g. 'I must always look both ways before crossing the road'). Rules are part of how society is organised. National constitutions, political ideologies, legal frameworks, religious beliefs, professional ethics and school codes of behaviour – all these are rules.

Figure 25. Changing the Rules:
Headings for a Written Summary

My old Rule is:	State the Rule in your own words
This Rule has had the following impact on my life:	Summarise the ways in which your old Rule has affected you
I know that the Rule is in operation because	Note the clues that tell you your old Rule is active (thoughts, feelings, body sensations, patterns of behaviour)
It is understandable that I have this Rule because	Summarise the experiences which led to the development of the Rule and have reinforced it
However, the Rule is unreasonable, because:	Summarise the ways in which your Rule does not fit the way the world works or asks more of you than can reasonably be asked of any normal, imperfect human being
The payoffs of obeying the Rule are:	Summarise the advantages of obeying the Rule and the risks of letting it go. Check to see if these are more apparent than real
But the disadvantages are:	Summarise the harmful side effects of obeying the Rule
A more realistic and helpful Rule would be:	Write out your new Rule, in your own words
In order to test-drive the new Rule, I need to:	Write down how you plan to strengthen your new Rule and put it into practice in everyday life

Parents pass on rules to their children, so that they will be able to deal with life independently (e.g. 'Make sure you eat a balanced diet'). Children also absorb rules from their families and parents purely by observation. They notice connections (e.g. 'If I don't tidy my room, Mum will do it for me') and these can become a basis for more general rules (e.g. 'If things go wrong, someone will be there to pick up the pieces'). They tune in to expectations that may never be put into words. They notice what is praised and what is criticised, what brings a smile to a parent's face and what causes a frown. All these experiences can become a basis for personal Rules with a lasting impact on how people live their lives.

Helpful rules tend to be tried and tested, based on a solid foundation of experience. They are flexible, and allow the person to adapt to changes in circumstances and to respond differently to different people. So, for example, a person from one culture who travels to another will be able to adapt successfully to local social conventions, so long as their rules for how to relate to people are flexible and open. But if their social rules are rigid, and especially if they are viewed as the *right and only* way to behave, the person may run into difficulties.

Some rules, instead of helping us to make sense of the world and negotiate its demands successfully, trap us in unhelpful patterns and prevent us from achieving our life goals. They are designed to maintain self-esteem – in fact, they undermine it, because they place demands on us that are impossible to meet. They make no concessions to circumstances or individual needs (e.g. 'You must always give 110 per cent, no matter what the cost'). These extreme and unbending rules create problems. They become a strait-jacket, restricting freedom of movement and preventing change.

Personal Rules that make you vulnerable to low self-esteem may operate in many areas of life. They may determine the performance you expect of yourself in a range of different situations. Perfectionist Rules like Rajiv's, for example, might not only require high-quality performance in the work environment, but might also require perfection in your physical appearance, in where you live and how you decorate and furnish your house, what sort of car you drive, where you go for your holidays – in fact, in how you carry out the most mundane of everyday activities.

Rules can restrict your freedom to be your true self with other people. Like Kate, you may have the sense that approval, liking, love and intimacy are all dependent on your acting (or being) a certain way. Rules may even influence how you react to your own feelings and thoughts. Like Mike, you may base your good opinion of yourself on being fully in control of your emotions, your thoughts and what life throws at you. Unhelpful Rules like these imprison you. They build a wall of expectations, stand-ards and demands around you. Here is your chance to break out.

The relationship between Rules for Living and the Bottom Line

At the heart of low self-esteem is your belief that your Bottom Line is true. Unhelpful Rules for Living are like 'escape clauses', ways to get round the Bottom Line. For example, at heart, you might believe yourself to be incompetent. But *so long as* you work very hard all the time and set yourself high standards, you can override your incompetence and feel OK about yourself. Or you might believe yourself to be unattractive. But *so long as* you are a fount of funny stories, the life and soul of the party, maybe no one will notice and so again you can feel OK about yourself.

Rules like these can work very well, much of the time – which is why we carry on obeying them. For long periods, they may protect you from the pain of low self-esteem, allow you to feel reasonably good about yourself, even if you have underlying doubts. Unfortunately, however, there is a fundamental problem with them. Rules allow you to wallpaper over what you feel to be the real truth about yourself (your Bottom Line). But they do not change it. Indeed, the more successful they are, and the better you are at meeting their demands, the less opportunity they give you to stand back and take stock, question your Bottom Line and adopt a more accepting and appreciative point of view. So the Bottom Line stays intact, waiting to be wheeled into place whenever your Rules are in danger of being broken. You can see how this system worked for Rajiv on page 252.

Figure 26. Rules For Living and the Bottom Line: Rajiv

Bottom Line

I am not good enough

Rules For Living

Unless I get it right, I will never get anywhere in life
If someone criticises me, it means I have failed

Policy

Go for perfection every time
Do everything you can to avoid criticism

Advantage

I do a lot of really good work and get good feedback for it

BUT: Problem

At heart, I still believe my Bottom Line 100%
Obeying the Rules keeps it quiet but it doesn't go away

Plus:

However hard I try, it's not possible to be perfect
and avoid criticism all the time

The more I succeed, the more anxious I get
I feel a fraud – any minute now, I'm going to fall off
the tightrope. And whenever something goes wrong,
or someone is less than wholly positive about me,
I feel terrible – straight back to the Bottom Line

What are Rules like?

Rules are learned

Unhelpful personal Rules are rarely formally taught but rather absorbed through experience and observation. This is rather like a child learning to speak without learning the formal rules of grammar. As an adult, you speak grammatically (if not, you could not make yourself understood) but, unless you have made a special study of it, you are probably quite unaware of the grammatical rules you are obeying. Consequently, you might find it difficult or impossible to put them into words.

Personal Rules for Living are often the same – you may consistently act in accordance with them, without having ever expressed them in so many words. This is likely to be because they reflect decisions you made about how to operate in the world when you were too young to have an adult's broader perspective. Your Rules probably made perfect sense when you drew them up, but they were based on incomplete knowledge and the limited experience available to you at the time, and so may be out of date and irrelevant to your life in the present day.

Rules are part of the culture we grow up in

Rules are part of our social and family heritage. Think, for example, about gender stereotypes, the rules society has evolved about what men and women should be like. We absorb these ideas from our earliest years and, even if we disagree with them, it may be difficult to act against them. We may be punished for attempting to do so by social disapproval – or worse. The difficulties women still have in reaching senior positions in the workplace, the struggle to establish a meaningful role for men in childcare, and the problems gay and transgender people of both genders still encounter in many settings would be examples of this.

Personal Rules for Living are often like exaggerated versions of the rules of the society we grew up in. Western society, for example, places a high value on independence and achievement. In a particular individual, these social pressures might be expressed through Rules like: 'I must never ask for help' and 'If I'm not on top, I'm a flop'. Social and cultural rules can change, and such changes (via the family) will have an impact on personal Rules. The English, for example, used to be famous for their 'stiff upper lip' stoicism. In the individual, this might be expressed as: 'If I show my feelings, people will write me off as a wimp' or 'Rise above it'. More recently, however, things have changed, and the value of openly expressing vulnerability and emotion has come to the fore. In the individual, this might become: 'If I do not follow my heart, it means I am hard and inhuman.' The culture from which personal Rules derive operates at all levels – political systems, ethnic and religious groups, class, community, school. Whatever your background, the chances are that your personal Rules reflect the culture you grew up in and the culture in which you now live, not just your immediate family.

Your Rules are unique to you

Although your personal Rules may have much in common with those of other people growing up in the same culture, no one else will exactly share your experiences of life. Even within the same family, each child's experience is different. However careful parents are to be fair to their children, each one will be treated a little differently, loved in a different way. So your Rules are unique.

Rules are rigid and resist change

This is because they shape how you see things and how you make sense of what happens to you on a day-to-day basis. The negative biases in perception and in interpretation discussed in Chapter 2 reinforce and strengthen them. Rules encourage you to behave in ways that make it difficult for you to discover just how unhelpful they are.

Think back to the work you have done on checking out anxious predictions. You saw how unnecessary precautions prevent you from finding out whether your fears are accurate. Rules work in the same way, but at a more general level. So Rajiv, for example, not only strives to be '100 per cent great' when completing his high-profile assignment, but in a more general sense has perfectionist standards for everything he does. This means that he has no opportunity to discover that, given his natural talents and skills, he has no real need to place such pressure on himself.

Rules are linked to powerful emotions

Strong emotions are a signal that you have broken your Rules or that you are at risk of doing so. You feel depressed or despairing, not sad. You experience rage, not irritation. You react with fear, not apprehension or concern. These powerful emotions are a sign that a Rule is in operation, and that the Bottom Line is gearing up for activation. In this sense, they are useful clues. However, their strength may also make it difficult to observe what is going on with curiosity, from an interested, detached and open-minded perspective.

Rules are unreasonable

Like anxious predictions and self-critical thoughts, personal Rules for Living do not match the facts. They do not fit the way the world works, or what can reasonably be expected of any normal, imperfect human being. Rajiv (page 252) recognises this when he acknowledges that it is not always possible to be perfect or to avoid criticism. We shall return to this point in more detail when we come to reformulate your personal Rules.

Rules are excessive

Unhelpful Rules are overgeneralisations. They do not recognise that what is helpful and adaptive changes according to the circumstances in which you find yourself. They do not respond to variations in time and place, or recognise that what works in one situation or at one time in your life will not work in another. This is reflected in their language: 'always'/'never', 'everyone'/'no one', 'everything'/'nothing'. They prevent you from attending to moment-to-moment changes in your circumstances, from taking each situation on its merits, and from adopting a flexible approach and selecting the best course of action, according to your particular needs at a particular moment in time.

Rules are absolute; they do not allow for shades of grey. Again, this is reflected in their language: 'I must . . .', 'I should . . .', 'I ought to . . .', rather than 'It would be in my interests to . . .' or 'I prefer . . .'; 'I need . . .' rather than 'I want . . .' or 'I would like . . .' This all-or-nothing quality may reflect the fact that they were developed when you were very young, before you had the breadth of experience to see things from a more complex perspective.

Rules guarantee continued low self-esteem

The sequence Rajiv identified on page 252 illustrates an important point. He noticed that his Rules required something that was in fact impossible: unfailing 100 per cent performance and never encountering criticism of any kind. This is characteristic of unhelpful Rules linked to low self-esteem. They mean that your sense of your own worth is dependent on things which are impossible (e.g. being perfect, always being in full control of what happens to you), or outside your control (e.g. being accepted and liked by everyone). People hang self-esteem on a whole range of pegs:

- Being young
- Being beautiful
- Being fit and healthy
- Being in paid employment
- Being a parent
- Money
- Status
- Being at the right school
- Having a partner
- Being a particular weight and shape
- Being top dog
- Achieving success
- Being famous
- Being loved
- Having children who are doing well
- Being secure
- Being sexually attractive . . .

The list is endless and ever-changing. The problem is that none of these things can be guaranteed. We all get old; we all get sick from time to time; we may be damaged or disabled; we may lose our employment (whether through company relocation, economic downturn or even planned retirement); our children leave home (or if they don't, that becomes a cause of concern); there are times in our lives when we have no one special to love us or when our futures are insecure; and so on. All these things are fragile, and could be taken away. This means that, if we depend on them in order to feel good about ourselves, our self-esteem is also fragile. To be happy with yourself simply for existing, to accept yourself just as you are, regardless of your circumstances, puts you in a far stronger position.

How to identify your Rules for Living (Awareness)

What am I looking for?

You are looking for general Rules that reflect what you expect of yourself, your standards for who you should be and how you should behave, your sense of what is acceptable and what is not allowed, and your idea of what is necessary in order to succeed in life and achieve satisfying relationships. In essence, you are defining what you have to do or be in order to feel good about yourself, and what your self-esteem depends on. If you have low self-esteem, the chances are that these standards are demanding and unrealistic (more, for example, than you would expect of any other person) and that, when you explore their impact, you will discover that they actually prevent you from having a secure sense that it is OK to be you.

What form do unhelpful Rules take?

Rules for Living can usually be expressed in one of three ways: assumptions, drivers and value judgements.

1. ASSUMPTIONS

These are your ideas about the connections between self-esteem and other things in life (for example, those listed on page 258). These usually take the form of 'If . . . , then . . .' statements (they can also be phrased as 'Unless . . . , then . . .'). If you look back at the list of Rules for Living on pages 72–3 in Chapter 2, you will find a number of examples of assumptions, for example:

Briony	If I allow anyone close to me, [then] they will hurt and exploit me
Rajiv	If someone criticises me, [then] it means I have failed
Kate	Unless I do everything people expect of me, [then] I will be rejected
Lin	Nothing I do is worthwhile unless it is recognised by others (i.e. Unless what I do is recognised by others, [then] it is not worthwhile)

Sometimes the 'If . . . /Unless . . ., then . . .' is not immediately obvious, but you will see it if you look carefully. For example, Aaron's 'Survival depends on hitting back' could be understood as an assumption: '*Unless* I hit back, *then* I will be destroyed.'

Assumptions like these are rather like negative predictions writ large. They describe what you think will happen if you act (or fail to act) in a certain way. This immediately provides a clue to one important way of changing them: experiments. They can be tested by setting up the 'if . . .' and seeing if the 'then . . .' really happens. As you learned in relation to anxious predictions, the threat could be more apparent than real.

2. DRIVERS

These are the 'shoulds', 'musts' and 'oughts' that compel us to act in particular ways or be particular kinds of people, in order to feel good about ourselves. There are some examples of 'drivers' in the list on pages 72–3:

Briony	I must never let anyone see my true self
Jack	I must always keep myself under tight control
Mike	I should be able to cope with anything life throws at me

Drivers usually link up with a hidden 'or else'. If you can find the 'or else', you will be able to test out how accurate and helpful they are. For Briony, the 'or else' was 'they will see what a bad person I am and reject me'. For Jack, it was 'I will go over the top and spoil things'. For Mike, it was 'I am pathetic'.

You can see from these examples that the 'or else' may be very close to the Bottom Line. In fact, the 'or else' may be a simple statement of the Bottom Line: 'or else it means that I am inadequate/unlovable/incompetent/ugly' or whatever. In this case, the driver is a very clear statement of the standards on which a person bases his or her self-esteem.

3. VALUE JUDGEMENTS

These are statements about how it would be if you acted (or did not act) in a particular way, or if you were (or were not) a particular kind of person. In a sense, these are rather similar to assumptions, but their terms are less clear and they may need to be unpacked to be fully understood. Examples would be: 'It's terrible to make mistakes', 'Being rejected is unbearable', 'It's vital to be on top of things'. If you find rules that take this form, you need to ask yourself some careful questions in order to be clear about the demands they are placing on you. Try to find out what exactly you mean by these big, vague words ('terrible', 'unbearable', 'vital'). For example:

- What's 'terrible' about mistakes? If I did make one, what then? What would it say about me? What is the worst that could happen? What would the consequences be?
- What do I mean by 'unbearable'? If I imagine being rejected, what exactly comes to mind? What do I imagine would happen? How do I think I would feel? And for how long?

- 'Vital' in what way? What would happen if I was not on top of things? What does being on top protect me from? What is the worst that could happen if I was not? Where would that put me? What sort of person would it make me? What impact would it have on my place in the world?

How will I know when I have found my Rules?

Discovering your Rules can be a fascinating process. You become like a detective, searching for the clues that give you the key to the story, an explorer hunting for the map that will show you the paths through the jungle. So once more see if you can approach this investigation in a spirit of interest and curiosity – even playfulness perhaps. Just what is going on here? What *are* your repeating patterns? What do they mean? What do they tell you about what you must do or be in order to feel OK about yourself?

Because you may never have expressed your personal Rules in so many words, they may at first be less easy to spot than anxious and self-critical thoughts, which you can often observe running through your mind at particular moments in time.

You may even feel quite surprised to discover what your Rules are ('Oh, that's nonsense, I don't believe that'). If this is your first reaction, stop for a moment and consider. It may be hard to believe your Rule when you are sitting calmly with it written down in front of you. But what about when you are in a situation relevant to it? For example, if your Rule is to do with pleasing people, what about situations where you feel you have not done so? Or if your Rule is to do with success, what about situations where you feel you have failed? And what about times when you are upset and feeling bad about yourself? Even if the Rule you have identified does not seem fully convincing to you in the cold light of day, do you in fact *act as if it were true*? If so, then unlikely as it may seem, you've struck gold.

When it comes to identifying your Rules, you already have a wealth of relevant information from the work you have done on anxious predictions, self-critical thoughts and enhancing self-acceptance and self-esteem. You may already have observed that certain situations reliably spark off uncomfortable emotions and cause you problems. These are likely to be the situations relevant to your own personal set of Rules.

The key situations for Rajiv, for example, were times when he might be unable to perform to standard and feared he would attract criticism. Your observation of repeating patterns in your reactions may have already given you a pretty clear idea of what your Rules are. If not, do not worry. If you have never put your Rules into words, then it may take a while to find the right formula. Be creative and open-minded. Approach the task from different angles, using the ideas below to develop hunches about what they might be. Try different Rules on for size, experiment with different wordings, and use all the clues at your disposal, until you find a general statement that seems to have been influencing you more or less consistently for some time, and which has affected your life in many different situations.

Identifying Rules for Living: Sources of information

You can use a number of sources of information to identify your Rules. Some of these are summarised below and described in more detail on pages 266–272. You will probably find the process most rewarding and thought-provoking if you explore a range of different sources.

It's worth realising that you may have a number of Rules. Make a note of any you discover. But it is probably best to work systematically on one at a time. Otherwise, you may lose track of what you are doing. Choose a Rule to work on that relates to an area of your life that you particularly want to change (e.g. relationships with other people). When you have completed the process of formulating an alternative Rule and testing it out, you can use what you have learned to tackle other unhelpful Rules that you also wish to change.

**Figure 27. Identifying Unhelpful Rules for Living:
Sources of Information**

- Direct statements
- Themes
- Your judgements of yourself and other people
- Memories, family sayings
- Follow the opposite (things you feel really good about)
- Downward arrow

Direct statements

Look through the record you have kept of your anxious predictions and self-critical thoughts. See if you can identify any Rules masquerading as specific thoughts. On reflection, do any of your predictions in particular situations reflect broader issues? Are any of your self-critical thoughts specific examples of a more general Rule?

Rajiv, when rushing to complete his assignment, has the thought: 'This has got to be 100 per cent great.' On reflection, he could see that this statement could also apply in many other situations – it was a general Rule.

Themes

Even if no Rules for Living are directly stated in your record sheets, can you pick out continuing preoccupations and concerns? Themes that run through the work you have done? What kinds of situations reliably make you doubt yourself (for example, noticing you have not done something well, or having to encounter people you are unfamiliar with)? What aspects of yourself are you most hard on? What behaviour in other people undermines your confidence? Repeating themes can give you some idea of what you require of yourself, other people and the world in order to maintain your sense of self-esteem.

Lin noticed from recording her anxious and self-critical thoughts that she was hard on herself whenever someone showed any sign whatsoever of disliking a painting she had done. On reflection, this helped her to identify a new Rule: 'If someone disapproves of me, there must be something wrong with me.' Rajiv, in contrast, noticed when he recorded his activities in the Daily Activity Diary that he tended to dismiss any activity which did not receive an Achievement rating of 8 or above. He realised after consideration that this all-or-nothing thinking reflected one of his perfectionist Rules: 'If it's not 100 per cent, it's pointless.'

Your judgements of yourself and other people

Look at your self-critical thoughts. Under what circumstances do you begin to put yourself down? What do you criticise in yourself? What does that tell you about what you expect of yourself? What might happen if you relax your standards? How could things go wrong? If you do not keep a tight rein on yourself and obey the Rule, where will you end up? What sort of person might you become (e.g.

stupid, lazy, selfish)? What are you never allowed to do or be, no matter what?

Consider, too, what you criticise in other people. What standards do you expect them to meet? These may reflect the demands you place on yourself. Rajiv, for example, noticed that he was always impatient with people who took a relaxed attitude to their work, allowed themselves lunch breaks and went home at a reasonable hour. 'Useless,' he would say to himself. 'Might as well not bother to come in at all.' This harsh judgement of other people was another clue to the high standards he set himself.

Memories, family sayings

As has been said, Rules have their roots in experience. Sometimes people can trace them back to particular early experiences, or to sayings that were current in the household where they grew up. Identifying these may help you to understand the policies you have adopted. Your Rules may now be outdated and unhelpful, but there was a time when they made perfect sense.

When I asked for something as a child, I was often told in disapproving tones: 'I want doesn't get.' The message I took away from this was that if I wanted something, I would not be allowed to have it, or it would be taken away from me. In order to avoid disappointment, it was probably better not to want anything, and it was certainly not a good policy to be open about what you wanted.

I realised only many years later, after having children of my own, that 'I want doesn't get' was actually intended to convey an entirely different message: 'If you want something, say please' or, more broadly, 'Be polite'. Despite this new understanding, I still sometimes feel awkward and uncomfortable asking directly for what I want, and apprehensive about committing myself to wanting anything wholeheartedly – indeed I can still have trouble defining what I want at all.

This example shows how statements can have one meaning for the people who make them, and another for the people on the receiving end. What was intended as a lesson in manners was understood in a less benign way. As a child, not knowing any different, I took what I was told absolutely literally. The policy I developed as a consequence has stuck with me through thick and thin. Even insight into the difficulty and its origins has not eliminated it completely. As you will discover, identifying your Rules is only the first step to changing them.

Think back to when you were young, as a child and in your teens, and consider the messages you received about how to behave and what sort of person you should be. Ask yourself:

When I was growing up:

- What was I told I should and should not do?
- What were the consequences if I did not go along with what I was told? What sort of person did that make me? What was I told to expect?

What were the implications for my relationships with other people, or for my future?

- What was I criticised, punished or ridiculed for?
- What did people say or do when I did not make the grade, or failed to meet expectations?
- How did people important to me react when I made mistakes, or was naughty, or did not do well at school?
- What was I praised and appreciated for?
- What did I have to do or be in order to receive warmth and affection?
- What family proverbs and sayings can I remember (e.g. 'better safe than sorry', 'present pain for future gain', 'stupid is as stupid does')?

To help you search out memories of particular experiences, look at your thought records again, and pick out feelings and thoughts that seem typical to you (themes). Ask yourself:

- When did I first have those feelings, or notice myself thinking and behaving in that way? What were the circumstances?
- When I look at something that typically makes me anxious or triggers self-criticism, does this

remind me of anything in my past? Whose voices or faces come to mind?

- When did I first grasp that certain things were expected of me, or get the sense that approval or love were dependent on something I was required to do or be, rather than simply on the fact that I existed?

- What particular memories or images or sayings come to mind? Kate's desire to please, for example, was reinforced by her mother's repeated statement: 'If you're naughty, Mother won't love you any more.' She also had a clear (and still upsetting) memory of a particular time when her mother unexpectedly left the house after an argument. Kate could still see herself running down the street, begging her mother to come back, convinced that she was being abandoned.

Follow the opposite

Your knowledge of situations which you find difficult is one valuable source of information about your Rules for Living. You may also find clues by looking carefully at the times when you feel particularly good. These may be the times when you have obeyed the Rules, done as you should and got the reactions from others that you need in order to feel good about yourself. You *did* reach those high standards, you *did* look absolutely stunning in every detail, everyone *did* like you, it was tough but you *did* keep things under control. So, ask yourself:

- What makes me feel really, really good?
- What are the implications of this? What Rule might I have obeyed? What standards have I met?
- What qualities and actions do I really admire and value in other people? What does this tell me about how I am supposed to act or be?

Downward arrow

This is a way of using your awareness of how you think and feel in specific problem situations to get at general Rules. It was first described in David Burns's book, *Feeling Good*, a self-help CBT manual for depression. You will find an example (Rajiv's downward arrow) on page 277. These are the steps involved:

YOUR STARTING POINT

Think of a kind of problem situation that reliably upsets you and makes you feel bad about yourself (for example, being criticised, failing to meet a deadline, avoiding an opportunity). These are the situations where your Bottom Line has been activated because you are in danger of breaking your Rules, or have actually broken them. Now find a recent example which is still fresh in your memory.

THE DETAILS

Call the example vividly to mind. What was the situation? Exactly what happened? What thoughts or images were running through your mind? What emotions did you experience? What was going on in your body? What did you do? And what was the outcome? Write down what you remember, in detail.

When you have done so, identify the thought or image that seems to you to be most important, and which most fully accounts for your experience, how you felt and what you did.

THE DOWNWARD ARROW

Then, instead of searching immediately for alternatives, ask yourself: 'Supposing that thought or image were true, what would it mean to me?' When you find your answer to this question, rather than trying to work out alternatives to it, ask the question again: 'And supposing *that* were true, what would it mean to me?' And again. Continue on, step by step, until you discover the general underlying Rule that makes sense of your thoughts and feelings in the specific problem situation you started from. There is no particular number of steps it takes to get from situation to Rule. Sometimes people get there very quickly, sometimes not – especially perhaps if your Rule has never been put into words.

'What would that mean to you?' is only one possible question you can use to pursue the downward arrow. You will find others that may be helpful in teasing out the rule behind the problem listed below.

You may find it interesting to pursue downward arrows from a number of different starting points. This is especially important if you have difficulty identifying your Rule when you first approach the downward arrow, and if you have the sense that there may be other Rules around – people very often have more than one. It is both a way of verifying that you are on the right track, and also a route to discovering other Rules within your system if there are any. Experiment with asking different questions, too. The answers may be illuminating.

Figure 28. Downward Arrow Questions

- Supposing that were true, what would it mean to me?

- Supposing that were true, what would happen then?

- What's the worst that might happen? And what would happen then? And then?

- What would be so bad about that? (n.b. 'I would feel bad' is not a helpful answer to this question. You probably would feel bad, but that on its own will not tell you anything useful or interesting about your Rules. So if your immediate answer is something about your own feelings, ask yourself why you would feel bad.)

- How would that be a problem for me?

- What are the implications of that?

- What does that tell me about how I should behave?

- What does that tell me about what I expect from myself, or from other people?

- What does that tell me about my standards for myself?

- What does that tell me about the sort of person I should be in order to feel good about myself?

- What does that tell me about what I must do or be, in order to gain the acceptance, approval, liking or love of other people?

- What does that tell me about what I must do or be in order to succeed in life?

If, when you do the downward arrow, you have a sense of going round in circles after a certain point, the chances are that you have reached your Rule, but that it is not in a form you can easily recognise. Stop questioning, stand back and reflect on your sequence. What Rule for Living do the final levels suggest to you? When you have an idea, a draft Rule, try it on for size. Can you think of other situations where this might apply? Does it make sense of how you operate elsewhere?

Try another similar starting point. Does it end up in the same place? Take a few days to observe yourself, especially your anxious predictions and self-critical thoughts. Does your draft Rule make sense of your everyday reactions? If so, you are in a position to start looking for a more helpful alternative. If not, what Rule might better account for what you observe? Don't be discouraged; have another go.

You may find at first that you have a good general sense of what your Rule might be, but that the way you have expressed it doesn't feel quite right. Play around with the wording until you find a version that 'clicks' with you. Try out the different possible forms a Rule can take: assumptions, drivers and value judgements. When you get the right wording, you will experience a sense of recognition – 'Aha! So that's what it is.'

Assessing the impact of your Rules for Living

Rules are not like anxious predictions or self-critical thoughts. They do not pop into your head under specific circumstances at specific moments. They are much broader, more general in their impact, and may influence how you think, feel and act across a whole range of different situations, and across time. As we said, you may well have learned them when you were very young.

Once you have identified an unhelpful Rule, it is worth considering the impact it has had on your life. When you come to change it, you will not only need to formulate an alternative, more realistic and helpful Rule for Living, but also to reduce the continued influence of the old Rule on daily living.

Recognising its impact will help you to achieve this. You will already have much of the information you need from the work you have done on anxious predictions, self-critical thoughts and enhancing self-esteem.

Start by looking at your life now. What aspects of it does your Rule affect? For example, relationships? Work? Study? How you spend your leisure time? How well you look after

Figure 29. The Downward Arrow: Rajiv

Situation:
Was asked a question I could not answer in a meeting

Emotions:
Anxious, self-conscious, embarrassed

Body Sensations:
Hot, tight jaw and hands

Thought:
'I should know the answer to that'

What does it mean to me that I don't?

'That I'm not doing my job properly'

And if that was true, what would it mean to me?

'That sooner or later people will notice that I'm not up to it'

And supposing they did, what would follow on from that?

'I would lose credibility. I might be demoted'

And what are the implications of all that for my performance?

*'I really can't afford not to have the answers to everything.
I've got to come up with the goods, all the time, no matter what'*

So what's the Rule?
Unless I always get it right, I will never get anywhere in life

yourself? How you react when things do not go well? How you respond to opportunities and challenges? How good you are at expressing your feelings and making sure your needs are met? How do you know your Rule is in operation? What are the clues? Particular emotions, or sensations in your body, or trains of thought? Things you do (or fail to do)? Reactions you get from other people?

Now look back over time. Can you see a similar pattern extending into your past? From a historical perspective, what effect has the Rule had on you? What unnecessary self-protective policies and precautions has it led to? What have you missed out on or failed to take advantage of, or lost or jeopardised because of the Rule? What restrictions has it placed on you? How has it undermined your freedom to appreciate yourself and to relax with others? How has it affected your capacity for pleasure? Look back at the work you have already done in previous chapters. How much can the day-to-day reactions you have observed be accounted for by this Rule?

Consolidating your discoveries

You should now have a good sense of what your Rule (or Rules) might be. Consolidate by summarising in writing what you have discovered:

- My Rule is:

- This Rule has had the following impact on my life:

- I know that the Rule is in operation, because (note thoughts, feelings, body sensations, behaviour):

You may find it helpful to increase your awareness of how the Rule operates by watching it in action for a few days. Collect examples (probably very similar to what you have already been recording) and fine-tune your understanding of how it influences you and the signals that tell you that it is in operation. Once you have identified it, you may discover it popping up all over the place.

Changing the Rules: Rethinking and experiments

Your Rules for Living may have been in place for some considerable time. They will not change overnight. However, you are not at square one. The core skills you have already mastered in dealing with anxious predictions and self-critical thoughts, in focusing on your good points and treating yourself with respect and kindness, are all central to changing the Rules. Now that you know what they are, you will move on to questioning the Rules in their own right (rethinking), and then to experimenting with doing things differently. You will find some helpful questions listed on page 281 and discussed in more detail below.

Your aim is to find new Rules which will encourage you to adopt more realistic and compassionate standards for yourself and help you to get what you want out of life. As we said earlier, you may have discovered more than one unhelpful Rule that keeps your self-esteem low (for example, you need approval, and you are also something of a perfectionist). If so, start with the one you would most like to change, and then use what you learn to reformulate the others. You will gain more from working systematically on one Rule at a time than from jumping around from one to another, doing a little bit here and a little bit there. You may find it helpful to summarise your line of argument and how you plan to test-drive your new Rule as suggested overleaf.

Figure 30. Changing the Rules: Helpful Questions

- Where did the Rule come from?
- In what ways is the Rule unreasonable?
- What are the payoffs of obeying the Rule?
- What are the disadvantages?
- What alternative Rule would be more realistic and helpful?
- What do I need to do to 'test-drive' my new Rule? How can I go about putting it into practice on a day-to-day basis?

Where did the Rule come from?

The purpose here is not to wallow in the past, but rather to put your Rules in context, to understand how they started and what has kept them going. This will help you to step back from them and see them simply as out-of-date strategies which you no longer need to obey. Keep these questions in mind:

- To what extent does my past experience make sense of my Rules?
- How well does it explain the strategies I have adopted?
- How well does it help me to understand how I operate in the present day?

You may already have a good idea of where your Rules come from. Understanding their origins will help you to see that they were your best options, given the knowledge available to you at the time. This compassionate insight in itself will not necessarily produce substantial change, but it can be a helpful first step towards updating your Rules. However, if you cannot think where they have come from, do not despair. This information is not essential to changing them. It just means that the questions which follow are likely to be more helpful to you.

If you know what they are, summarise the experiences in your life that led to the Rule you are working on. Remind yourself when you first noticed the cues that tell you it is in operation. Was the Rule part of your family culture, or part of the wider culture in which you grew up? Did you adopt it as a means of dealing with difficult and distressing circumstances? Was it a way of ensuring the closeness and caring you needed as a child? Or of managing unkind or unpredictable adults? Or coping with the demands of school, or the transition to adult life? Or perhaps of protecting yourself from teasing and ridicule?

You may also want to take account of later experiences that have contributed to keeping the Rule in place. For example, have you found yourself trapped in abusive relationships? Have other people taken over your parents' demanding and critical stance towards you? Have you repeatedly found yourself in environments that reinforce the policies you have adopted? Rajiv, for example, had particular problems in one job where he had a bad-tempered and critical boss. Under this pressure, he redoubled his efforts to get it right.

Granted that the Rule did make sense at one point, how relevant is it to you now, as an adult? If you come from a broadly Christian culture, there was probably a time in your life when you believed in Santa Claus. You had every reason to do so. People you trusted told you he existed, and you saw the evidence with your own eyes on Christmas morning. It made perfect sense to adopt a policy of trying to be especially good in the days before Christmas and putting out a stocking (or pillowcase) for your presents. When I was a child, we also left a glass of brandy and a mince pie out for the old man, and some carrots for the reindeer. In the morning, nothing was left but crumbs.

But things move on, and you now have a broader experience of life and a different understanding of what happened on Christmas Eve. It is unlikely that, as an adult, you are still convinced that Santa Claus exists and behave accordingly. It would be odd if you still put out your stocking – unless, of course, you have good reason to suppose that someone else in your household will fill it, or you are playing Santa Claus for a new generation of children.

If you come from a cultural background which does not recognise Santa Claus, you may be able to think of other myths or stories which you believed in as a child but which now, as an adult, you understand differently. Maybe the same is true of your personal Rules. Are they still necessary or beneficial? Or might you in fact be better off with an updated perspective?

In what ways is the Rule unreasonable?

This question is a little like questioning negative thoughts by assessing the evidence for and against them. Unhelpful Rules for Living are extreme in their demands. In this sense, they depart from the facts and refuse to recognise the richness and variety of experience. Call on your adult knowledge to consider in what ways *your* Rule fails to take account of how the world works. How does it go beyond what is realistically possible for an ordinary, imperfect human being, or what you would expect from another person you respected and cared about? In what ways are its demands over the top, exaggerated or even impossible to meet?

Remember, this was a contract you made with yourself as a child. Would you now allow a child to run your life for you? Why not? What can you see as an adult that you could not grasp when you were very young? Given their limited experience of life, how good are children at seeing that one situation is different from another, that what works with one person does not work with another, that everything passes, that what is true at one time and in one place may not be true at another?

What are the payoffs of obeying the Rule?

However unhelpful they are in the long run, Rules for Living have genuine payoffs. These help to keep them in place.

Rajiv, for example, knew that his high standards did genuinely motivate him to produce excellent work, for which he was respected and praised and which had helped to advance his career. This was not something he wished to lose.

It is important to be clear about the payoffs for your own Rules, because alternatives you formulate will need to give you the advantages of the old Rule, without its disadvantages. Otherwise, you may be understandably reluctant to let go of the old system – after all, better the devil you know than the devil you don't.

Make a list of the payoffs and advantages of your Rule. What benefits do you gain from it? In what ways is it helpful to you? And consider too what you might risk if you were to let go of it. What does it protect you from?

People often have an uneasy feeling that if they were to abandon their Rules, catastrophe would follow. Rajiv suspected that if he were not a perfectionist, he might never again do a decent piece of work. It felt to him as though perfectionism was the only thing that guaranteed acceptance by other people. Ideas like these can be tested out through experiments at a later stage. For the moment, the important thing is to identify payoffs and fears that keep the old Rule in place.

When you have listed all the payoffs of your Rule, take a careful look at them. Some of them may be more apparent than real. For example, the Rule that you must always put others first may encourage you to be genuinely helpful, and dispose others to feel kindly towards you. But there is a downside. Your own needs are not met, and you may end up feeling increasingly resentful and drained, so that in the end you are no longer in a fit state to look after others.

Rajiv realised, on reflection, that his excellent work did not in fact always guarantee acceptance. He was sometimes so driven and tense that people found him unapproachable and thought him arrogant.

Do not take the payoffs you have identified for granted. Look at them closely: To what extent do they genuinely work for you in practice? Do the same for your concerns about dropping your Rule. How do you know these things would actually happen? How could you find out?

What are the disadvantages of obeying the Rule?

You have explored the payoffs; now for the downside. Basically, unhelpful Rules make it impossible to relax into simply being who you are, because there is a constant pressure to be somebody else – somebody more intelligent, or thinner, or more hard-working, or more sociable, or whatever. Examine the ways in which your Rule restricts your opportunities, robs you of pleasure, contaminates and sours your relationships with other people, undermines your sense of achievement or stands in the way of getting what you want out of life. Use the information you have already collected when you were assessing its impact on your life and observing it in action from day to day.

It may help to clarify the impact of the Rule on your chances of living the kind of life you want for yourself. Make a list of what you most value, what life goals are most important to you. Examples might be: to have a satisfying career; to take pleasure in what I do; to be relaxed and confident with people; to use my talents to give something of value to others; to make the most of every experience. Then ask yourself: Does this Rule help me to reach these goals? Is it the best strategy for getting what I most value in life? Or does it in fact stand in my way?

Charting payoffs and disadvantages

It can be helpful to summarise the payoffs and disadvantages you have identified by recording them in two side-by-side columns. In the left-hand column, write down the payoffs attached to your Rule and the apparent risks of letting it go. In the right-hand column, list its disadvantages. Weigh up the two lists and, at the bottom, write your conclusions about just how helpful your Rule is to you. If you decide that, on balance, it is helpful and takes you where you want to go, then you need take this exercise no further. If, on the other hand, you conclude that it is *un*helpful, and stands in the way of a fulfilled life, lived according to your deepest values, the next step is to formulate an alternative that will give you the advantages of the old Rule without its disadvantages.

What alternative Rule would be more realistic and helpful?

New Rules can transform everyday experiences. They allow you to deal comfortably and confidently with situations which, under the old system, would have been code violations, triggering anxiety or self-criticism. What would have been disasters become passing inconveniences. What have seemed matters of life and death become exciting challenges and opportunities. New Rules open the door to attaining what is most important to you in life.

To help you to free up your thinking, consider whether you would advise another person to adopt your old Rule. If, for example, an alien from outer space came to you for advice on how to ensure a happy and fulfilled life in your part of the planet, what would you say? Or again, would you want to pass on your Rule to your children, if you had any? If not, what would you prefer their Rule to be?

Your task is to find a new Rule which as far as possible allows you to enjoy the payoffs of the old, but eliminates its disadvantages. The new Rule will probably be more flexible and realistic than the old one, more able to take account of variations in circumstances, and to operate in terms of 'some of the people, some of the time'. It will inhabit the middle ground rather than the extremes. So it will be phrased in terms of 'I want . . .', 'I enjoy . . .', 'I pre-fer . . .', 'It's OK to . . .', rather than 'I must . . .', 'I should . . .', 'I ought to . . .', or 'It would be terrible if . . .' You may find that the new Rule starts with the same 'if . . .', but ends with a different 'then . . .'. For example, Rajiv replaced 'If someone criticises me, it means I have failed' with 'If someone criticises me, I may or may not deserve it. If I have done something worthy of criticism, that's not failure − it's all part of being human, and an opportunity to learn, and there's nothing wrong with that.'

This example illustrates something typical of new Rules: they are often longer and more elaborate than old ones. This reflects the fact that they are based on your adult ability to understand how the world works at a deeper level and to take account of variations in circumstances. Sometimes it is nice, however, to capture their essence in a slogan, the sort of snappy statement you might find on a badge or T-shirt. Some time after he had formulated his new Rule, Rajiv watched a film in which a young boy was struggling to please his father on the mistaken grounds that only something exceptional would win his approval. Rajiv decided to adopt the father's loving response as a slogan for himself: 'You don't have to be great, to be great.'

You may find it difficult at first to find an alternative you feel comfortable with. Once you have what feels like a good draft, it can be very helpful to use your imagination to get a feel for how it might work in practice before you try it in the real world. Take yourself back to the problem situation which was the starting point for your downward arrow. Supposing your new Rule had been in place at that time, how would it have changed things? Imagine as vividly as you can what sort of thoughts, feelings and body sensations might have been present, and how you might have acted differently. Would things have played out differently and better if you had been operating from your new Rule? If yes, then time to experiment. If no, then time to think again.

Once you have something that feels workable, write it down, and then try putting it into operation for a week or two to find out how well it works for you in real situations. Here is where experiments once more come to the fore – exploring through direct experience what the impact of your new Rule is and using that experience to reinforce it, or to change it for the better if you need to.

It may also be worth your while to talk to and observe other people. What do you think their Rules might be? Your observations will give you an opportunity to discover the variety of positions people adopt, and to clarify what stance might work best for you.

What do you need to do to 'test-drive' your new Rule? How can you go about putting it into practice on a day-to-day basis? (Experiments)

Your old Rule may have been in operation for some considerable time. In contrast, the new one is fresh from the lathe, and it may take a while for it to become a comfortable fit. What can you do to consolidate your new policy, check out how well it works for you, and learn how to put it into practice on an everyday basis? This takes us back to all the work you have already done, and to the central idea of finding things out for yourself by setting up experiments and examining their outcome. The most important thing you can do to strengthen your new Rule (and indeed to discover if you need to make further changes to it) is to act as if it was true and observe the outcome. The next section will provide some ideas on how to go about this.

Consolidating what you have learned

The written summary

This is a good time to complete your written summary, and using the headings on page 248 if you wish on paper or electronically. You will find an example (Rajiv's written summary) on pages 297–9. You have already summarised what you discovered when you were identifying your unhelpful Rule; now you can summarise what you learned when you worked on changing it.

Like your list of positive qualities and good points, a written summary on its own is not enough. The line of argument you have pursued, and the new Rule you have formulated, need to be part of your everyday awareness, so that they have the best possible chance of influencing your feelings and thoughts and what you do in problem situations. So when you have completed your summary, make sure it is somewhere easily accessible and, over the next few weeks, read it carefully every day, letting it sink in – perhaps more than once a day, to begin with. A good time is just after you get up. This puts you in the right frame of mind for the day. Another good time is just before you go to bed, when you can think over your day and consider how the work you have done is changing things for you.

The objective is to make your new Rule part of your mental furniture so that eventually, acting in accordance with it becomes second nature. Continue to read your summary regularly until you find you have reached this point.

The flashcard

Another helpful way to encourage the changes you are trying to make is to write your new Rule on a stiff card (an
index card, for example) small enough to be easily carried in
a wallet or purse. Or you could have it as wallpaper on your
computer, or programme it to pop up at intervals on your
mobile phone. You can use these as reminders of the new
strategies you aim to adopt, for example reading them carefully when you have a quiet moment in the day, and before
you enter situations you know are likely to be problematic
for you.

Dealing with the old Rule

Even when you have a well-formulated alternative and you
are beginning to put it into practice, your old Rule may
still rear its ugly head in the usual situations for some while.
After all, it has been around for a long time and might not
just slink quietly away as soon as you expose it to the light
of day. If you are prepared for this, you will be able to
tackle the old Rule calmly when you see it in operation,
realising that it is a chance to deepen your new learning
instead of getting discouraged and wondering if you will
ever be rid of it. Here is where the work you have done
on anxious predictions and self-critical thoughts will pay
off. Remember that these are the signs that the old Rule is
in danger of being broken or has been broken. Continue
to use the core skills you have learned to question your
thoughts, find alternatives to them, and experiment with

acting in different ways. Over time, you will find you have less and less need to do so.

Experimenting with the new Rule

As well as tackling the old Rule when it comes up, you need to develop a clear plan of action to help you experiment with acting in accordance with the new Rule and observing the outcome. Do the 'if . . .' or 'unless . . .' and see if the 'then . . .' follows. If you look back over earlier chapters, you may well find that in fact you have already been doing so when you checked out anxious thoughts, countered self-criticism by being kinder towards yourself, focused on your good points, gave yourself credit for your achievements, and treated yourself as you would treat a good friend. Examine what you have already done, and identify things which will help with changing your Rules. You can put them in your action plan.

In addition, ask yourself what else you could do to ensure that your new Rule is indeed a useful policy, and to explore the impact of adopting it on your everyday life. This means expanding your boundaries, discovering that it is still possible to feel good about yourself even if you are less than perfect, even if some people dislike and disapprove of you, even if you sometimes put yourself first, or even if you are sometimes gloriously out of control.

Make sure that you include specific changes in how you go about things, not just general strategies. Not just 'to be more assertive', for example, but 'ask for help when I need it', 'say no when I disagree with someone', 'refuse requests when to carry them out would be very costly for me', 'be open about my thoughts and feelings with people I know well'. Then consider how to plan these changes into your life. You could, for instance, use the Daily Activity Diary to plan experiments at specific times, with specific people, in specific situations.

You will also need to be sure that you know how to go about assessing the results of your experiments. This is rather like what you learned to do when you were checking out anxious predictions. What exactly do you need to be on the lookout for? What would be the signs that your new policy was paying off – or not? What would you observe in yourself (your thoughts and feelings, your body state, changes in your behaviour) if the new Rule was working (or not)? What would you see in others' reactions to you? Just as, at the level of specific thoughts, you specified your predictions and how you would know if they were true, so you need to be specific when carrying out experiments to consolidate and strengthen new Rules for Living.

Don't be surprised if acting in accordance with your new Rule feels uncomfortable at first. You may well feel quite apprehensive before you carry out experiments. If so, work out what you are predicting and use your experiment to check it out (remember to drop unnecessary precautions, otherwise you will not get the information you need). Equally, you may find you feel guilty or worried after you have carried out an experiment, even if it has gone well. This happens, for example, with people who are experimenting with being less self-sacrificing or with dropping

Figure 31. Experimenting with New Rules Worksheet

Date/Time	The situation	What I did	The outcome

their standards from '110 per cent' to 'good enough'. Or again, you may get angry with yourself and become self-critical if you plan to carry out an experiment and then chicken out. If you experience uncomfortable feelings like these, look for the thoughts behind them and answer them, using the core skills you have already practised.

Be prepared

It could take some months for your new Rule to take over completely. As long as it is useful to you and you can see it taking you in useful and interesting directions, don't give up. You may find it helpful to review your progress regularly and to set yourself targets. What have you achieved in the last week? The last month? What do you want to aim for in the next week? The next month?

Keeping written records of your experiments and their outcome, and of unhelpful thoughts that you have tackled along the way, will help you to see how things are progressing. Use either paper or electronic records – whatever suits you best. The 'Experimenting with New Rules' worksheet on page 295 may help you to do this work systematically. You will find extra copies in the Appendix, and you can also download them from the 'Overcoming' website. You can look back over what you have done and use it as a source of encouragement. It may also be helpful to work with a friend – ideally, someone who does not share your particular Rule and whose particular Rule you do not share. Two heads are better than one, but not when you both have identical perspectives.

Figure 32. Changing the Rules:
Written Summary – Rajiv

- *My old Rule is:*

  Unless I get it right, I will never get anywhere in life.

- *This Rule has had the following impact on my life:*

  I have always felt inadequate, not good enough. This has made me work tremendously hard, to the extent that I have been constantly under pressure, tense and stressed. This has affected my relationships. I have not had enough time for people, and I have lost out because of it. At times, it has made me quite ill.

  And I have sometimes run away from opportunities because I didn't think I would measure up.

- *I know the Rule is in operation because:*

  I get anxious about failing and put myself under more and more pressure. I go over the top in how I go about things – try to dot every 'i' and cross every 't'. I feel sick with anxiety. And if I think I've broken the Rule, I become very self-critical, get depressed, and give up altogether.

- *It is understandable that I have this Rule because:*

  When I was young, my father's disappointment with how his life has turned out made him very keen that we should all make the most of ourselves. Instead of encouraging and praising us, he gave us all the message that we were not up to it if we did not perform the way he wanted us to. That message sank in, and I have tried to compensate by being a perfectionist.

- *However, the Rule is unreasonable because:*

  It simply is not humanly possible to get it right all the time. Making mistakes and getting things wrong are all part of learning and growth.

- *The payoffs of obeying the Rule are:*

  Sometimes I do really good work, and get praise for it. This is partly why I have done so well in my career. People respect me. When I do get it right, I feel great.

- *But the disadvantages are:*

  I am constantly tense. Sometimes my work is not as good as it could be, because I get in such a state about it. I can't learn from my mistakes, because they upset me so much, nor can I learn from constructive criticism. When things do not work out, I feel dreadful and it takes me ages to get over it. I avoid anything that I might not be able to get right, and miss all kinds of opportunities because of that. People may respect me, but it keeps them at a distance. They see me as a bit inhuman, unapproachable – even arrogant. The pressure I place on myself is bad for my health. Plus all my time and attention goes on my work – I don't allow myself to relax or do things I enjoy. In short, the Rule leads to stress, misery and fear on all fronts.

- *A more realistic and helpful new Rule would be:*

  Good enough is good enough – I don't have to be great, to be great. I enjoy doing well – there's nothing wrong with that. But I'm only human and I will get it wrong sometimes. Getting it wrong is the route to growth.

- *In order to test-drive the new rule, I need to:*

  - Keep reading this summary

  - Put my new rule on a flashcard and on my mobile phone and read it several times a day

- Cut my working hours and plan pleasures and social contact

- Take time for myself

- Revise my standards and give myself credit for less-than-perfect performance

- Experiment with getting it wrong and observe the outcome. For example, practise saying 'I don't know' when people ask me questions

- Plan my day in advance, and always plan less than I think I can do

- Focus on what I achieve, not on what I failed to do. Tomorrow is another day

- Remember: criticism can be useful – it doesn't mean I am a complete failure

- Watch out for signs of stress – they mean I am going back to my old ways

- Deal with the old pattern, when it comes up, using what I have learned to tackle anxious predictions and self-criticism

Chapter summary

1. *When you have low self-esteem, unhelpful Rules for Living prevent you from getting what you want out of life and accepting yourself as you are.*

2. *Rules are learned through experience and observation. They are part of the culture we grow up in, and are usually transmitted to us by our families.*

3. *Many rules are helpful. But the unhelpful Rules linked to low self-esteem are rigid, demanding and extreme, restrict freedom of movement, and make change and growth difficult or impossible.*

4. *Rules represent a way of coping with the apparent truth of the Bottom Line, but they do nothing to change it. In fact, they help to keep it in place.*

5. *Using the core skills you have already learned, you can learn to identify your unhelpful Rules, to question and rethink them, to create new Rules that are more realistic and give you more freedom to be yourself, and to experiment with testing them out in everyday life.*

8

Creating a
New Bottom Line

Introduction

You have now laid the foundations for tackling your Bottom Line, the negative beliefs about yourself that underpin low self-esteem. Here is your chance to capitalise on all the work you have done and go to the heart of the matter. Chapter 2 described how these beliefs develop. They are understandable conclusions you reached, probably as a child, on the basis of experience – opinions, not facts. Once established, they are kept in place by biases in how you perceive and interpret what happens to you, and by unhelpful Rules for Living which are designed to help you cope in the world (given that you believe the Bottom Line is true), but which in fact merely wallpaper over your insecurities while leaving them intact. Chapter 3 described how the Bottom Line is activated in situations where your personal rules are in danger of being broken, or have been broken, giving rise to a vicious circle fuelled by anxious predictions and self-critical thoughts.

Chapters 4 to 7 have addressed the key elements that keep low self-esteem in place, one by one. You have learned how to check out anxious predictions, how to answer self-critical thoughts, how to focus on your good points, how to treat yourself with kindness and consideration, and how to allow yourself to enjoy life to the full. You have formulated new, more realistic and helpful Rules for Living, and begun to put them into practice.

You may find that, by the time you have completed these chapters and reduced the impact of your Bottom Line on everyday life, your ideas about yourself have already changed. It may be that your old, negative Bottom Line already seems less convincing than it did, even though you have not yet addressed it directly.

Some people find that, once they have broken the vicious circle that keeps low self-esteem going and started acting in accordance with more realistic Rules for Living, the problem of low self-esteem is pretty much resolved. Others find it harder to use specific day-to-day changes in thinking and behaviour to alter entrenched negative beliefs about themselves. However things stand for you at this point, this chapter will help you to consolidate what you have learned and bring it to bear on your Bottom Line, using the core skills you have already practised (awareness, rethinking and experiments).

You have, perhaps for many years, assumed your Bottom Line reflects the real truth about you. Time now to take a fresh look and to find a new, more appreciative and kindly view, capitalising on the work you have already done as you take the final steps in your journey towards self-acceptance. These steps are:

- Identifying your old, negative Bottom Line
- Creating a new, more positive Bottom Line
- Reviewing the evidence you have used to support the Old Bottom Line and looking for other ways of understanding it
- Searching for counter-evidence that supports the New Bottom Line and contradicts the old one
- Devising experiments that will consolidate and strengthen your New Bottom Line.

Identifying the Bottom Line (Awareness)

As you have made your way through the book, you may already have gained a very good sense of what your Bottom Line is. This section will present some possible sources of information to help you identify it clearly (a summary can be found on page 309). You may find it helpful to consider each source of information in turn. Each will give you a slightly different take on things, so that your idea of what your Bottom Line might be will become increasingly clear.

Even if you are already pretty sure, reviewing this section will give you an opportunity to confirm your hunches, fine-tune the wording and perhaps discover other negative beliefs about yourself that you were less aware of. It is quite possible that you have more than one Bottom Line (like Lin, who saw herself as both unimportant and inferior). If so, do as you did with your Rules for Living. Choose the Bottom Line that seems most important to you, the one that you would most like to change, and use the chapter to work systematically on that. You can then use what you have learned to change other negative beliefs about yourself if you wish (and, indeed, to change unhelpful negative beliefs you may have about other people, the world in general and life).

Write down whatever hunches about your Bottom Line come to mind as you consider each potential source of information. When you feel you have a clear sense of what it is, summarise it for yourself ('My Bottom Line is: I am . . .'). On the belief scale below, rate how strongly you believe it (0–100 per cent), just as you rated belief in your anxious and self-critical thoughts. One hundred per cent would mean that you still find it fully convincing, 50 per cent that you are in two minds, 5 per cent that you now hardly believe it at all, and so on.

My Bottom Line is:

I believe it:

_____

0%   100%

You may notice that to what extent you believe your Bottom Line varies. If your self-esteem is relatively robust, your Bottom Line may only become convincing in particularly challenging situations. If so, make two ratings: first, how strongly you believe it when it is at its strongest, and second, how strongly you believe it when it is least convincing. Alternatively, you may find that your Bottom Line is more or less consistently present and convincing. In this case, you may only need one rating, or the difference between most convincing and least convincing may be smaller.

You may also find that your degree of belief has changed since you began to work on overcoming low self-esteem. This is especially likely if you have systematically followed through the ideas for change described in previous chapters. If this is the case for you, record how strongly you believed your Bottom Line before you started the book, and how strongly you believe it now. Consider too what accounts for any changes you have observed. Was it learning to face things that frightened you and discovering the worst did not happen? Was it learning to escape the trap of self-critical thinking? Was it making the effort to focus on what is strong and good in yourself, and beginning to see yourself as someone who is worthy of kindness and deserves to enjoy life? Or was it the work you did on formulating new Rules for Living and putting them into practice? Or perhaps it was some combination of these. If you can spot what helped, this will tell you what you need to continue doing for yourself.

When you have rated your degree of belief, take a moment to focus on your Bottom Line and notice what feelings emerge, just as you observed your feelings when you learned to spot anxious and self-critical thoughts. Write down any emotions and body sensations you experience (e.g. sadness, anger, tension, weight on your shoulders), and rate them according to how powerful they are (0–100). Again, you may notice that, although you can still call up your Bottom Line, your feelings in its presence have changed. If the Bottom Line is now less convincing to you than it was, then your distress when you focus on it should also be less intense.

Sources of information on your Bottom Line

As we saw in Chapter 2 (pages 39–74), there are many possible sources of low self-esteem. What they all have in common is the doubtful logic of seeing them as accurate measures of your worth. All of them can be questioned, re-evaluated, re-thought. All of them can be understood in fairer, kinder, more compassionate ways.

Your knowledge of your own history

This draws on the work you did when you were puzzling out how your low self-esteem developed. When you read the stories of the people described in Chapter 2 (pages 43–62), did any of them ring bells for you? Did any of the experiences described echo experiences you had when you were growing up? Even if not, did you find yourself thinking back to when you were young and remembering things that happened to you, and the impact they had on how you felt about yourself?

You can use these memories to clarify your Bottom Line, just as you may have used memories of earlier times to help you to identify your Rules for Living. In particular, consider:

- What early experiences encouraged you to think badly of yourself? What events in your childhood and adolescence – or later – led you to the conclusion that in some way you were lacking as a person?

- When did you first have this feeling about yourself? What images and memories come to mind when you are feeling anxious or low, or bad about yourself? See if you can recall specific experiences. Like Briony, when her stepfather first abused her, you may find one key memory of an event when your sense of yourself crystal-lised. Or it may be that (as was the case for Lin) no one event was important, but rather there was an ongoing climate of unkindness, or disap-proval and criticism, or lack of affection, or not quite fitting in.

- Whose voice do you hear when you are being hard on yourself? Whose face comes to mind? What messages did this person (or these people) give you about the kind of person you are?

> • What words were used to describe you when you failed to please or attracted criticism? The words used by others may have become your own words for yourself.

**Figure 33. Identifying the Bottom Line:
Sources of Information**

- • Your knowledge of your own history
- • The fears expressed in your anxious predictions
- • Your self-critical thoughts
- • Thoughts that make it hard for you to focus on your good points, treat yourself kindly and allow yourself to enjoy life
- • The imagined consequences of breaking your old Rules
- • The Downward Arrow

The fears expressed in your anxious predictions

Think back to the work you did on your anxious predictions. It could be that your fears, and the unnecessary precautions you took to keep yourself safe, will give you clues about your Bottom Line.

- • Supposing what you most feared had come true: what would that have said about you as a person? What sort of person would that have made you? Kate, for example, felt that to ask her boss for the money she was owed (page 106) would have demonstrated just how mean, grasping and fundamentally unlovable she was.

- And what about your unnecessary precautions? Especially if your anxieties are often about the impression you make on other people, your precautions may well have been designed to hide the real you. If so, what 'real you'? What sort of person did you fear might be revealed if you did not take steps to protect and conceal yourself? Tom's avoidance of challenges, for example, was designed to disguise the fact that (as he saw it) he was basically stupid.

Your self-critical thoughts

Look back over the work you did on questioning your self-critical thoughts. These thoughts may be a direct reflection of your Bottom Line.

- What words did you use to describe yourself when you were being self-critical? What names did you call yourself? Look for repeating patterns and automatic knee-jerk ways of addressing yourself. What negative beliefs about yourself do your self-critical thoughts reflect?

- Are the words you use similar to words that were used about you by other people when you were small? If so, they have probably been in place since then, and may well reflect lasting beliefs about yourself rather than momentary reactions.
- When you do things that trigger self-criticism, what do those things suggest about you as a person? What sort of person would do things like that? Mike, for example, thought that his inability to control his emotions must mean he was pathetic.

Thoughts that make it hard to accept your good points, treat yourself kindly and allow yourself to enjoy life

Examine the doubts and reservations that came to mind when you were trying to list your good points and observe them in action when you attempted to experience pleasure, give yourself credit for your achievements and treat yourself kindly. Your doubts and reservations may have reflected the fact that these new ways of relating to yourself were not a good fit with your Bottom Line. Rajiv, for example, recognised on reflection that his reluctance to give himself credit for what he did or allow himself time to relax reflected his belief that he was simply not good enough.

The imagined consequences of breaking your old Rules

In Rules for Living (pages 260–1), sometimes the 'then . . .' that follows an 'if . . .' or an 'unless' is more or less a direct statement of the Bottom Line (e.g. 'If I make mistakes, then *I am a failure*'). Go back to the Rules you have identified, and look at what you imagined would result from breaking them.

- If you break your Rules for Living, what does that say about you as a person?
- What kind of person makes mistakes, fails to win everyone's approval or liking or love, loses their grip on their emotions, or whatever?
- If your Rule is a 'should', would the 'or else' be a reflection of you as a person (e.g. 'I should always be constructively occupied [or else I am lazy]')?

The downward arrow

You can also use the 'downward arrow' technique (pages 274–5) to identify your Bottom Line. The process is much the same as the process of identifying Rules for Living, but the sequence of possible questions has a different emphasis and is designed to focus your attention on your negative

beliefs about yourself, rather than your standards and expectations. The main change is to enquire what each level of
questioning says *about you*, rather than what it means *to you*
in terms of how you should behave and the sort of person
you should be.

As before, start from a specific incident when you felt
bad about yourself. Call it vividly to mind – relive it in
detail if you can. What was the situation? What thoughts
or images were running through your mind at the time?
What feelings and body sensations were present? And what
did you do? Write down what happened in as much detail
as you can recall. As with the search for Rules for Living, it
may be helpful to focus in particular on whatever thought
was most powerful and accounted for most of the emotion
you experienced. Then, rather than searching for alternatives to your thoughts, ask yourself a sequence of questions,
for example:

* Supposing that were true, what would it mean
  about me?
* Supposing that were true, what would it tell me
  about myself?
* What does that say about me as a person?
* What kind of person does that make me?
* What beliefs about myself does that reflect?
* What are the implications of that for how I see
  myself?

It may be helpful to use a range of different questions to help you find your Bottom Line. You are looking for a blanket statement about yourself ('I am_____'), which not only applies in the particular situation you are working with, but more broadly, across the board. Do not stop at a specific self-critical thought, present at a particular moment. You will recognise your Bottom Line as an opinion you have held about yourself over time and across many different situations. You may wish to confirm your findings (or have another go, if you are having trouble finding the Bottom Line or putting it into words) by using a number of different situations in which you typically feel bad about yourself as your starting point. You will find an example of a downward arrow leading to a Bottom Line on page 315 (Briony).

Creating a new Bottom Line (Rethinking)

Once you have identified your Bottom Line, it is worth moving on right away to formulate a more positive and realistic alternative to it, even before you begin to think it through and undermine it. This is because, over time, you have probably accumulated a sizeable bank account of experiences that seem to you to support your Bottom Line, given the biases in thinking and memory that keep low self-esteem in place. You can call on your 'Old Bottom Line Account' any time you want, add new deposits, withdraw items and dwell on them like a miser counting and recounting money.

In contrast, you may not even have a 'New Bottom Line Account'. Or, if you have, it may be more or less empty, and difficult to access. Items get lost in transfer, and you keep forgetting your account number and code. This means that you have nowhere safe, solid and lasting to put 'New Bottom Line' deposits.

Creating a New Bottom Line opens an account in favour of yourself. It gives you a place to store experiences that contradict the Old Bottom Line and support a new, more kindly and accepting perspective. You have somewhere you can deposit new ideas and new experiences and keep them safe, knowing that they will be there for you when you need them.

This analogy illustrates the purpose of creating a New Bottom Line. It gives you somewhere to put positive information about yourself, experiences that support a more appreciative point of view. This means that you are not merely attempting to undermine your old negative beliefs ('Maybe I'm not completely useless, after all'), but actively setting up an alternative and beginning to scan for information and experiences which support it ('Maybe, in fact, I am *useful*').

The work you have already done in earlier chapters, besides providing you with information about your Old Bottom Line, may also have given you some idea of what your preferred alternative might be. As you have worked through the book, checking out anxious predictions, questioning self-critical thoughts, focusing on your good points, and changing your Rules, what new, kinder ideas about

Figure 34. The Downward Arrow: Identifying the Bottom Line – Briony

Situation:
New friend promised to phone and did not do so

Emotions:
Rejected, despairing

Body Sensations:
Sick to my stomach

Thought:
'He's forgotten'

If that was true, what would it mean about you?

'That I'm not worth remembering'

And what would that tell you about yourself?

'That he's backed off because he's seen the real me'

If he had, what would he have seen?

'Something he didn't like'

What would that be? What would he not like?

'The real me, that doesn't deserve to be liked or loved by anybody'

If that was true, what would it say about you as a person?

'I'm bad'

yourself have come to mind? When you look back over all you have done in each of these areas, what do the changes you have made tell you about yourself? Are they entirely consistent with your old negative view?

Look in particular at the qualities, strengths, assets and skills you have identified and observed, day by day. Do they fit with your Old Bottom Line? Or do they suggest that it needs updating, that it is a biased, unfair point of view, which fails to take account of what is good and strong and worthy in you? What perspective on yourself would better account for *everything* you have observed? What New Bottom Line would acknowledge that, like the rest of the human race, you are short of perfect, but that along with your weaknesses and flaws you have strengths and good qualities, that it is fundamentally OK to be you?

You are the judge and jury here, not the counsel for the prosecution. Your job is to take *all* the evidence into account, not just the evidence in favour of condemning the prisoner. When you have a sense of what your new Bottom Line is, write it down (on the Summary Sheet on pages 352–3 at the end of the chapter, if you wish). Rate to what extent you believe it, just as you rated your belief in your Old Bottom Line, including variations in how convincing it seems to you and how your belief has changed since you began to work on overcoming your low self-esteem. Then take a moment to focus your attention on it and note what emotions and body sensations come up and how strong they are. As you continue through the chapter, come back to the Summary Sheet from time to time, and observe how your belief in the New Bottom Line changes as you focus on evidence that supports and strengthens it.

Looking at the examples on pages 344–5, you will see that the New Bottom Line is sometimes simply the opposite of the old one (e.g. Evie, Jack, Kate). In some cases, on the other hand, the New Bottom Line 'jumps the tracks', as it were, and goes off in a new direction which makes the old one almost irrelevant (e.g. Briony, Aaron, Tom, Mary). Sometimes the New Bottom Line is somewhere between these (e.g. Rajiv, Lin, Mike). The point here is that your New Bottom Line should reflect a point of view that makes sense to you personally, will eventually change how you feel about yourself, and offers opportunities for a fresh perspective on your experiences that will allow you to begin noticing and giving weight to your good qualities and strengths. The correct wording is the wording that feels right to *you*.

You may find a New Bottom Line immediately springs to mind when you think back over everything you have done. Or you may find that your mind is pretty much a blank, especially if your low self-esteem has been in place for a long time and you have a strong taboo on thinking well of yourself which still needs to be addressed. Do not worry if this is the case. Your ideas may become clearer as you work through the chapter. For the moment, it may be helpful to ask yourself a question that Christine Padesky, the cognitive therapist I mentioned in Chapter 2, suggests: 'If you were not (your Old Bottom Line), what would you really, really like to be?' For example, 'If I were not incompetent, I would really, really like to be competent.' If you can come up with an answer to the question, however tentative, then even if it seems largely theoretical to you at the moment, write it down. It will give you a starting point for collecting evidence in favour of a new perspective (in this case, 'I am competent'), even if it does not yet seem at all convincing to you. Conviction may come as you continue to work through the chapter.

At this point, the old idea that it is wrong to think well of yourself may surface – once again, 'yes, buts' pop up. Remember that we are not talking here about having an inflated self-image ('I am totally wonderful in every way', 'Every day in every way I am getting better and better'). You are not aiming to forget your human weaknesses and flaws, to ignore aspects of yourself you would like to change or improve on, and pretend that they do not exist. Healthy self-esteem is not about the power of positive thinking, or about encouraging you to become as unrealistically positive about yourself as you were unrealistically negative. It is about achieving a balanced, unbiased view of yourself which puts your weaknesses and flaws in the context of a broadly favour-able perspective, and cheerleads for 'good enough' rather than 'perfect', allowing you to accept yourself just as you are. So resist the temptation to censor your emerging New Bottom Line. Let your imagination roam free, and allow yourself to connect with your deepest wishes about yourself.

It is unlikely that you will ever be 100 per cent lovable, 100 per cent competent, 100 per cent worthy, 100 per cent intelligent, 100 per cent attractive, or whatever. Why, after all, should you be the only member of the human race, ever, who is? The work you have been doing and will do asks you to make your flaws and weaknesses simply a part of yourself, rather than a basis for your assessment of your worth. You may decide you can live with them or you may decide you wish to change them – it is up to you.

To make this point clearer, let us consider it in relation to 'likeable'. Imagine a 10cm line representing likeability:

Likeable

0%   100%

Someone at the right-hand end of the line would be 100 per cent likeable. Superficially, this might appear to be a good thing. Someone at the left-hand end would be 0 per cent likeable. Right now, put a 'x' on the line where you think you fall. If you have doubts about how likeable you are, you probably fall towards the left-hand end of the line. Now let us consider what '100 per cent likeable' and '0 per cent likeable' would actually mean. In order to be '100 per cent likeable', you would have, for example:

- To be likeable all the time
- To be completely likeable (no aspect of you could be at all unlikeable)
- To be likeable to everyone

It will be immediately clear that 100 per cent likeable is just not possible. Nobody could be such a paragon. Think about people you know. With the extremes (0 and 100 per cent) clearly in mind, where would you put them on the line? And, again, keeping the extremes in mind, where would you now put yourself? When you decide on your New Bottom Line, keep this point in mind. You are not looking for the unattainable 100 per cent; you are looking for 'good enough'.

To check if you are on the right track, it may be helpful at this point to return to the specific problem situation that was your starting point when you followed the Downward Arrow to identify your Bottom Line. Once again, bring the situation vividly to mind, in high-definition detail. Then ask yourself: How would this situation have played out if my New Bottom Line had been in place? Would things have been different in the way I would wish them to be? If the answer is yes, then continue to work with your first draft. If the answer is no, you may need to think again.

Do not worry if, at the moment, your degree of belief in your New Bottom Line is low. If the Old Bottom Line has been in place for some considerable time, it will take patience, persistence and practice to make the new one powerfully convincing. We shall now move on to consider how to undermine your Old Bottom Line further, and how to strengthen the new one you have tentatively identified. You will find that the work you have already done will stand you in good stead here.

Undermining the Old Bottom Line (Rethinking)

Your negative beliefs about yourself are based on experience — an attempt to make sense of what happened to you in the past. This means that, given the biases in thinking and memory that keep them in place, as you look back over your life you will find 'evidence' that appears to support them. Examining this 'evidence' — and searching for other ways to explain it — is the next step towards overcoming low self-esteem. This is similar to what you did when you learned to question self-critical thoughts, and the ideas you used at that point may also be helpful to you here. However, the scale is broader: the focus is on your general beliefs about yourself, rather than on specific thoughts that arise at a particular moment in time. The key questions to bear in mind are:

- What 'evidence' supports your Old Bottom Line?
- How else could this 'evidence' be understood?

What 'evidence' supports your Old Bottom Line?

I have put 'evidence' in quotation marks here to indicate that, although you may have accepted a range of experiences as support for your Old Bottom Line, signs that what you believed about yourself was indeed true, these experiences may in fact be open to quite different interpretations. It could be that, if you look at them closely, you will realise that they do not reflect badly on you at all. The first step towards understanding this is to identify the experiences you have been taking as supporting evidence.

Reflect for a moment on your Old Bottom Line. This powerful idea did not come out of nowhere. What experiences, past and present, come to mind? What events appear to support it? What makes you say that you are inadequate, unlikeable, incompetent or whatever your Bottom Line may be? What leads you to reach such unkind conclusions about yourself?

Supporting 'evidence' varies from person to person. Sometimes most of it is located in the past, in relationships or experiences like those described in the stories in Chapter 2 (page 39). More recent events can also be used as sources of evidence. Some common sources of 'evidence' are described below. As you read, see if any of the 'evidence' rings bells for you.

The list is not exhaustive. The 'evidence' that you have used to back up your poor opinion of yourself may not be on it. Use this section nonetheless as an opportunity to reflect on what it might be. Bear in mind that you may well be using more than one source of 'evidence' to support your Old Bottom Line, and make a note of as many as you can find. Your next task will be to stand back and examine the 'evidence' carefully. When you take a good look at it, does it really confirm your negative view of yourself, or could it be understood in a different way?

Figure 35. Sources of 'Evidence' Supporting the Old, Negative Bottom Line

- *Current difficulties and symptoms of distress*
- *Failure to overcome them without help*
- *Past errors and failures*
- *Specific shortcomings*
- *Personal characteristics, physical or psychological*
- *Differences between yourself and other people*
- *Other people's behaviour towards you, past or present*
- *The behaviour of others for whom you feel responsible*
- *Loss of something which was a part of your identity*
- *Emotional reactions ('It just feels true')*

CURRENT DIFFICULTIES AND SYMPTOMS OF DISTRESS

Briony, for example, became quite depressed at one point. As is characteristic of people who are depressed, she became lethargic and found it hard to gear herself up to do anything. Briony took this to mean that she was a lazy good-for-nothing. In other words, it was yet another sign of what a bad person she was, rather than a temporary symptom of an understandable state which would disappear once her mood lifted.

FAILURE TO OVERCOME CURRENT DIFFICULTIES WITHOUT HELP

Mike's difficulty in talking openly to his wife and asking for outside help is an example of this. He saw being unable to manage independently as a sign of weakness, rather than a sensible recognition that talking things through with another person who knows us well can help to free up thinking, and that everybody needs loving support in life, especially when times are tough.

PAST ERRORS AND FAILURES

Given human frailty, it is impossible to get through life without doing things we regret. From time to time, we are all selfish, thoughtless, irritable, short-sighted or less than fully honest. We all take short cuts, make mistakes, avoid challenges and fail to achieve objectives. Such normal human weaknesses are often seen by people with low self-esteem as yet further evidence of their fundamental worthlessness.

This was true for Aaron. During his teens, he often operated on the fringes of the law. At times, he took part in fights in which other people were hurt, once very badly. He was repeatedly in trouble with the police and appeared in court more than once. As he got older, Aaron decided that this way of life was doing him no good. He was afraid to change, however, as this seemed to him the only way to survive in a hostile world. Still, he found the courage to move away from his home city, made new friends and found a job he liked (supporting young people from deprived backgrounds), and eventually married and had children of his own. Despite these very positive changes, he still found it hard to feel good about himself. His past haunted him. Whenever he looked back, he felt utterly worthless.

SPECIFIC PROBLEMS

No one is perfect. We all have shortcomings and aspects of ourselves that we would like to change or improve. People with low self-esteem may see these shortcomings as further proof that there is something fundamentally wrong with them, rather than as specific problems it might be possible to resolve and which bear no relation to their real worth. Every time Tom had problems with reading or writing, for example, he saw this as further evidence of his stupidity, rather than as an unrecognised specific learning difficulty that was no reflection of his intelligence and which, with proper help, could be overcome.

PHYSICAL CHARACTERISTICS

People with low self-esteem may feel that they are too tall, too short, too fat, too thin, the wrong colour, the wrong shape or the wrong build. They may use these observations to undermine their sense of self-esteem. Evie's belief that her worth depended on how she looked and what she weighed is an example of this. If her weight exceeded what she thought it should be, she immediately felt completely fat, ugly and unattractive. Nothing else counted. She ignored all the other things that made her attractive – for example, her sense of style, her ability to enjoy life and her intelligence.

PSYCHOLOGICAL CHARACTERISTICS

Psychological characteristics, too, can lead people with low self-esteem to feel bad about themselves. Jack, for example, even as an adult, was afraid that his high energy, curiosity and inventiveness would be seen as showing off. Expecting disapproval and criticism, he did what he could to blend in, become part of the furniture, and dampen himself down. Instead of accepting his qualities as gifts, he saw them as further evidence that he was unacceptable.

DIFFERENCES BETWEEN YOURSELF AND OTHER PEOPLE

However talented you are, it is likely that there are other people who are more talented. However much you have, there are probably others who have more. People with low self-esteem may use comparisons with other people as a source of evidence to support their poor opinions of themselves. They may compare themselves with people they know, or with images they see in the popular press or on social media. Lin, for example, was always comparing her work to that of other artists. In these comparisons, she usually felt she came off worst. Rather than judging herself on her own merits, regardless of the quality of other people's work, she used negative comparisons to fuel her sense of inferiority.

OTHER PEOPLE'S BEHAVIOUR TOWARDS YOU, PAST OR PRESENT

People who were treated badly as children may see this treatment as evidence of their own lack of worth, whether the treatment came from family, schoolmates or the society in which they lived. Equally, dislike, rejection, disapproval or abuse in the present day can be used to bolster low self-esteem. For example, the treatment she had received from her step-parents was Briony's main source of evidence that she was bad. Why else would they have been like that? Even as an adult, if someone treated her badly, her immediate assumption was that she must have deserved it in some way. So any unkindness or lack of consideration or disagreement became further evidence of her essential badness.

THE BEHAVIOUR OF OTHERS FOR WHOM YOU FEEL RESPONSIBLE

This is a particular trap for people with low self-esteem who become parents. They may blame themselves for anything that goes wrong in their children's lives, even long after the children have grown up and left home. This was true for Briony. When she discovered that her adolescent daughter had been drinking excessively and had occasionally taken street drugs at parties, her immediate reaction was that this must be entirely her fault. She was a bad parent. Her own essential badness had somehow leaked out and contaminated her daughter. This perspective made it difficult for her to handle the situation constructively, to discuss with her daughter the possible consequences of what she was doing and how best to resist peer pressure.

LOSS OF SOMETHING WHICH WAS A PART OF YOUR IDENTITY

Chapter 7 (pages 245–300) showed how people hang self-esteem on a range of different pegs. If the peg on which you have hung your sense of worth is taken away, this exposes you to the full force of negative beliefs about yourself. Rajiv, for example, was once made redundant because the firm he worked for was going through hard times. His work was one of the pegs on which he had hung his self-esteem. Although the company made it clear that they had no wish to lose him, he took the redundancy very personally. It was another sign that he was not good enough. Mary's inability to care for others as she had always loved to do, even though it was through no fault of her own, led to her seeing herself as completely useless.

How else can the 'evidence' be understood?

Each source of 'evidence' that is used to support the Bottom Line is open to different interpretations, just as specific self-critical thoughts that run through your head in particular situations are open to different interpretations. Once you have identified the evidence that you feel backs up your Old Bottom Line, your next task is to examine it carefully and assess to what degree it truly supports what you have been in the habit of believing about yourself. Make a note of your conclusions, on the Summary Sheet at the end of the chapter if you wish. You may find the questions listed below useful to you. You will see that they relate directly to the various sources of evidence outlined above. It may also be worth your while to bear in mind the questions you used to tackle self-critical thoughts (page 177). The particular questions that make sense to you will depend on the nature of the 'evidence' you use to support your Old Bottom Line.

Figure 36. Reviewing the 'Evidence' that Supports Your Old Bottom Line: Useful Questions

- Aside from personal inadequacy, what explanations could there be for current difficulties or signs of distress?

- Although it is useful to be able to manage independently, what might be the advantages of being able to ask for help and support?

- How fair is it to judge yourself on the basis of past errors and failures?

- How fair is it to judge yourself on the basis of specific shortcomings?

- How helpful is it to let your self-esteem depend on rigid ideas about what you should do or be?

- Just because someone is better at something than you, or has more than you do, does that make them better as a person?

- What reasons, besides the kind of person you are, might there be for others' behaviour towards you?

- How much power do you actually have over the behaviour of people you feel responsible for?

ASIDE FROM PERSONAL INADEQUACY, WHAT EXPLANATIONS COULD THERE BE FOR CURRENT DIFFICULTIES OR SIGNS OF DISTRESS?

If this is a time when you are having difficulties or experiencing distress, rather than taking this as a sign that there is something fundamentally wrong with you, look at what is going on in your life at the moment. Is anything happening that might make sense of how you are feeling?

If someone you cared about was going through what you are going through right now, might they feel similar? If so, what would you make of that? Would you assume that they, too, must be inadequate, bad or whatever? Or would you consider their reactions to be understandable, given what was going on, and respond to them with compassion? Even if nothing very obvious is happening in your life right now to explain how you feel, could it be understood in terms of old habits of thinking which are a result of your past experiences? If so, then perhaps you will find it more helpful to be compassionate and understanding to yourself, to encourage yourself to do whatever needs to be done and to get whatever help you need, rather than adding to your distress by beating yourself up about it.

ALTHOUGH IT IS USEFUL TO BE ABLE TO MANAGE INDEPENDENTLY, WHAT MIGHT BE THE ADVANTAGES OF BEING ABLE TO ASK FOR HELP AND SUPPORT?

Like Mike, you may feel that asking for help is a sign of weakness or inadequacy. You should be able to stand on your own two feet. But perhaps being able to ask for help when you genuinely need it actually puts you in a stronger position, not a weaker one, because it may give you a chance to deal successfully with a wider range of situations than you could manage on your own. How do you feel when other people who are in difficulties come to you for help or support? Do you automatically conclude they must be feeble or pathetic? People who have difficulties in asking for help themselves are often very good at giving help to others.

They do not judge others unkindly. On the contrary, being able to offer help makes them feel useful, wanted and warm towards the person who needs them. This is how other people who care about you might feel about you, if you gave them half a chance.

Alternatively, you may fear (like Kate) that if you ask for help, you will be disappointed. Other people may take a dim view of it. They may refuse, or be scornful, or not be able to give you what you need. In fact, people may be more helpful than you anticipate – and, if someone is not, that may say more about their limitations than yours. Nonetheless, of course it makes sense to select people who you have no particular reason to suppose will react in this way. The best way to test out how others will react is to try it. Work out your predictions in advance and check them out, just as you learned to do in Chapter 4 (pages 101–146).

HOW FAIR IS IT TO JUDGE YOURSELF ON THE BASIS OF PAST ERRORS AND FAILURES?

People with low self-esteem sometimes confuse what they do with what they are. They assume that a bad action is a sign of a bad person, or that to fail at something means to be a failure through and through. If this were true, no one in the world could ever feel good about themselves. We may regret things we have done (like Aaron), but it is not helpful or accurate to move on from that to complete self-condemnation. If you do one good thing, does that make you a totally good person? If you have low self-esteem, you probably don't believe this. But when you do something wrong, no doubt it's probably a different story. There you are, it just goes to show that what you have always believed about yourself is indeed true.

Believing that you are thoroughly bad, worthless, inadequate, useless or whatever can act as a self-fulfilling prophecy. It makes it difficult to make reparation for things you regret, to learn from the experience and ensure you don't make the same mistake again, and to work out how to do things differently – how to act in accordance with your true values. What's the point, if it is dyed in the wool? Understanding your past failings in terms of natural human error and early learning may be more constructive. It will allow you to treat yourself more compassionately – to condemn the sin but not the sinner.

This is not the same as letting yourself off the hook. It is a first step towards putting right whatever needs to be put right, and thinking about how you might avoid making the same mistakes in future. What you did may have been the only thing you could do, given your state of knowledge at the time. Now you can see things differently, so take advantage of your broader current perspective. And remember: you may have done a bad or stupid thing, but that does not make you a bad or stupid person.

HOW FAIR IS IT TO JUDGE YOURSELF ON THE BASIS OF SPECIFIC SHORTCOMINGS?

Just because you have difficulty asserting yourself, or being punctual, or organising your time, or talking to people without anxiety, does it follow that there is something

fundamentally wrong with you as a person? Having something about yourself that you would like to improve makes
you part of the human race. If you are using specific difficulties as a basis for low self-esteem, you may be employing
a double standard (see page 178). Would you judge another
person with the same specific difficulty in the same way? If
not, experiment with using a kinder approach to yourself.
Again, this may help you to move forward rather than mir-
ing you in self-criticism.

Remember that your shortcomings, whatever they
are, are only one side of you (your list of good qualities
may already have begun to make this clear). Albert Ellis,
the originator of a form of psychological treatment called
'Rational Emotive Therapy', used an analogy to make this
point. Imagine a basket of fruit. In the basket are a magnifi-
cent pineapple, some good apples, a rather mediocre orange
or two, a bunch of grapes with the bloom still fresh upon
them, some pears which are probably past their best and,
lurking underneath, a banana which is completely black and
rotten. Now, the question is: how do you judge the basket
as a whole? It is impossible to do so. You can only judge its
contents one by one.

The same is true of people. You cannot judge them as
a whole – you can only judge individual aspects of them,
and individual things they do. Think of Aaron. Is he a bad
person because of his behaviour as a young man? Or is he
a good person because of how he turned out in the end?
Maybe he's just another normal, fallible human being, capable of behaving both well and badly.

HOW HELPFUL IS IT TO LET YOUR SELF-ESTEEM DEPEND ON RIGID IDEAS ABOUT WHAT YOU SHOULD DO OR BE?

Hanging self-esteem on particular pegs, which may well not be under your control, inevitably makes you vulnerable to low self-esteem. You may have always been aware that your self-esteem was based on a particular aspect of yourself (e.g. your ability to make people laugh, your physical strength, or your capacity to earn a high salary). Or (like Mary, as she became unwell and was no longer able to do things for others in the way she had done) you may have only recognised how much you depended on something to feel good about yourself after you lost it. You need now to ask yourself what your worth depends on, *apart from* the one thing you have accepted as your be-all and end-all.

Your list of good qualities may be a useful starting point here. Take another look at it. How many of the qualities, strengths, skills and talents on the list depend on the peg on which you usually hang your self-esteem? If you find it difficult to get a clear perspective on this, think about people you know, like and respect. Write down what attracts you to them. When you consider why you value each person, how important is the one thing your own self-esteem depends on? Evie found this line of enquiry very helpful in reassessing the contribution of her physical appearance to her self-esteem. Many of the positive qualities she had listed about herself (sense of style, ability to enjoy life, intelligence) bore no relation to her weight or shape. On the other hand, she could see how these qualities might be compromised by the *belief* that only weight and shape mattered. It was difficult to enjoy life, for example, when she was preoccupied with eating and not eating.

She also made a list of people she liked and respected, and wrote down what she saw as attractive in each one. She had some admiration for people who were thin and fit, but it was outweighed on a personal level by other qualities such as sense of humour, sensitivity, thoughtfulness and common sense. Compared to these, physical appearance was trivial. Evie concluded that she would do better to accept and appreciate herself just as she was, fat or thin, rather than making how she thought about herself dependent on some irrelevant standard.

JUST BECAUSE SOMEONE IS BETTER AT SOMETHING THAN YOU, OR HAS MORE THAN YOU DO, DOES THAT MAKE THEM BETTER THAN YOU AS A PERSON?

The fact that some people are further along a particular dimension than you are (competence, beauty, material success, career progression), does not make them any better than you as people. It is impossible to be best at everything. And (apart from very specific comparisons like height, weight and income) people cannot meaningfully be compared, any more than volcanoes and porcupines can be compared. Your sense of your own worth is best located within yourself, regardless of how you stand in relation to other people, or to the sort of idealised images promoted by social media and the popular press.

WHAT REASONS, BESIDES THE KIND OF PERSON YOU ARE, MIGHT THERE BE FOR OTHERS' BEHAVIOUR TOWARDS YOU?

People with low self-esteem often assume that if others treat them badly or react to them negatively (face-to-face or in cyberspace), this must in some way be deserved. This can make it difficult to set limits as to what you will allow others to do to you, to feel entitled to others' time and attention, to assert your own needs, and to end toxic relationships that damage you and stand in the way of feeling better about yourself.

Taking what others think of you, or how they behave towards you, as a measure of your personal worth does not make sense for a number of reasons. For example:

* People's judgements are not always reliable. Hitler, for example, was widely revered in the 1930s and even later in his own country. History has shown this opinion to be wrong.
* The fact that someone does not like something does not mean that it has no worth. If I did not like chocolate ice cream, for example, would that make it a bad thing?
* If your opinion of yourself rests on others' opinions of you, it is difficult (if not impossible) to have any stable sense of yourself. If someone likes you on a particular day, then that means you are OK as a person. If the following day you have an

argument and fall out, all of a sudden you are not OK. How on earth can both of these be true? You are still the same person. And again, if you were with two people, one of whom liked you and the other did not, you would then be both OK and not OK at the same time. Relying on others' opinions for your sense of yourself is a recipe for confusion.

- It is impossible to get everyone's approval or liking or love all the time. People's tastes are too varied. If you try to please everyone, you will be faced with constant conflicting demands. Even if you manage to please most of the people most of the time, you will still have no real sense of worth, because any moment you could displease someone or attract criticism or unkindness. Basing your good opinion of yourself on others' good opinions of you is like building your house on quicksand.

There are many possible reasons why people behave as they do. In the case of the particular person (or people) whose behaviour to you seems to back up your Old Bottom Line, what reasons could there be? For example, it could be that their own early learning has made it difficult for them to behave any differently (just as children who are abused or treated violently often become abusers or violent themselves). It could be that they are behaving badly for purely circumstantial reasons (stress, pressure, illness, fear).

It could be that, without them necessarily being aware of it, you remind them of someone they do not get on with. It could be that you are simply not their cup of tea. It could be that there is nothing personal about how they treat you – their manner is critical or sharp or dismissive with everyone, not just with you.

If you find it difficult to detach yourself from your usual self-blaming perspective and to think of other reasons why people behave towards you as they do, observe how you explain bad behaviour or unkindness towards people other than yourself. For example, in recent years, child abuse has jumped into the headlines. When a case is reported, do you always immediately assume that the child in question must have been to blame? Or do you place responsibility squarely on the adult abuser? Similarly, if you read about intimidation, persecution, rape or assault, is it your automatic conclusion that the person on the receiving end must have deserved it? Or can you see that the perpetrator is responsible for what he or she did? Do you consider that civilian victims of war are to blame for their fate? Or do you see them as innocent victims of violence carried out by others for their own reasons? In each of these cases, is it your automatic reaction to explain what happened in terms of there being something wrong with the person treated badly – it must in some way be their fault? Or do you explain what happened in some other, more compassionate way? If so, try applying similar explanations to your own experiences.

HOW MUCH POWER DO YOU ACTUALLY HAVE OVER THE BEHAVIOUR OF PEOPLE YOU FEEL RESPONSIBLE FOR?

To feel bad about yourself because someone you feel responsible for is not OK assumes a degree of power over others which, realistically, you may not have. At the relatively trivial end of the scale, if you have a supper party, you can make your home warm and welcoming, you can provide good food and drink, you can play music you know your guests are likely to appreciate, and you can ask a mix of people who you have good reason to believe will get on with one another – but you cannot guarantee that everyone will enjoy themselves. Only they can do that.

Turning to the more serious example of Briony's daughter, there is much Briony can do to show how distressed she is, to explain to her daughter why what she is doing may cause her harm, and to help her to think for herself rather than going along with the crowd. But she cannot (without completely removing the independence her daughter needs as a young adult) organise twenty-four-hour surveillance and forbid her to leave the house. In other words, Briony is responsible for managing the situation in the most caring and careful way she can, but she cannot ultimately be responsible for what her daughter does when elsewhere – she simply does not have that much power.

Try to be clear about the limits of your responsibility towards other people, in the sense of separating out what you can realistically do to influence them from what is beyond your control. It is reasonable partly to base your good opinion of yourself on your willingness to meet your responsibilities. It is not reasonable to base your self-esteem on things over which you have no control.

Summary

When you have identified the evidence you use to support your Old Bottom Line and found other ways of understanding it, briefly note your findings, using the Summary Sheet at the end of the chapter if you wish. Then, once again, rate how strongly you believe your Old and New Bottom Lines, and how you feel when you consider them. Can you see any change? If so, what made a difference? If not, is it that you have not yet discovered a convincing alternative way of interpreting the 'evidence'? Or is there more 'evidence' that you have not yet addressed? If so, have another try.

The other side of the story: What evidence supports the New Bottom Line and contradicts the old one?

You have identified the evidence you have used to back up your Old Bottom Line, weighed it up and looked for other ways of interpreting or explaining it. What is the other side of the story? What evidence directly contradicts the Old Bottom Line and supports your new alternative? (If you have not yet defined an alternative, stick with looking for evidence that is not consistent with your Old Bottom Line.) These two different angles on undermining the Old Bottom Line are equivalent to answering self-critical thoughts and focusing on your good points. They complement each other. Additionally, just as your work on self-criticism may have helped you to re-evaluate the evidence supporting the Old Bottom Line, so the work you have done on highlighting your strengths, skills and qualities and becoming more aware of them on a day-to-day basis will help you to look in a more focused way for information that supports your New Bottom Line.

There are two main ways of collecting new evidence that supports the New Bottom Line and contradicts the old one: observation, and behavioural experiments.

1. Observation

Chapter 2 (pages 39–74) described how the Old Bottom Line is kept in place by systematic biases in perception. These make it easy for you to notice and give weight to information consistent with the Bottom Line, while encouraging you to screen out or dismiss information that contradicts it. You have already worked on correcting this bias when you made your list of good points and set about recording examples of them in practice. So a good starting point is to review your list and the records you have kept and to highlight anything that contradicts your old self-critical Bottom Line. Don't forget to include the fact that you are working your way through this book; it is a reflection of your courage and resourcefulness.

The next step is to begin actively to seek out and record information that directly contradicts your old ideas about yourself, and supports the New Bottom Line you have identified. Keeping a record, and reviewing it regularly, will once again be helpful here. It will sharpen your focus on your good qualities, and confirm and strengthen your new Bottom Line.

It is important to have a clear sense of exactly what you are looking for before you begin your observations, just as you learned to be specific about what you feared might happen when you were checking out anxious predictions. Otherwise, you may waste time on observations that have no real relevance to the issue you are working on, and so will do nothing to weaken the Old Bottom Line and strengthen the New. You may also miss information that could genuinely have made a difference.

The information (or evidence) you need to look for will depend on the exact nature of your Bottom Line. If, for example, your Old Bottom Line was 'I am unlikeable' and your New Bottom Line is 'I am likeable', then you would need to collect evidence that supported the idea that you are indeed likeable (for example, people smiling at you, people wanting to spend time with you, or people saying that they enjoyed your company). If, on the other hand, your Old Bottom Line was 'I am incompetent' and your New Bottom Line is 'I am competent', then you would need to collect evidence that supported the idea that you are indeed competent (for example, completing tasks to deadline, responding sensibly to questions, or handling crises at work effectively).

In order to find out what information you personally need to look for, make a list of as many things as you can think of in answer to the following related questions:

- What evidence would you see as inconsistent with your Old Bottom Line?
- What information or experiences would suggest to you that it is inaccurate, unfair or invalid?

---

and, conversely:

- What evidence would you see as consistent with your New Bottom Line?
- What information or experiences would suggest to you that it is accurate, fair and valid?

Make sure the items on your list are absolutely clear and specific. If they are vague and poorly defined, you will have trouble deciding if you have observed them or not. This is why 'likeable' and 'competent' above have been broken down into small elements, rather than left as global terms that might mean different things to different people.

To give you some sense of what the possibilities are, here are examples from the people you first met in Chapter 2 (pages 39–74). They are a result of each person thinking carefully about what exactly would count as supporting evidence for his or her New Bottom Line.

Figure 37. Evidence Supporting the New Bottom Line: Examples

	Old Bottom Line	New Bottom Line	Supporting evidence to look for
Briony	I am bad	I am worthy	Things I do for other people
			Things I contribute to society (e.g. my charity work, political activism)
			My good points, day to day (from list)
			My relationships – signs that people love me (e.g. phone calls, letters, invitations, people stopping to talk to me)
Rajiv	I am not good enough	I am OK as I am	Signs that people value what I do (smiles, praise, thanks) even when it is not up to my old standard
			The good things about me that are nothing to do with how I perform (e.g. enjoying being sociable, appreciating music)
			My friendships – things people say and do that show they like me for myself, not for how good a job I do
Evie	I am fat and ugly	I am attractive	All the good qualities I have that are nothing to do with physical appearance (from my list – note daily examples)
			Signs that men are interested in me (being asked out, glances of appreciation, being chatted up)
			People responding warmly to me (smiling, laughing at my jokes, people sitting next to me, looking pleased to see me)
Jack	I am unacceptable	I am acceptable	Positive responses when I dare to be myself, when I indulge in flights of fancy, get loud, pursue issues to the end, give my energy full rein (people joining in, being fired

	Old bottom line	New bottom line	Evidence and examples
Aaron	I am worthless	I belong	by my enthusiasm, wanting to know more, asking me back, wanting to spend time with me
			Everything that shows I am a part of things (the football club, workmates inviting me out for a drink, my kids running to say hello when I come in, my wife giving me a hug)
Kate	I am unlovable	I am lovable	My friends' affection for me. The practical things my parents do for me (it's their way of showing it)
			The good things in me that mean I am a lovable person (my loyalty, my thoughtfulness, my ability to tune in to other people's needs)
Lin	I am inferior	I am as good as anyone	My positive qualities (keep recording examples)
			The good things in my life, that I deserve (my flat, my friends, the countryside I love, my new kitten)
Tom	I am stupid	I am open-minded	The way I expose myself to opportunities to learn
			My curiosity
			The fact that I am now facing my dyslexia and doing something about it
Mike	I am strong and competent → I am pathetic	I am as strong and competent as needs be	Daily signs of my ability to manage my life (handling crises at home and work; running family finances; doing my job well)
			Recognising when I need help and asking for it
Mary	I am kind and caring → I am completely useless	I am loved and accepted as I am	People phoning to ask how I am
			People obviously pleased to see me when they visit
			Seeing how my support and affection are still valued by those I care about

2.Behavioural experiments

You have already gained experience of how to set up and carry out experiments to check out whether your anxious predictions hold water, to act against self-critical thoughts and to test-drive new Rules for Living. Now is the time to push back the walls of the prison low self-esteem has built around you by experimenting with acting as if your New Bottom Line were true, daring to break out and begin to move freely and extend your range. If you wish, you could use the 'Acting in Accordance with my New Bottom Line' worksheet (page 405) to record what you do and the outcome of your experiments. Despite the work you have already done on rethinking your old position, you may still feel uncomfortable or even fearful of doing this. It is absolutely natural to have doubts. If your Old Bottom Line were not so well embedded and compelling, you would have escaped its clutches long ago.

Notice what thoughts run through your mind when you contemplate operating differently, when you feel apprehensive about entering new situations, and perhaps also when you have succeeded in being your new self and then afterwards began to doubt how well it went. The chances are, you will find anxious predictions and self-critical thoughts behind these feelings. If so, you know what to do about them.

Once again, the experiments you need to carry out depend on the exact nature of your New Bottom Line. Consider what experiences would confirm and strengthen your new perspective on yourself.

What do you need to do in order to discover that this new perspective is useful and rings true? Remember the situations you found yourself avoiding when you were working on anxious predictions, and the situations where you felt you needed to use unnecessary precautions. You have experimented with approaching what you avoided and dropping your precautions – how does what you discovered fit here? What other experiments could you carry out on similar lines?

Equally, consider the changes you made when you were learning to treat yourself kindly and build rewards and pleasures into your life. How does *that* fit with what you are doing now? Are there are other similar things you could do now to strengthen your belief in your New Bottom Line? Or more of the same?

Work out in detail what someone who believed your New Bottom Line would do, how they would operate on a day-to-day basis. Make a list of as many things as you can think of in different areas of life – work, leisure time, close relationships, social life, looking after yourself. Then translate your list into specific experiments and begin to put them into practice in your daily life. Over the previous few pages, you will find some examples, to give you a sense of the variety of experiments that is possible.

Summary

It will be important to record what you observe at this stage. Make sure, too, that you assess the outcome of your experiments carefully, just as you assessed the outcome of

Figure 38. Building a New Bottom Line – Behavioural Experiments

	New Bottom Line	Experiments
Briony	I am worthy	Make the first approach to people I trust, rather than waiting for them contact me Be more open about myself with people, step by step Plan treats and pleasures for myself
Rajiv	I am OK as I am	Drop my standards – spend less time preparing assignments and documents Leave minor errors and observe the impact Admit ignorance Practise saying, 'I have no opinion on that'
Evie	I am attractive	Go swimming, even if I do feel fat Wear bright colours that suit me rather than hiding behind drab clothes
Jack	I am acceptable	Stop suppressing myself – show my feelings and see how people react Express my ideas rather than waiting for someone else to speak Say whatever comes into my head instead of rehearsing everything
Aaron	I belong	Take the risk of making the first move towards people Look for a house to buy, instead of always living in rented rooms

Kate	I am lovable	Say 'no' Ask for what I need – otherwise there's no way I'll get it
Lin	I am as good as anyone	Act as if I was entitled to people's time and attention Look for opportunities to exhibit my work, rather than avoiding them Read the critics – I don't have to agree with what they say
Tom	I am open-minded	Make up for lost opportunities – look into adult education and see what facilities there are for people with dyslexia Tell people about the problem instead of trying to pretend it doesn't exist
Mike	I am as strong and competent as needs be	Make a point of asking for help, even when I do not really need it When something upsets me, talk about it
Mary	I am loved and accepted as I am	Keep seeing the people I care about. Even if I am no longer physically strong, I can still be a good listener and offer loving support and advice – do so, and notice the effect of this

experiments when you checked out your anxious predictions. Keep a careful record of what you notice, exactly what you did, and how it turned out. You could perhaps write this information down in your Positives Portfolio, along with examples of your good points. If you do not record it, it may be forgotten or lost, and will not be available to you in the future when you feel doubtful about yourself.

Experiment by experiment, keep asking yourself: How do these results fit with my New Bottom Line? And from time to time, as you accumulate new evidence, check how strongly you *now* believe both the Old and the New Bottom Lines, and how you now feel. You could use the Summary Sheet at the end of the chapter for this. The more you translate your new perspective into action, the stronger it will become, especially if you stay open-minded and curious and willing to have a go and to learn.

Taking the longer view

Building and strengthening a New Bottom Line can be a lengthy process. It may take weeks (or even months) of systematic observation and experimentation before you find the alternative you have identified fully convincing. You have accumulated a lifetime of evidence that supports the Old Bottom Line, collected and stored it, mulled it over and mused on its implications for yourself. You will not need a similar lifetime of evidence in support for your New Bottom Line (that would be a discouraging thought!). But you should expect to make some investment in time and energy, some regular commitment to record-keeping and practice, in order to reach the point where thinking and acting in accordance with your New Bottom Line becomes second nature. When you reach this point, you will have made the final step towards overcoming low self-esteem and accepting and valuing yourself just as you are. The last chapter of the book will give you some ideas on how to get to this point.

Chapter summary

1. *Your final step towards overcoming low self-esteem is to identify your old negative Bottom Line, in your own words. You can use a number of different sources of information to become aware of it.*

2. *Then you can move on right away to formulate a kinder, more balanced alternative. This will help you to notice information you have screened out and discounted which contradicts your old beliefs about yourself.*

3. *The next step is to identify the 'evidence' you have used to support your Old Bottom Line, and to find other ways to understand it, rather than assuming it must reflect your real self (rethinking).*

4. *Finally, it's time for experiments. Decide what experiences and information would support your New Bottom Line and begin to seek them out, acting as if your New Bottom Line was true and observing the results.*

Figure 39. Bottom Line Worksheet

My Old Bottom Line: 'I am _____

	Belief (%)	Emotions (0–100)
When the Old Bottom Line is most convincing:		
When the Old Bottom Line is least convincing:		
When I started the book:		

My New Bottom Line: 'I am _____

	Belief (%)	Emotions (0–100)
When the New Bottom Line is most convincing:		
When the New Bottom Line is least convincing:		
When I started the book:		

'Evidence' supporting the Old Bottom Line and How I Now Understand it :

'Evidence'	New understanding

In the light of this new understanding, I now believe my Old Bottom Line: _____ %

In the light of this new understanding, I now believe my New Bottom Line: _____ %

CREATING A NEW BOTTOM LINE

Evidence (past and present) which supports my New Bottom Line:

_____
_____
_____
_____
_____
_____
_____
_____
_____
_____
_____

In the light of this new understanding, I now believe my Old Bottom Line: _____ %

In the light of this new understanding, I now believe my New Bottom Line: _____ %

Observation. Information and experiences I need to be alert to, in order to gather more evidence to support my New Bottom Line:

_____
_____
_____
_____
_____
_____
_____
_____
_____
_____

Experiments. Specific things I need to do, in order to gather more evidence to support my New Bottom Line:

_____
_____
_____
_____
_____
_____
_____
_____
_____
_____
_____

Figure 40. Bottom Line Worksheet: Briony

My Old Bottom Line: 'I am _____ bad _____'

	Belief (%)	Emotions (0–100)
When the Old Bottom Line is most convincing:	70%	Despair 75, Guilt 60
When the Old Bottom Line is least convincing:	45%	Despair 50, Guilt 40
When I started the book:	100%	Despair 100, Guilt 100

My New Bottom Line: 'I am _____ worthy _____'

	Belief (%)	Emotions (0–100)
When the New Bottom Line is most convincing:	50%	Hope 30, Relief 40
When the New Bottom Line is least convincing:	20%	Hope 10, Relief 10
When I started the book:	0%	Hope 0, Relief 0

'Evidence' supporting the Old Bottom Line and How I Now Understand it :

'Evidence'	New understanding
My parents died – blamed myself	They loved me dearly and would never have left me if they could have helped it.
My step-parents' behaviour	Not my fault – their behaviour was vicious and cruel, and there was no reason for it. No child deserves to be treated like that.
My step-father's abuse	It was a wicked tihng to do. He knew it: that is why he concealed it. He was the adult: I was the child. He should never have abused my trust like that. It was sick.
My first marriage – husband ridiculed and criticised me constantly, wore me down.	I now know that he was like that in other relationships. Given what had already happened to me, I was in no position to fight back. My belief that I was bad was a self-fulfilling prophecy. I thought I deserved it.
People being irritable or unkind or putting me down.	Bound to happen sometimes – can't please everyone. Does not mean I am bad.

In the light of this new understanding, I now believe my Old Bottom Line: _____ 30% _____ %

In the light of this new understanding, I now believe my New Bottom Line: _____ 75% _____ %

CREATING A NEW BOTTOM LINE

Evidence (past and present) which supports my New Bottom Line:

My parents loved me. I know that from my own memories and from photos and things I have. My grandmother loved me. She couldn't protect me but she made me feel worthwhile and lovable. I made some friends at school, though I was too prickly and unhappy to have many (not my fault). Even when I was being abused in my first marriage, I managed to hold down a job and then, after having the children, I protected them from their father. When he began to show signs of abusing them I got the courage to leave, even though I never thought I would make it alone. I found a second husband who loves and supports me. He is a good man, and he chose me and stuck by me in spite of all my difficulties. I have struggled to overcome what happened to me. It has been really hard sometimes, and I've had lots of ups and downs. It's taken courage and persistence, and in the end I have made a good fist of it. All the good points on my list.

In the light of this new understanding, I now believe my Old Bottom Line: _____20%_____ %

In the light of this new understanding, I now believe my New Bottom Line: _____85%_____ %

Observation. Information and experiences I need to be alert to, in order to gather more evidence to support my New Bottom Line:

Things I do for other people, especially all the time and care I put into the children. My love for them and my husband. The pleasure I take in them. My creativity and imagination in looking after them and helping them to develop into good people. Things I contribute to society (my charity work, my political activism). My good points as they show themselves day to day. My relationships – signs that people love me such as phone calls, letters, invitations, people stopping to talk to me and wanting me to get involved in things. My intelligence – at last I am starting to think I am worth educating, and doing something about it.

Experiments. Specific things I need to do, in order to gather more evidence to support my New Bottom Line:

Begin making the first approach to people I trust, rather than leaving it up to them. Be more open about myself with people, step by step – see if they really do back off. Plan treats and pleasures for myself – I deserve it. Make time to study. Start saving for a proper course. Give more responsibility to the others at home to keep the show on the road. Look for a better job, one which really uses what I have to offer.

9

Planning for the future

Introduction

In working through this book, you have tackled the various thinking habits that keep low self-esteem going. You have created new Rules for Living and a new Bottom Line, and worked out how to put them into practice and act as if they were true on a day-to-day basis. In this chapter, the practical ideas for overcoming low self-esteem that you have been working with will be related back to the flow chart in Chapter 2 (page 42), so that you can see how what you have been doing fits with the understanding of low self-esteem that was your starting point. We shall then move on to consider ways of ensuring that the changes you have made are consolidated and carried forward, rather than left behind when you close the book. The chapter will close with some ideas on how to seek outside help if you find the ideas you have read about here interesting and relevant, but feel you need someone to help you put them into practice successfully.

Overcoming low self-esteem: Where does everything fit?

On pages 358–9, you will find the flow chart that explains the development and persistence of low self-esteem. You are already familiar with this, from previous chapters. Here, however, instead of mapping how low self-esteem develops and what keeps it going, you will see that the different methods you have used to undermine your Old Bottom Line and to establish and strengthen a New Bottom Line have been entered under the different headings. This is so that you can see clearly how the changes you have made fit together as parts of a coherent plan for overcoming low self-esteem. The cognitive behavioural understanding of low self-esteem, illustrated in the flow chart, consistently emphasises the influence of thoughts and beliefs on everyday feelings and behaviour. This emphasis has informed every step of the route you have followed.

Planning for the future

You may have been highly successful at dealing with anxious predictions and self-critical thoughts, focusing on your good qualities, giving yourself credit for what you do, treating yourself to relaxation and pleasure, and creating and acting on new Rules and a new, more accepting and generous Bottom Line. However, it is possible that, unless you continue to put what you have learned into practice on a regular basis, what now seem like blinding insights will become vague and hard to credit, and your new ways of treating yourself more kindly will decay.

Figure 41. Overcoming Low Self-esteem: A Map of the Territory

Undermining the negative beliefs that lie at the heart of low self-esteem:

(Early) Experience

What experiences (events, relationships, living conditions) contributed to the development of your negative beliefs about yourself?

What experiences contributed to keeping them going?

Are these experiences part of the 'evidence' that supports your low opinion of yourself?

The Bottom Line

On the basis of experience, what conclusions did you draw about yourself?

What were your old, negative beliefs about yourself?

What perspective on yourself would make better sense?

What is your New Bottom Line?

What 'evidence' did you use to support your Old Bottom Line? How else could you understand this 'evidence'?

What experiences (evidence) support your New Bottom Line and contradict the Old one?

What new information (things you have screened out/discounted) do you need to be alert to?

What experiments do you need to carry out?

Changing unhelpful rules:

Rules For Living

What are your Rules for Living? In what ways are they unreasonable and unhelpful?

What alternatives would be more reasonable and helpful?

Put them into practice

Breaking the Vicious Circle:

Trigger Situations

In what situations do you risk breaking your Rules for Living? Or feel that you have indeed broken them?

PLANNING FOR THE FUTURE

Activation of the Old Bottom Line

What thoughts, emotions, body sensations and behaviours
tell you your Old Bottom Line is activated?
What do you need to do to short-circuit activation
and bring your New Bottom Line and
new Rules for Living into play?

Depression
Minimised or
nipped in the bud.

Negative Predictions
Identify, question and
test (experiments).

Unhelpful Behaviour
Treat yourself kindly
and allow yourself
to relax and enjoy life.

Anxiety
Minimised or
nipped in the bud.

Self-critical Thinking
Identify and question.
Experiment with encouraging and
praising yourself.

Recognise your good points
and give yourself credit
for your achievements.

Unhelpful Behaviour
Face things you avoid,
drop unnecessary
precautions, give weight
to your successes.

Confirmation of the Bottom Line
Are you ignoring or discounting the times when things go well?

Are you giving too much weight to the times when
things do not go well, and assuming they say something
about you as a person?

As we have said before, old habits die hard. Particularly at times when you are stressed or pressurised, or when you are feeling low or unwell or tired or under par, you may find that your Old Bottom Line will surface again. As that happens, old patterns of thought and action may begin to re-establish themselves. You may become aware that your harsh and unforgiving standards for yourself are emerging once again, and with them old habits of expecting the worst, screening out positives and focusing on negatives, criticising yourself and forgetting to allow yourself relaxation and pleasure, to give yourself credit for what you do or to treat yourself kindly.

There is no need to worry about this. Long-established thought habits are probably never deleted from the brain's 'hard disc'. So given the right circumstances they may well pop up again. But now things are different. You know how to break the vicious circle that keeps low self-esteem going, and you have established and practised new Rules for Living and a New Bottom Line. So you are no longer stuck with only one, unkind and painful, point of view – you have somewhere else to go. It is simply a question of going back to what you already know and practising it systematically until you are back on an even keel.

If you have a healthy awareness that a setback could occur, you will be in the best possible position to spot early warning signals that your Old Bottom Line is resurfacing and to deal with it without delay. You may be able to put it back in its place almost immediately (with little more than 'Uh-oh, here I go again' and a swift change of gear). Or it may take you a little time.

Either way, the experience (even if unpleasant) will be a valuable one. It will give you an opportunity to refine your awareness of the early warning signals that tell you your sense of yourself is losing its balance, to discover again how new ideas and skills can help, and to work at fine-tuning and strengthening your new, kinder perspective on yourself. By planning ahead and considering how setbacks might come about and what to do when they do, you will ensure that the changes you have made endure over the long term.

On the other hand, you may feel that you have learned a lot, but that new ways of thinking and acting towards yourself are still fragile. This is especially likely to be true for you if your low self-esteem has been in place for many years, and if it has had a substantial impact on your life. Here again, it will be worth your while summarising what you have learned, to look ahead and plan how to consolidate your discoveries and make sure that they continue to influence how you go about your daily life, strengthening your belief in your New Bottom Line and ensuring that changes you have made are carried forward.

In the section that follows, you will find some questions to help you to formulate an action plan for the future (see page 372 for a summary, and pages 383–5 for an illustrative example). These questions are designed to help you to make a short summary of key points you have learned, to consider how best to continue putting new ideas into practice on a daily basis, and to prepare for setbacks so that they will not knock you sideways and you can manage them in the best possible way. Think of solidly grounded, healthy self-esteem as your marker on the horizon. Your learning summary and action plan are the kit you need in your backpack to support you on your continuing journey.

Steps towards a water-tight action plan

The first draft

Write down your answers to the questions, together with any other helpful points that occur to you as you follow them through. This is the first draft of your Action Plan. When you have completed the draft, review it and see if you have left anything important out. Go back through the book, and any records you have kept, to remind yourself of everything you have done. When you are satisfied that you have the best possible version for the time being, put your Action Plan into practice for two or three weeks.

Make sure you have it somewhere easily accessible, whether on paper or electronically, and that you regularly remind yourself what it says and keep it at the back of your mind, so that you can capitalise on any useful experiences that come up. You may find it helpful to give yourself some simple cues to help you remember – for example, sticky coloured dots where you can easily see them (e.g. on the fridge or the mirror you use in the morning), or perhaps reminders on your phone or pop-ups on your computer.

The second draft

Two or three weeks of putting your first draft into practice should give you a good idea of how helpful your Action Plan is. Now is a good time to review it and refine it, if you wish to do so. You may find that you have omitted something vital, or that things arise that you have not bargained for, or that what seemed clear to you when you wrote it down seems less helpful to you when you try to apply it in real life, or when you look back on it after a time.

Make whatever changes seem necessary to you, and then write out a revised version for a longer test-drive. Decide for yourself how long you will practise applying this version – three months? Six? You need long enough to find out how helpful the plan is in the longer term. You need an opportunity to discover how well established your New Bottom Line is, and how consistently it influences how you feel about yourself in everyday life. You also need some sense of how well your Action Plan helps you to deal with ups and downs, and times when the old Bottom Line resurfaces. So it may be helpful to decide in advance when you will review how things are going and to make any changes you need. Put reminders in your diary or on your computer or smartphone.

The final draft

After a longer period of practice, once again conduct a thorough review of your Action Plan. How helpful has it been to you? How well did it keep you on track? Has it enabled you to continue to grow and develop and move towards that marker on the horizon – healthy self-esteem?

Has it ensured that you have dealt with setbacks in the best possible way?

If all is well, your second draft may be your final draft. If, on the other hand, your Action Plan still has shortcomings, make whatever changes are necessary, and test-drive your new version for a limited period you agree with yourself. Then review again.

It is worth noting that, unless you have superhuman powers to foretell the future, your Action Plan will never cover everything. Even your final draft will still be a *draft*, not an ultimate truth engraved on tablets of stone. However good a fit it is, and however helpful, be prepared to change and fine-tune it at any future point when you realise it could be extended, elaborated or improved.

Getting SMART

When devising an Action Plan, it is important to ensure that what you plan to do will get you where you want to go. If your plan is too ambitious, you will not be able to put it into practice successfully, and this is likely to discourage and demoralise you. If your plan is too vague, you may find that after a week (or month) or two you have no real idea of what you are supposed to be doing. If your plan is too limited, you may feel you are not making any real progress towards becoming the person you want to be. So, whichever stage you are at – first, second or final draft – make sure that your Action Plan meets these **SMART** criteria:

Figure 42. Action Planning: Smart Criteria

S	Is it	Simple and Specific enough?
M	Is it	Measurable?
A	Is it	Agreed?
R	Is it	Realistic?
T	Is the	Timescale reasonable?

S: Is it Simple and Specific enough?

Can you explain what you plan to do in words of one syllable? Is it so straightforward that even a child could understand it? To check this, try reading it out to a trusted friend or a member of your family. Do they ask you to explain or clarify any part of it? If so, that part of it needs redrafting. When you have redrafted your plan, check out how it sounds to them now.

M: Is it Measurable?

How will you know when you have achieved what you set out to do? For example, in six months' time, if you have successfully acted on your Action Plan, how will you be feeling? Which of your new habits will still be in place? What specific targets will you have reached? How will you know that your New Bottom Line is still going strong? And if you still have changes to make, experiments to carry out, what will you be doing then that you are not doing now?

If you can specify clearly what you are going for, it will make it much easier for you to judge whether your plan is within your grasp, to observe how well you are doing at putting it into practice and where it falls down, and to assess how helpful it is to you. As you do this, beware of self-criticism sneaking in if your plan is not going as well as you wish or think it should. The point is to learn and develop your skills in consolidating and strengthening your new ways of operating, and of course this will take time and practice. You are learning new life skills, and learning life skills is a lifelong process.

A: Is it Agreed?

Have you taken into account the opinions and feelings of people who will be affected by your plan? Do you have their agreement (or at least their understanding) of what it implies?

I certainly do not mean by this that you should only proceed if other people are in favour of what you are trying to do – you do not need permission to feel better about yourself and make changes in your life that will improve your self-esteem. However, it is worth acknowledging that changes in you will mean changes for other people. For example, if you are planning to become more assertive about voicing your opinions and getting your needs met, then this will inevitably have an impact on those around you. If you are planning to change how you organise your working life (e.g. to reduce your working hours, in the interests of having more leisure and social time, or looking for more challenging assignments), again this will have an impact on other people, both at work and at home.

When you make your Action Plan, it is important to take this into account. Are there things about your intentions that you need to communicate to others? Would it help to negotiate some of the changes you want with your nearest and dearest? What about asking for help in sticking to your plan?

And, even if you do not wish to directly involve others, consider what impact changes in you will have on them. Are they likely to react negatively in any way? What do you predict? You could, of course, be wrong – but you will be in a stronger position to stay on course if you have considered what might realistically happen, and planned how you will deal with it (if necessary, with outside support).

Part of Briony's plan, for example, was to give herself more time to do things she enjoyed. She realised that this meant she could not continue to manage domestic tasks single-handedly. In order to feel like a good mother, she had always felt she must do all the shopping, cooking, washing and cleaning for her family, even though her husband was quite capable of helping her out and her children were now old enough to contribute.

Briony realised that she had educated her family to leave all the housework to her. She decided that it would be a good idea to fill them in on the work she had been doing to improve her self-esteem, and to tell them that she planned to start a fairer system of sharing the housework. She predicted that, in theory, her family would be able to see the justice of this, and would be in favour of what she was trying to do. She also predicted that, in practice, they would be reluctant to do their bit and would understandably prefer to leave things as they were. After all, why soil your hands if you have a servant willing to do the dirty work for you? So, in her plan, she included careful details of what to do when her family failed to change along with her. This included reminding herself of her reasons for making the change: she was a worthy person who deserved more out of life than to be a skivvy.

R: Is it Realistic?

When you plan ahead, take into account:

- Your state of emotional and physical health and fitness
- Your resources (e.g. money, time, people who care about and respect you)
- Other demands on your time and energy
- The level of support you have from friends, family, colleagues and others (for example, groups you belong to, such as a woman's group or a church fellowship group).

Your Action Plan will be most solid and realistic if it takes account of these factors. And keep it short. It will be most helpful to you if it is not too long. The longer and more elaborate your plan, the less likely you are to return to it and use it as time goes on. If there are points you want to go into in more detail, put them on separate pages which you can refer to in the Action Plan and keep along with it. It's also helpful to use colour to emphasise key points – highlighting, different typefaces, coloured sticky notes.

T: Is the Timescale reasonable?

Finally, make sure that you have considered carefully how much time you are willing to devote to putting your Action Plan into practice, and what timescale makes sense for achieving whatever targets you have set yourself. This may well include deciding what changes are most important to you, and which are less of a priority. Ask yourself:

- What are your priorities? If you could only complete 20 per cent of your plan, which 20 per cent would you want it to be?
- How much time every week do you need to ensure that your Action Plan becomes a reality? If you believe it would still be helpful to you to be regularly writing down and questioning your thoughts, how much time will you need to set aside every day to ensure that you do this in

the most helpful way and without feeling pressurised or rushed? (This may involve deciding how many examples you wish to work on every day.) You may, on the other hand, be at the stage of tackling upsetting thoughts in your head by now, and be routinely noticing evidence that supports your New Bottom Line without needing to write it down. Even so, it could be helpful to plan regular reviews. How much time might you need every week (or month) to assess how things are going and set yourself new challenges to master?

- What are your personal objectives, as far as self-esteem is concerned (your milestones on the journey to healthy self-esteem)? Where do you want to be after three months? After six months? After one year?

- How frequently will you review progress (successes, difficulties, what helped you, and what got in your way)?

- Have you set a date for your first review? This could be next week, or next month, or further away. Whenever it is, decide on a definite date and make an appointment with yourself. Make your review a special occasion. Take yourself out for lunch, give yourself a day out in the country, a health spa or at the seaside. At the very least, find a peaceful space in your home, somewhere

> you feel comfortable and at ease, and choose a
> time when you will not be interrupted. Create
> a relaxed space where you can reflect on what
> you have achieved and think ahead.

Note the date and time when you will review right now.
And do not allow yourself to put it off or be diverted. This
is something you are doing for yourself. It is important. And
you deserve it.

A note of caution

Action Plans can be filed away and forgotten. If you do not
know where it is, you will not be able to make use of it.
Leaving it lying around to end up all stained and dog-eared,
or buried in a part of your computer or phone that is difficult to access and whose password you have forgotten, is
like a message to yourself that it does not really matter – *you*
do not really matter. So make sure that you know where
your Action Plan is, and that you can find it easily when
you need to. Put it somewhere easy to find, somewhere
special, if you can: somewhere that is yours and yours alone.

Action planning: Helpful questions

Here are some questions to help you with developing your
action plan. Each is explained in more detail below.

Figure 43: Action Planning: Helpful Questions

1. How did my low self-esteem develop?

2. What kept it going?

3. What have I learned as I worked my way through the book?

4. What were my most important unhelpful thoughts, rules and beliefs? What alternatives did I find to them?

5. How can I build on what I have learned?

6. What might lead to a setback for me?

7. How will I know that all is not well?

8. If I do have a setback, what will I do about it?

1. How did my low self-esteem develop?

Briefly summarise the experiences that led to the formation of your Old Bottom Line. Also include later experiences that have reinforced it, if this is relevant.

2. What kept it going?

In response to this question, summarise the unhelpful Rules for Living that you developed as an attempt to cope with your Bottom Line, and the thinking that fuelled your vicious circle (anxious predictions and self-critical thoughts that have been typical of you). Also include any biases in what you noticed and gave weight to. What aspects of yourself did you automatically home in on? What did you automatically screen out, ignore or discount? Finally, note any unnecessary precautions and self-defeating behaviour that prevented you from discovering that your predictions were not accurate and conspired to keep you down.

3. What have I learned as I worked my way through the book?

Make a note of new ideas you have found helpful (for example, 'My beliefs about myself are opinions, not facts'). Also include particular methods you have learned for dealing with anxious and self-critical thoughts, Rules and the Bottom Line (for example, 'Review the evidence and look for the bigger picture', 'Don't assume – check it out'). Look back over what you have done and make a note of whatever made sense to you, and whatever you personally found useful in practice.

4. What were my most important unhelpful thoughts, rules and beliefs? What alternatives did I find to them?

Write down the anxious predictions, self-critical thoughts, Rules for Living and Bottom Lines that caused you most trouble. Against each, summarise the alternatives you have discovered. It may be helpful to give this space of its own, outside the main action plan, if you have a number of items it would be useful to summarise. You could use this format:

Unhelpful thought/rule/belief	Helpful alternative

5. How can I build on what I have learned?

Here is your opportunity to think ahead and consider in detail what you need to do in order to ensure that the new ideas and skills you have learned are consolidated and made a routine part of how you go about your life. This is also your chance to work out what changes you still want to make. This could include going back to particular parts of the book and working through some sections again, or using the methods you have learned to change unhelpful Rules for Living or beliefs about yourself that you have not yet addressed. It might also include further reading, or a decision to seek help in order to take what you have discovered further or put it into practice more effectively (see below).

Specifically, taking it chapter by chapter:

- Are there parts of your understanding of how your low self-esteem developed and what kept it going that you have not yet mapped out fully? If so, how could you go about clarifying them?
- Are there still situations where you feel anxious, but you are not clear why? If so, what do you need to do to see clearly the predictions you make in those situations? Are there situations where you understand very well what your predictions are, but you have not yet faced them fully without dropping all your unnecessary precautions? If so, how could you make a step-by-step plan to tackle them? Even if you have successfully faced the situations that made you anxious and discovered that your predictions were unrealistic, it could well be that you will experience other anxieties in the future (indeed, it would be extraordinary if this were not the case, since anxiety is a normal part of human experience). How will you use what you have learned to deal with future anxieties?
- How will you ensure that you continue to extend your ability to spot and answer self-critical thoughts? What self-defeating behaviours do you still need to watch out for? What do you plan to do instead?

- How good are you at keeping your good points in mind and noticing examples of your qualities, strengths, skills and talent on a day-to-day basis? Do you still need to keep a written record? Even if you do not, might it be rewarding to do so? Might it also be a useful resource to look over, if you have a setback at some point in the future?

- When you look at the pattern of your day and your week, are you achieving a good balance between 'A' activities (duties, obligations, tasks) and 'P' activities (pleasure, relaxation)? If so, how will you ensure that you continue to do so? And if not, then what do you need to do to build on changes you have already made?

- Are you routinely giving yourself credit for what you do and appreciating your achievements? If so, how can you ensure that you continue to do so? If not, why not? Are self-critical thoughts creeping in, for example, or are you still hanging on to perfectionist standards for yourself? If so, what do you need to do about it?

- How convincing do you now find your new Rules for Living? How easy is it to put them into practice? If they make complete sense to you, and you have no difficulty acting in accordance with them, then how can you ensure that this continues to be the case, even when the going gets tough and circumstances trigger off the old Rules? To what extent should you still deliberately be acting against the old Rules and observing the consequences? How frequently should you read your 'Changing the Rules' summary in order to ensure that what you have written stays fresh in your mind? If you still have some doubts about your new Rules or find it difficult to put them into practice, what do you need to do to strengthen your belief in them and make acting on them second nature? What experiments do you still need to carry out? What thoughts are getting in your way and how can you tackle them?

- How strongly do you now believe your New Bottom Line? And your old one? To what extent are you able to act as if the New Bottom Line were true? If you believe the New Bottom Line strongly and act routinely as though it were true, how can you ensure that it stays rock solid, even in times of pressure or distress? What information do you need to continue to notice (even if you no longer routinely write it down)? What experiments do you need to continue to carry out and make a part of your life? How frequently should you read your 'Bottom Line' summary, so as to ensure that it remains at the front of your mind?

6. What might lead to a setback for me?

Consider what experiences or changes in your circumstances might still cause you problems by activating your Old Bottom Line. Your knowledge of situations that have activated your Bottom Line in the past will be helpful here (see Chapter 3, page 77–9). You are probably in a position now to deal with these situations much more constructively. However, supposing you were confronting a high level of stress, or your life circumstances had become very difficult, or you were tired or unwell or upset for some other reason, this might still make you vulnerable to self-doubt. Working out what your own personal vulnerabilities might be will prepare you to notice quickly when things go wrong and do something about it.

7. How will I know that all is not well?

The signs that all is not well, and that your new sense of yourself is losing its balance, are unique to each person – much like a fingerprint or signature. Here are some questions you could ask yourself to help you identify your personal pattern:

What clues would tell you your Bottom Line was back in operation?

- How would you feel (your emotions)?
- What body sensations might you experience?

- What thoughts would be running through your mind?
- What images would appear in your mind's eye?
- What would you notice about your behaviour (e.g. beginning to avoid challenges, dropping pleasurable activities, ceasing to stand up for yourself and meet your own needs)?
- What might you notice in others (e.g. irritation, reassurance, apologies)?

Make a note of the signals that would tell you your self-esteem is beginning to slip – your personal setback signature.

If there is someone who knows you very well and whom you trust, it might be useful to ask for their help with this. Shifts in mind and mood states can be quite subtle and hard to spot, especially if you are inside them. People who care for us and know us very well can sometimes see these subtle warning signals of setback before we do. You could even, if you feel confident of their good will, make an agreement that it's OK for this person to say something if they think all is not well, and discuss how they might most helpfully go about that.

8. If I do have a setback, What will I do about it?

The next thing is to consider in detail what you should do if you do see the early warning signals of a setback. How can you best care for yourself in this difficult situation, short-circuit the spiral down into low self-esteem, and make sure you get whatever support you need as you do so? The first thing to say to yourself is the emergency instruction from Douglas Adams's *Hitchhiker's Guide to the Galaxy*: DON'T PANIC. It is quite natural to have setbacks on your journey towards overcoming low self-esteem, especially if the problem has been with you for a long time.

A setback does not mean you are back to square one, or that there is no point in doing anything further to help yourself. On the contrary, you simply need to return to what you have learned and begin putting it into practice systematically until your self-esteem is back in balance. This may mean going back to basics – for example, starting to record things regularly again, perhaps after you have stopped needing to do so for some time. This may feel like a backwards step. In fact, it is simply a sensible recognition that, for a limited period, you need to put some extra time and effort into consolidating your New Bottom Line. This is rather like what you might need to do if you had learned a language, not spoken it for a long time, and then revisited the country concerned. Even if you had become quite fluent, it would still make good sense to revise what you knew, in order to meet the challenge successfully.

What to do if you need outside help

If the ideas in this book make good sense to you, but you have difficulty putting them into practice (perhaps because your Old Bottom Line is so strong or because it has had such a disabling effect on your life), then it may be useful to look for a therapist who could help you to take things further than you can initially manage on your own. If you like this particular way of understanding low self-esteem and overcoming it, then your best bet is probably to look for a cognitive-behavioural therapist. If, on the other hand, you would prefer a more reflective, less structured approach, with a greater emphasis on developing insight than on practical techniques for achieving changes in daily living, then a counsellor or psychotherapist may suit you better. You will find some useful addresses at the end of this book.

As I said in Chapter 1 (pages 3–35), there is nothing shameful about seeking psychological help. It is not an admission of defeat, but rather a step towards taking control of your life and doing what needs to be done in order to become the person you would like to be. Supposing you were on a journey that involved travelling in the dark through unknown territory: you might well be glad of a guide, and be less likely to fall into swamps and lose your way than if you had ventured out alone. A therapist is like a guide. He or she will help you to acquire the map-reading skills you need in order to complete your journey successfully, and will teach you how to detect pitfalls and challenges and deal with them constructively on your own.

Similarly, if you were learning a new skill (for example, driving a truck or mastering a sport), it would probably seem reasonable to you to have some lessons or seek out a coach. Therapists are also like coaches. Their prime objective is to help you to develop your own skills to the point where the therapist becomes redundant, because you are able to do it for yourself.

Chapter summary

1. *The ideas and techniques you have learned as you worked through the book form a coherent programme for change, each related to a particular aspect of the cognitive-behavioural understanding of low self-esteem.*

2. *To ensure that you carry forward what you have learned and make it part of how you go about the business of living, make a written Action Plan for the future.*

3. *Make your Action Plan straightforward and realistic. Ensure that you are clear about how to measure your progress in carrying it out, and that it considers the impact of changes in you on those around you. It should also take account of limitations on your time and resources, and the timescale should be realistic.*

4. *In the Action Plan, summarise your understanding of how your low self-esteem developed and what kept it going. Note what you have learned as you worked your way through the book, and how you plan to build on new ideas and skills. Identify future events and stresses that might lead to a setback and the early warning signs that will tell you that all is not well. Then work out what to do about it, how best to take care of yourself if a setback does occur.*

Figure 44. Action Plan for the Future: Briony

1 *How did my low self-esteem develop?*

When my parents died, I felt it was my fault. When my step-parents treated me so badly, that confirmed it. Finally, when my stepfather began to abuse me, I came to the conclusion that everything that had happened was a result of something in me. It all meant I was BAD. This was my Old Bottom Line. Once this idea was in place, other things happened that seemed to confirm it. For example, my first marriage was to a man who constantly criticised and ridiculed me. Because of what had happened earlier on, I thought this was just what I deserved.

2 *What kept it going?*

I kept on acting and thinking as if I really was a bad person. I never paid attention to good things about myself; I kept my true self hidden from people, because I was convinced that if they found out what I was really like, they would want nothing further to do with me. I was always very hard on myself. Anything I got wrong filled me with despair – yet more evidence of what a bad person I was. I could not have close relationships, except with the few people who persisted even when I held back. I allowed people to dismiss me and treat me badly. I didn't think I deserved anything better.

3 *What have I learned as I worked my way through the book?*

To understand things better – it's my belief that I'm bad that's the problem, not the fact that I really am bad. I have learned that it is possible to change beliefs about yourself that have been around for a long time, if you work on them. I have learned to still my critical voice and focus on the good things about me. I am changing my rules and taking the risk of letting people see more of the true me.

4 *What were my most important thoughts, rules and beliefs? What alternatives did I find to them?*

I am bad → I am worthy

If I let anyone close to me, they will hurt and exploit me → If I let people close to me, I get the warmth and affection I need. Most people will treat me decently – and I can protect myself from those who don't.

I must never allow anyone to see my true self → Since my true self is worthy, I need not hide it. If some people don't like it, that's their problem.

5 *How can I build on what I have learned?*

Read the Summary Sheets for my new rules and Bottom Line daily – I need to drum them in. Keep acting as if they were true and observe the results. When I notice myself getting apprehensive and wanting to avoid things or protect myself, work out what I am predicting and check it out.

Watch out for self-criticism – it's well entrenched and I need to keep fighting it.

Keep on recording examples of good things about me – it's already made a difference.

Make time for me – don't be afraid to remind the family when they go back to their old ways.

6 *What might lead to a setback for me?*

Getting depressed for any reason. Being consistently badly treated by someone. Something going very wrong for someone I cared about (I would tend to blame myself).

7 *How will I know that all is not well?*

Wanting to shut myself away and avoid people. Getting snappy and irritable with my husband and children. Rise in tension — especially in my neck and shoulders.

8 *If I do have a setback, what will I do about it?*

Try to notice the early warning signals, for a start. Ask my husband to help with this — he's sensitive to when I start hiding myself away and being irritable and defensive, and he notices when I start to be down on myself. Then get out my notes, especially the Summary Sheets and this Action Plan, and follow through on what I know works. Don't be hard on myself for taking a backwards step — it's bound to happen from time to time, given how long I have felt bad about myself and how I came to be that way. Be encouraging, compassionate and kind to myself — that's what I would do for anyone else in distress. Get all the support I can, and go back to the basics.

Useful books and addresses

Useful books

Ruth A. Baer, 2014. *Practising Happiness: How Mindfulness Can Free You From Psychological Traps and Help You Build the Life You Want*. Robinson.

David Burns, 2000. *Feeling Good: The New Mood Therapy*. Avon Books (2nd edition).

Gillian Butler, 2008. *Overcoming Social Anxiety and Shyness: A Self-Help Guide Using Cognitive Behavioural Techniques*. Basic Books.

Gillian Butler and Tony Hope, 2007. *Manage Your Mind: The Mental Fitness Guide*. Oxford University Press (2nd edition).

Paul Gilbert, 2009. *Overcoming Depression: A Self-Help Guide Using Cognitive Behavioural Techniques*. Robinson (3rd edition).

Paul Gilbert, 2013. *The Compassionate Mind*. Robinson.

Dennis Greenberger and Christine A. Padesky, 2016. *Mind Over Mood: Change How You Feel By Changing the Way You Think*. Guilford Press (2nd edition).

Steven Hayes (with Spencer Smith), 2005. *Get Out of Your Mind & Into Your Life: The New Acceptance & Commitment Therapy*. New Harbinger Publications.

Helen Kennerley, 2014. *Overcoming Anxiety: A Self-Help Guide Using Cognitive Behavioural Techniques*. Robinson (2nd edition).

Helen Kennerley, 2009. *Overcoming Childhood Trauma: A Self-Help Guide Using Cognitive Behavioural Techniques*. Robinson (2nd edition).

Matthew McKay, Patrick Fanning, Carole Honeychurch and Catherine Sutker, 2005. *The Self-Esteem Companion*. New Harbinger.

Susan Nolen-Hoeksma, 2004. *Women Who Think Too Much: How to Break Free of Overthinking and Reclaim Your Life*. Piatkus

Mary Welford, 2012. *Building Your Self-Confidence Using Compassion Focused Therapy*. Robinson.

Mark Williams and Danny Penman, 2011. *Mindfulness: A Practical Guide to Finding Peace in a Frantic World*. Piatkus.

Useful addresses

Great Britain

British Association for Behavioural Cognitive Psychotherapies
Imperial House
Hornby Street
Bury, Lancashire BL9 5BM
Tel: (0044) 161 705 4304
Website: www.babcp.com

British Association for Counselling & Psychotherapy
BACP House
15 St John's Business Park
Lutterworth, Leicestershire LE17 4HB
Tel: (0044) 1455 883300
Website: www.bacp.co.uk

British Psychological Society
St Andrews House
48 Princess Road East
Leicester LE1 7DR
Tel: (0044) 116 254 9568
Website: www.bps.org.uk

Mental Health Foundation (Headquarters)
Colechurch House
1 London Bridge Walk
London SE1 2SX
Tel: (0044) 20 7803 1100
Website: www.mentalhealth.org.uk

MIND: The National Association for Mental Health
15-19 Broadway
Stratford
London E15 4BQ
Tel: (0044) 20 8519 2122
Website: www.mind.org.uk

Newcastle Cognitive & Behavioural Therapies Centre
Benfield House
Walkergate Park
Benfield Road
Newcastle upon Tyne, NE6 4PF
Tel: (0044) 191 287 6100
Website: www.ntw.nhs.uk

Oxford Cognitive Therapy Centre
Warneford Hospital
Oxford OX3 7JX
Tel: (0044) 1865 902801
Website: www.octc.co.uk

Australia
Australian Association for Cognitive & Behaviour Therapy
AACBT Ltd
15 Haig Avenue
Georges Hall
New South Wales NSW 2198
Email: info@aabct.org
Website: www.aabct.org

Australian Centre for Clinical Interventions
223 James Street
Northbridge
Western Australia 6003
Tel: (0061) 08 9227 4399
Website: www.cci.health.wa.gov.au

Canada

Canadian Association of Cognitive & Behavioural Therapies
CACBT – ACTCC
260 Queen Street West
PO Box 60055
Toronto, ON
M5V 0C5
Website: www.cacbt.ca

Europe

European Association of Behavioural & Cognitive Therapies
EABCT Office
PO Box 14081
3508 SC Utrecht, The Netherlands
Tel: (0031) 30 254 30 54
Website: www.eabct.eu

New Zealand

Aotearoa New Zealand Association for Cognitive
Behavioural Therapies
Website: www.cbt.org.nz

United States

Academy of Cognitive Therapy
245 N. 15th Street, MS 403
17 New College Building
Department of Psychiatry
Philadelphia, PA 19102
Tel: (001) 215 831 7838
Website: www.academyofct.org

American Institute for Cognitive Behavior Therapy
136 E. 57th Street, Suite 1101
New York City, NY 10022
Tel: (001) 212 308 2440
Website: www.cognitivetherapynyc.com

The Association for Behavioral & Cognitive Therapies
(ABCT) (Formerly the Association for the Advancement
of Behavior Therapy)
305 7th Avenue, 16th Floor
New York, NY 10001
Tel: (001) 212 647 1927/0019
Website: www.abct.org

Institute for Behavior Therapy
20 E. 49th St, 2nd Floor
New York, NY 10017
Tel: (001) 212 692 9288
Website: www.ifbt.net

Appendix

Figure 10. Predictions and Precautions Worksheet.

Date/Time	Situation What were you doing when you began to feel anxious?	Emotions and body sensations (e.g. anxious, panicky, tense, heart racing) Rate 0–100 for intensity	Anxious predictions What exactly was going through your mind when you began to feel anxious? (e.g. thoughts in words, images) Rate 0–100% for how strongly you believed each one	Precautions What did you do to stop your predictions coming true? (e.g. avoid the situation, safety-seeking behaviours)

Figure 10. Predictions and Precautions Worksheet

| Date/Time | Situation

What were you doing when you began to feel anxious? | Emotions and body sensations (e.g. anxious, panicky, tense, heart racing) Rate 0–100 for intensity | Anxious predictions

What exactly was going through your mind when you began to feel anxious? (e.g. thoughts in words, images) Rate 0–100% for how strongly you believed each one | Precautions

What did you do to stop your predictions coming true? (e.g. avoid the situation, safety-seeking behaviours) |
|---|---|---|---|---|
| | | | | |
| | | | | |

Figure 13. Checking Out Anxious Predictions Worksheet

Date/ Time	Situation	Emotions and body sensations Rate intensity 0–100	Anxious predictions Rate 0–100% for how strongly you believed each one	Alternative perspectives Use the key questions to find other views of the situation Rate belief 0–100%	Experiment 1 What did you do instead of taking your usual precautions? 2 What were the results? 3 What did you learn?

Figure 13. Checking Out Anxious Predictions Worksheet

Date/ Time	Situation	Emotions and body sensations Rate intensity 0–100	Anxious predictions Rate 0–100% for how strongly you believed each one	Alternative perspectives Use the key questions to find other views of the situation Rate belief 0–100%	Experiment 1 What did you do instead of taking your usual precautions? 2 What were the results? 3 What did you learn?

Figure 16. Spotting Self-critical Thoughts Worksheet

Date/Time	Situation What were you doing when you began to feel bad about yourself?	Emotions and body sensations (e.g. sad, angry, guilty) Rate each 0–100 for intensity	Self-critical thoughts What exactly was going through your mind when you began to feel bad about yourself? (e.g. thoughts in words, images, meanings) Rate 0–100% for degree of belief	Unhelpful behaviour What did you do as a consequence of your self-critical thoughts?

Figure 16. Spotting Self-critical Thoughts Worksheet

Date/Time	Situation What were you doing when you began to feel bad about yourself?	Emotions and body sensations (e.g. sad, angry, guilty) Rate each 0–100 for intensity	Self-critical thoughts What exactly was going through your mind when you began to feel bad about yourself? (e.g. thoughts in words, images, meanings) Rate 0–100% for degree of belief	Unhelpful behaviour What did you do as a consequence of your self-critical thoughts?

Figure 16. Spotting Self-critical Thoughts Worksheet

Date/Time	Situation What were you doing when you began to feel bad about yourself?	Emotions and body sensations (e.g. sad, angry, guilty) Rate each 0–100 for intensity	Self-critical thoughts What exactly was going through your mind when you began to feel bad about yourself? (e.g. thoughts in words, images, meanings) Rate 0–100% for degree of belief	Unhelpful behaviour What did you do as a consequence of your self-critical thoughts?

Figure 16. Spotting Self-critical Thoughts Worksheet

Date/Time	Situation What were you doing when you began to feel bad about yourself?	Emotions and body sensations (e.g. sad, angry, guilty) Rate each 0–100 for intensity	Self-critical thoughts What exactly was going through your mind when you began to feel bad about yourself? (e.g. thoughts in words, images, meanings) Rate 0–100% for degree of belief	Unhelpful behaviour What did you do as a consequence of your self-critical thoughts?

Figure 18. Questioning Self-critical Thoughts Worksheet

Date/ Time	Situation	Emotions and body sensations Rate each 0–100	Self-critical thoughts Rate belief in each 1–100%	Alternative perspectives Use the key questions to find other perspectives on yourself. Rate belief in each 0–100%	Outcome 1 Now that you have found alternatives to your self-critical thoughts, how do you feel (0–100)? 2 How strongly do you now believe your self-critical thoughts (0–100%)? 3 What can you do now (action plan, experiments)?

Figure 31. Experimenting with New Rules Worksheet

Date/Time	The situation	What I did	The outcome

Figure 45. Acting in Accordance with My New Bottom Line

Date/Time	Experiment (what I did)	Results (what I notice, my feelings and thoughts, others' reactions, what I learned)	My belief in my Old Bottom Line	My Belief in my New Bottom Line

Figure 22. Daily Activity Diary				
		Mon	Tue	Wed
M O R N I N G	6-7			
	7-8			
	8-9			
	9-10			
	10-11			
	11-12			
A F T E R N O O N	12-1			
	1-2			
	2-3			
	3-4			
	4-5			
	5-6			
E V E N I N G	6-7			
	7-8			
	8-9			
	9-10			
	10-11			
	11-12			

Thurs	Fri	Sat	Sun

Acknowledgements

With gratitude to all those from whom I have learned so much, especially John, Gillian, David, Anke, Paul, Ann, Joan, Christine and Kathleen, Ferris, Mark, and all the patients with whom I have been privileged to spend time over the years. And above all to Clive, Emily and Jacob.

Index

Aaron (case example) 52–3,
    63–4, 72, 79, 82, 260,
    324, 331, 333, 345, 348
abuse 326–7, 337–8
  online 49–50
  systematic 43–6, 354–5,
    383–4
accidents 59–60
achievements
  lack of 230–2
  listing your 203
Action Plans 362–80, 383–5
  agreeability 366–8
  caution regarding 371
  getting SMART 364–71
  helpful questions 371–80
  measurability 365–6
  realistic nature 368–9
  reviewing 370–1
  simplicity 365
  timescale 369–70
action replays 167
Adams, Douglas 380
adoption 44
advocates, inner 181

affection, difficulties showing
    54–5
all-or-nothing thinking 179, 267
alternative perspectives 168,
    169, 170–3, 175–6,
    184–6, 190
alternative views 126–34
Andersen, Hans Christian, *The
    Snow Queen* 196
anxiety 18
  and breaking the Rules for
    Living 77–81
  how anxious thinking
    works 105–9
  physical symptoms 114–16,
    117–19
  trigger situations 105
anxious predictions 81–9, 95–
    7, 242–3, 245–6, 301–2,
    373, 375
  alternative views to 126–34
  and avoidance behaviours
    85, 122, 124
  and awareness 101–2,
    111–23

and Bottom Lines 308–9

checking out 101–46

'Checking Out Anxious Predictions' worksheet 125, 127–9

and experiments 101–2, 109, 112, 122–3, 124, 135–44

identification 111–23

and identifying Rules for Living 263–4, 266

and rethinking 101–2, 112, 124–34, 143

tackling 101–2, 109, 111–44

and taking unnecessary precautions 109–23

treating like facts 103

writing down 119–21, 125, 127–9

artists 56–7

avoidance behaviours 85, 122, 124, 230

awareness 101–2, 111–23

and Bottom Lines 303–6

and changing your Rules for Living 246, 272

and enhancing self-acceptance 194, 198–208, 218–32

tackling anxious predictions with 101–2, 111–23

tackling self-critical thoughts with 156–67

bad feelings, and self-critical thoughts 148, 152, 157

bad, seeing oneself as being 44, 327, 331–3, 339, 383–5

Beck, Aaron T. 29

behaviour

impact of anxious predictions on 84–9

impact of low self-esteem on 12–13

impact of self-critical thoughts on 92–4

beliefs see self-beliefs

best case scenarios, envisioning 132

best friends, being your own 197–8

biases 67–70, 193

of anxious thinking 106–9, 125

and Bottom Lines 313, 321

of interpretation 68, 193–4

of perception 67, 193–4, 341

and Rules for Living 255

of self-critical thinking 176–83

blame
taking the 181–2
see also self-blame
bodily sensations
and Bottom Lines 206
impact of low self-esteem
on 13
writing down 114–16,
117–19, 160–1, 162
body image 47–8, 325, 334–5
Bottom Lines 42, 61–6, 72–3,
75, 78–82, 94–6, 106,
194, 245–6, 372–4
'Acting in Accordance with
my New Bottom Line'
worksheet 346, 352–5
activation 359
and anxious predictions
308–9
and bodily sensations 206
and childhood experience
306–8
and cognitive biases 313, 321
confirmation 89–90, 359
creating new 102, 197, 232,
301–55, 357–8, 360–1,
363, 377
definition 303–6
and the downward arrow
technique 311–13, 315,
320

and emotions 206, 256
evidence for 321–50
and experiments 346–50,
353, 355
identification 303–13, 320
observation 341–5, 353, 355
professional help with
380–1
rating the degree of your
belief in 304–6,
316–17, 320, 340, 377
and record-keeping 342,
346, 350, 352–5
and rethinking 313–40
reviewing the evidence
supporting 329
and Rules for Living 251–2,
256, 262, 272–3, 301,
311, 372–3
and self-criticism 186,
309–10, 359
and setbacks 378–80, 384–5
sources of information on
your 306–13
taking the longer view
350–1
undermining old 321–40
breathing rate 118
Briony (case example) 44, 46,
63–5, 71–2, 79, 105, 246,
260–1, 307, 313, 315,

323, 327, 339, 344, 348,
354–5, 367–8, 383–5
bullying 48–50
Burns, David 272

catastrophizing 108, 125
CBT see cognitive behavioural
therapy
celebrity, ideals of 47–8
challenges, listing your 203
Chesterton, G.K. 183
childhood experience 358
and the Bottom Line 306–8
and the development of low
self-esteem 43–5, 61–2,
65–6
and Rules for Living 249,
268–71, 282, 297
and self-criticism 151
cognitive behavioural
therapists 381
cognitive behavioural therapy
(CBT) 29–31, 43, 122
cognitive biases 67–70, 193
of anxious thinking 106–9,
125
biases of interpretation 68,
193–4
biases of perception 67,
193–4, 341
and Bottom Lines 313, 321

and Rules for Living 255
of self-critical thinking
176–83
comparison-making,
unfavourable 46–7,
228–9, 326, 335
consideration, treating yourself
with 214
see also self-kindness
counsellors 381
criticism 61–2
systematic 43–5
see also self-critical thoughts
culture, and Rules for Living
249, 253–4, 283
cyberbullying 48–50

Daily Activity Diary, The
(DAD) 215–27, 233–43,
267, 294
achievement ratings 220–4,
226–7, 233–6, 243
daily plans 234–43
and lack of achievement
230–2
pleasure ratings 215, 218,
219–20, 224, 226–7,
233–6, 243
reviews 224–5, 235–6
and self-observation 226–32
what you did 219

daily plans 234–43
delinquency 324
depressed path 94
depression 153, 359
    and the Bottom Line 323
    and losing pleasure in things
        229
    symptoms 15–17
    and the vicious cycle of low
        self-esteem 93–4, 97
diary-keeping 112–23, 125,
        158–67
    alternative perspectives 168,
        169, 170–3, 175–6,
        184–6
    and anxious predictions
        119–21
    and bodily sensations 114–
        16, 117–19, 160–1,
        162
    Daily Activity Diary 215–
        27, 233–43, 267, 294
    date and time 114–16, 159,
        160–1
    and emotions 114–17,
        160–1, 162
    outcomes 169, 170–3
    and self-critical thoughts
        160–1, 162–4
    the situation 114–16,
        159–62

and unnecessary precautions
        121–3, 160–1
dieting 48
difference 55–8, 326
difficulties, current 323–4,
        329–30
direct statements 266
discrepancy-based processing
        186–7
distress 323, 329–30
    being on the receiving end
        of other people's
        50–1
double standards 178, 205,
        333
downward arrow technique
        272–6, 277, 289, 311–13,
        315, 320
dyslexia 58

Ellis, Albert 333
emotions
    impact of anxious
        predictions on 83–4
    impact of low self-esteem
        on 13
    impact of self-critical
        thoughts on 92–4, 157,
        162
    rating the strength of your
        117, 162

and Rules for Living 256
writing down 114–17,
160–1, 162
see also feelings
end results 68–70
enjoying life 310, 367–8
see also pleasurable activities
errors, past 324, 331–2
evidence
against negative views of
yourself 175
for Bottom Lines 321–50,
352–5
for your anxious predictions
126, 130
for your self-critical
thoughts 174–5
evidence-based approaches 29
Evie (case example) 72, 79,
325, 334–5, 344,
348
experiments 25
and alternatives to
unnecessary
precautions 138–9
carrying out 139–40
and changing your Rules
for Living 246
and enhancing self-
acceptance 233–43
example 143–4

giving yourself credit for
142–3
how to conduct 136–43
outcomes 140–1
stating your predictions
137–8
tackling anxious predictions
with 101–2, 109, 112,
122–3, 124, 135–44
tackling self-critical
thoughts with 156,
183–91
thinking about what you
have learned 141–2

facts, treating thoughts like 10,
39, 103, 174
failure, past 324, 331–2
families
being the odd one out 55–6
place in society 52–3
scapegoats 44
family sayings 268–71
fear 109, 308–9
feelings
bad 148, 152, 157
upset 186
see also emotions
'fight or flight' response 119
flashbacks 62
flashcards 292

future planning 356–85
    Action Plans 362–80,
        383–5
    getting SMART 364–71

gastric system 118
gifts, listing your 204
Gilbert, Paul 229
'good enough', being 189,
        296, 298, 318, 320
    see also 'not good enough'
growth, blockers to 153–4
guilt 60

habits, persistence 360
heart rate 118
help, asking for 323–4, 330–1
hopelessness, sense of 90

ideas, new, putting into
        practice 25
identity
    loss of something that was a
        part of your 327–8
    online 49
'If..., then' statements 260–1,
        293, 311
inner advocates 181
inner judges 181
interpretation, negative biases
        in 68, 193–4

'it-should-be-different'
        thinking 186–7, 228–9

Jack (case example) 51, 62–4,
        72, 79, 82, 261, 325–6,
        344–5, 348
judgements 262–3, 267–8,
        326, 331–3, 336
judges, inner 181
'jumping to conclusions'
        176–7

Kate (case example) 54–5, 63,
        64, 72, 79, 82, 86, 106–8,
        112, 120, 123, 125,
        128–9, 131–2, 143–4,
        260, 271, 308–9, 331,
        345, 349
'killjoy' thoughts 218, 228, 229
kindness, treating yourself
        with 214, 310, 314–16

learning 43
    blockers to 153–4
leisure activities, impact of
        low self-esteem on 14
life, impact of low self-esteem
        on 13–15
life events
    and the development of
        low-self-esteem 39–74

overestimating the chances
of bad life events 106–7
overestimating the impact
of bad life events 107–8
underestimating outside
resources to deal with
bad life events 108–9
underestimating personal
resources to deal with
bad life events 108
see also worst case scenarios
likeability 319–20
likelihood of events,
envisioning 133
Lin (case example) 56–7,
61–4, 73, 79, 82, 207–10,
213, 219–23, 231–2, 260,
267, 304, 307, 326, 345,
349
low self-esteem 5, 6
causes/development 31,
39–74, 372, 383
definition 3–35
impact 10–15, 19–22
late onset 58–61
maintenance 31–2, 75–98,
372–3, 383
mapping the territory of
40–2
protective factors 22–7
recognition 7–9

variations in the role and
status of 15–19
see also overcoming low
self-esteem; vicious
circle of low self-
esteem

Mary (case example) 60–1,
63–4, 73, 80, 328, 334,
345, 349
memory
painful memories 62
recreating memories 214
and Rules for Living
268–71
unreliable nature 27, 165
see also childhood
experience
mental changes 118
Mike (case example) 59–60,
63–4, 73, 80, 82, 148–9,
172–3, 184, 250, 261,
323–4, 330, 345, 349
muscle tension 117
'musts' 230, 257, 261–2

needs, prioritising your 227–8
negative qualities, you don't
possess 206
negative self-beliefs 303–4,
311–12, 321, 328

at the heart of low self-
esteem 32–4, 39–41,
43, 67–70
and the maintenance of
low self-esteem 75–6,
81–2, 89, 91, 95
undermining 358
negative thoughts
patterns of 226
and Rules for Living 255
neglect, systematic 43–5
new ideas 25
new possibilities 23
new skills 25
'not good enough', being
treated as 42, 46–7, 63,
70, 72, 77, 96, 148,
228, 252, 297, 310,
328, 344

obligations 220–4, 226–7,
233–6, 240–1, 243
observation 112–13, 122,
218–233, 341–5
'odd one out', being the 55–8
online identities 49
openness 23
'or elses' 261–2, 311
other people
behaviour towards you
326–7, 336–40

being on the receiving
end of their distress
50–1
opinions of you 204, 206–8,
336–7
qualities 205
'oughts' 230, 257, 261–2
overcoming low self-esteem
99–385
changing the Rules for
Living 245–300
checking out anxious
predictions 101–46
creating new Bottom Lines
301–55
enhancing self-acceptance
193–244
future planning 356–85
questioning self-critical
thoughts 147–92
overgeneralisations 256–7

Padesky, Christine 69, 317
panic 18
parental standards, failure to
meet 46–7
peer pressure 47–8, 327
people-pleasing 14, 44,
271
perception, negative biases in
67, 193–4, 341

perfectionism 182–3, 189,
250, 252, 255–6, 267,
285–6, 297–9, 310,
318–19, 328
performance anxiety 87–8
personal growth, blockers to
153–4
personal relationships, impact
of low self-esteem on 14
personal resources,
underestimating 108
physical characteristics 47–8,
325, 334–5
pleasurable activities 215, 218,
219–20, 224, 226–7,
233–6, 238–41, 243
lack of 227–9
positive self-beliefs 10
positive self-esteem 6
positive thinking 318
positives, discounting 205
'Positives Portfolio' 211–14,
350
post-traumatic stress disorder
60
power imbalances 339–40
precautions *see* unnecessary
precautions
predictions *see* anxious
predictions
prioritising 269

problems
and low self-esteem 17–18
vulnerability to 18–19
procrastination, getting to
grips with 241–3
professional help 28–31,
380–2
protective factors 22–7
psychological characteristics
325–6
psychotherapists 381
psychotherapy 29
public-speaking 81–4, 86
punishment, systematic 43–5

Rajiv (case example) 46–7,
63–4, 71–2, 79, 86, 91–2,
95, 105, 250–2, 255–7,
260, 264, 266–8, 272,
277, 282–6, 288–9, 291,
297–9, 310, 328, 344,
348
rape 44
'Rational Emotive Therapy'
333
realism 154–5, 280, 368–9
record-keeping *see* diary-
keeping; worksheets;
writing things down
relationships, impact of low
self-esteem on 14

reliving 208–11, 214
resources
  underestimating outside
    108–9
  underestimating personal 108
respect, treating yourself with
  214
responsibility, sense of 327
rethinking (questioning)
  101–2, 112, 124–34, 143
  and Bottom Lines 313–40
  and changing your Rules
    for Living 246, 280–90
  and key questions 126–34,
    169–83
  tackling anxious predictions
    with 101–2, 112, 124–
    34, 143
  tackling self-critical
    thoughts with 156,
    168–83
reviews 224–5
Rules for Living 32, 42, 66,
  70–3, 75, 97, 372–4, 384
  alternative Rules 287–90
  assessing the impact of
    276–8
  assumptions 260–1
  and Bottom Lines 251–2,
    256, 262, 272–3, 301,
    311, 372–3

breaking the Rules 76–81,
  94, 96, 101, 103, 105,
  106, 109, 111, 122,
  246
changing the Rules 232,
  245–300, 302, 358,
  360, 376–7
and childhood experience
  249, 268–71, 282, 297
concessions 249–50
consolidating discoveries
  278–9, 291–9
and culture 249, 253–4, 283
dealing with old Rules
  292–3
developing less harsh Rules
  102
and direct statements 266
disadvantages of not
  obeying 286–7
and the downward arrow
  technique 272–6, 277,
  289
drivers 261–2
and emotions 256
and enjoyment 228
excessive nature 256–7
and experiments 280–90,
  293–6
and family sayings 268–9
and flashcards 292

and the 'follow the
opposite' tactic 271–2
and the guarantee of low
self-esteem 257–9
helpful questions to ask
regarding 281–90
identifying your 246,
259–76
idiosyncratic/unique nature
255
imagined consequences of
breaking 311
judgements 267–8
and a lack of a sense of
achievement 230
learnt nature 253
and memories 268–9
origins of 247–50, 281–3
payoffs of 284–6, 287
and perfectionism 182
preparations for change 296
and rethinking 246, 280–90
rigidity/resistance to change
249, 255, 334–5
and self-critical thoughts
263–4, 266–8
sources of information on
265–76
test-driving new 290–9
themes 266–7
unreasonable nature 256, 284

and value judgements 262–3
what are Rules like? 253–9
written summaries 291,
296–9
rumination 91, 92, 94, 97
rumination trap 187–9

safety-seeking behaviours 122,
124, 141
school
being the odd one out at
57–8
impact of low self-esteem
on 13–14
self
learning to pay more
attention to the
positive sides of 151
statements about 12
thoughts about 12
true 250
self-acceptance, enhancement
5, 32, 193–244
and awareness 194,
198–208, 218–32
and experiments 233–43
and key questions to
establishing your
strengths 201–8
making the most of
planning ahead 234–43

and 'Positives Portfolios'
211–14
recognising 198–208
and reliving 208–11, 214
and self-kindness 214
and the taboo against self-
acceptance 194–8
and The Daily Activity
Diary 215–18
self-beliefs 10–11
positive 10
see also Bottom Lines;
negative self-beliefs
self-blame 181–2, 336–8
self-care, impact of low self-
esteem on 14
self-commitment 25–6
self-compassion 280, 332
self-concept 3–4
self-condemnation, on the
basis of a single event
179–80
self-confidence 4–5, 31
self-critical thoughts 19–22,
90–4, 95–7, 134, 242–3,
245–6, 301–2
alternative perspectives 168,
169, 170–3, 175–6,
184–6, 190
as blocker of learning and
growth 153–4

and Bottom Lines 186,
309–10, 359
and childhood experience
151
cognitive biases of 176–83
evidence for 174–5
harmful nature 151–5
and identifying Rules for
Living 263–4, 266–8
impact 147–51, 176
key questions to finding
alternatives to 169–83
and a lack of feeling of
achievement 231–2
meaning 163–4
paralysing nature 152
questioning 147–92
'Questioning Self-critical
Thoughts' worksheet
168–74, 170–3, 184–91
and reality 154–5
and self-defeating behaviour
160–1, 164
and self-doubt 189–91
'Spotting Self-Critical
Thoughts' worksheet/
record sheet 158–67,
168
stopping 32
tackling with awareness
156–67, 199

tackling with experiments
156, 183–91
tackling with rethinking
156, 168–83
that kick you when you are
down 155
treating like facts 174
unfair nature 153, 180–1
writing down 158–74,
184–91
self-doubt 19–22, 78, 105,
189–91, 310
self-efficacy 4–5, 31
self-esteem 5
healthy 6–7, 31
lacking what you need to
develop 53–5
over-positive 6
pegs of 257–9, 327–8,
334–5
positive 6
see also low self-esteem
self-fulfilling prophecies 332
self-image 3–4, 31
self-kindness 214, 310, 314–16
self-observation 218–233
self-perception 3–4, 31
biases 67
self-prejudice 69–70
self-protection, unnecessary
86–7, 109–23

self-respect 5
self-worth 5, 31, 49, 60–1
setbacks 378–80, 384–5
shame 49, 53
shortcomings, natural 325,
332–3
'shoulds' 230, 257, 261–2, 311
skills
listing your 204
new 25
SMART goals 364–71
Smith, Sydney 153
society, family position in
52–3
step-by-step, taking things
23–5
step-families 44
strengths
ignoring your 180–1
key questions to establishing
your 201–8
making a list of your 199–
208
recording (your 'Positives
Portfolio') 211–14, 350
thoughts that make it
difficult to accept 310
stress, being on the receiving
end of other people's
50–1
stupid, being made to feel 58

success, discounting 88–9
suicide 50
support 26, 28, 330–1, 368

talents, listing your 204
talking therapies 30
therapists 28–31, 380–2
thoughts, treating like facts 10,
    39, 103, 174
threat perception 109
threat response 81–3, 118
Tom (case example) 58, 63–4,
    73, 80, 325, 345,
    349
trigger situations 42, 76–80,
    105

uncertainty 81
'Unless..., then' statements
    260–1, 293, 311
unlovable, being made to feel
    55
unnecessary precautions 86–7,
    109–23
  and alternatives 138–9
  and the Bottom Line 309
  spotting 111–23
  writing down 121–3, 160–1
ups and downs, preparedness
    for 27
upset feelings 186

value judgements 262–3
vicious circle of low self-
    esteem 32, 75–98, 246,
    301
  and anxious predictions
    103–4, 123–4
  breaking 32, 75–98, 358
  mapping 77, 95–7
  and self-criticism 150, 158
vulnerability to problems
    18–19

weaknesses
  concentrating on 180–1
  natural 325, 332–3
work, impact of low self-
    esteem on 13–14
worksheets
  'Acting in Accordance with
    my New Bottom Line'
    346, 352–5
  'Checking Out Anxious
    Predictions' 125, 127–9
  'Questioning Self-critical
    Thoughts' 168–74,
    170–3, 184–91
  'Spotting Self-Critical
    Thoughts' 158–67, 168
worst case scenarios
  dealing with 133–4
  envisioning 131–2

writing things down 26–7,
112–23, 125, 158–67
anxious predictions 119–21,
125, 127–9
Bottom Lines 342, 346,
350, 352–5
Daily Activity Diary 215–
27, 233–43, 267, 294
'Positives Portfolios' 211–
14, 350

and Rules for Living 291,
296–9
self-critical thoughts 158–
74, 184–91
unnecessary precautions
121–3, 160–1
see also worksheets
written summaries 291, 296–9

'yes, buts' 210, 318